J. Gordon McConville

A GOD OF FAITHFULNESS

Essays in Honour of J. Gordon McConville on His 60th Birthday

EDITED BY

Jamie A. Grant, Alison Lo

AND

Gordon J. Wenham

B L O O M S B U R Y

NEW YORK · LONDON · NEW DELHI · SYDNEY

Bloomsbury T&T Clark

An imprint of Bloomsbury Publishing Plc

175 Fifth Avenue   50 Bedford Square
New York   London
NY 10010   WC1B 3DP
USA   UK

www.bloomsbury.com

First published by T&T Clark International 2011
Paperback edition first published 2012

Library of Congress Cataloging-in-Publication Data
A catalog record for this book is available from the Library of Congress

ISBN: HB: 978-0-567-26436-7
PB: 978-0-567-64275-2

Typeset by Pindar NZ, Auckland, New Zealand
Printed and bound in the United States of America

CONTENTS

Chapter 6
PAUL'S SELF-UNDERSTANDING IN THE LIGHT OF
JEREMIAH: A CASE STUDY INTO THE USE OF THE OLD
TESTAMENT IN THE NEW TESTAMENT
Hetty Lalleman, Spurgeon's College, London

Chapter 7
'PROPHET TO THE NATIONS': MISSIONAL REFLECTIONS
ON THE BOOK OF JEREMIAH
*Christopher J.H. Wright, International Director, Langham
Partnership International*

Chapter 8
REMNANT MOTIF IN AMOS, MICAH AND ZEPHANIAH
Alison Lo, London School of Theology

Chapter 9
THE THREE SHEPHERDS: READING ZECHARIAH 11 IN
THE LIGHT OF JEREMIAH
Michael R. Stead, Moore Theological College, Sydney

Part III
POETRY

Chapter 10
THE GOLDEN CALF IN THE PSALMS
Gordon J. Wenham, Trinity College, Bristol

Chapter 11
THE HERMENEUTICS OF HUMANITY: REFLECTIONS ON
THE HUMAN ORIGIN OF THE LAMENTS
Jamie A. Grant, Highland Theological College UHI

Chapter 12
'I WILL HOPE IN HIM': THEOLOGY AND HOPE IN
LAMENTATIONS
Heath Thomas, Southeastern Baptist Theological Seminary

LIST OF CONTRIBUTORS

Jamie A. Grant is Vice Principal of the Highland Theological College UHI, Dingwall, Scotland, where he also teaches Biblical Studies.

Christine Hahn works in the Theology Faculty of the Université de Genève, Switzerland.

Herbert H. Klement is Professor of Old Testament at the Staatsunabhängige Theologische Hochschule Basel, Switzerland.

Hetty Lalleman is Lecturer in Old Testament at Spurgeon's College, London.

Alison Lo is Lecturer in Old Testament at London School of Theology.

Karl Möller is Senior Lecturer in Old Testament at the University of Cumbria.

Michael R. Stead is Rector of St James Anglican Church, Turramurra, and visiting lecturer in Old Testament at Moore Theological College, Sydney.

Heath A. Thomas is Assistant Professor of Old Testament and Hebrew at Southeastern Baptist Theological Seminary, Wake Forest, North Carolina and Fellow in Old Testament Studies at the Paideia Centre for Public Theology in Ontario, Canada.

Peter T. Vogt is Associate Professor of Old Testament at Bethel Seminary, St. Paul, Minnesota.

Gordon J. Wenham is Emeritus Professor of Old Testament at the University of Gloucestershire and research supervisor in Old Testament at Trinity College, Bristol.

Hugh G.M. Williamson is Regius Professor of Hebrew at Oxford University, on the faculty of the Oriental Institute, and a Fellow of the British Academy.

Christopher J.H. Wright is the International Director of the Langham Partnership International which is based in London but works throughout the world.

A Tribute to J. Gordon McConville

The idea of dedicating a Festschrift to Gordon McConville on the occasion of his 60th birthday came to mind in the summer of 2007 and work on this project has been continuing ever since. The age of 60, to some people, may seem a bit 'young' to merit a Festschrift. However, we hope that this volume will serve as a stimulus to encourage Gordon to continue his significant contribution to biblical scholarship while still in the first flush of youth! This collection incorporates 12 essays written by his colleagues, friends and former research students, addressing key interpretative issues in Pentateuch, History, Prophets and Poetry. The breadth of subject-matter discussed in this volume merely reflects Gordon's own wide-ranging research interests.

Now is not the time for a comprehensive biography of Gordon's life but a brief sketch will bring out something of Gordon's various 'personae' as scholar, colleague, teacher and friend. Gordon was born and raised in Lurgan, Northern Ireland. He and his wife Helen have four grown-up children and are now at the stage of enjoying the fun of being grandparents. After studying Modern Languages (French and German) at Cambridge (Emmanuel College) and Theology at Edinburgh (New College), Gordon undertook PhD studies at Queen's University, Belfast, focusing on cultic laws in Deuteronomy. A little-known fact is that Gordon McConville was Gordon Wenham's first doctoral student (the first of many, it has to be said!). In Wenham's eyes, Gordon was 'a very diligent, thorough student, who did not require much guidance, just the sort you need when you are supervising the first time'. After earning his PhD degree, Gordon taught Old Testament at Trinity College, Bristol (1980–89) and Wycliffe Hall in Oxford (1989–95).

To deal with their growing number of research students in OT, Gordon McConville was invited to join the Theology and Religious Studies Department of the University of Gloucestershire (formerly Cheltenham and Gloucester College of Higher Education) as a Senior Lecturer in 1995, becoming Professor of Old Testament Theology in 2002. It was in Cheltenham, at the University of Gloucestershire, that 'the Gordons' (Wenham and McConville) came to work together as colleagues. During the late 1990s numbers of research students in Cheltenham were well into double figures, making it one of the largest groups of OT research students in the UK. Looking back, Wenham comments, 'I never remember any awkwardness in him as a colleague. He was always helpful and obliging. He even took over two of the students who did not like my style of supervising and guided them to a successful conclusion'.

Over the past 30 years, Gordon has successfully supervised more than 20 PhD students to completion. Each of these graduates can testify to Gordon's tireless efforts in mentoring, advising and guiding them to successful completion. We firmly believe that he has set an example worthy of emulation through his own disciplined research, his unyielding integrity and his determination never to shirk the difficult questions of biblical investigation. As a teacher, he was always available to give wise counsel, to discuss research or to brainstorm ideas, and his academic rigour was always matched by a gentleness, kindness and graciousness of personality that made up for the copious amounts of 'red pen'. Gordon's scholarship is also marked by a strong degree of humility. He openly (and, sometimes, generously) comments on how much he learns from his students. And this willingness to listen and openness to new perspectives builds a bridge of friendship that is often missing from the doctoral supervisor-student relationship. His sense of humour is dry and witty and his students have found in Gordon not only an excellent teacher and mentor, but also a firm friend.

The title of this volume, *A God of Faithfulness*, comes from Gordon's 'beloved' Deuteronomy (Deut. 32.4). It is this God who is always the central focus of Gordon's life, as family man, scholar and churchman. Gordon's desire to respond to the faithfulness of God is revealed in his own devotion to scholarship and in his desire to fulfil this calling by bringing greater light to our understanding of the Scriptures. The way he has touched and inspired many lives to this end leaves a lasting legacy. With gratitude for his contributions to biblical scholarship and in anticipation of the fruit that his current and future endeavours will bear, we dedicate this Festschrift to Gordon McConville. It is but a small token of our sincere appreciation for his writing, teaching, friendship and support throughout the years.

Jamie A. Grant
Alison Lo
Gordon J. Wenham
Easter 2010

PUBLICATIONS

Books

1984

Law and Theology in Deuteronomy (Sheffield: JSOT Press, 1984).
1 and 2 Chronicles (Daily Study Bible; Edinburgh: St Andrew Press/
Philadelphia: Westminster Press, 1984).

1985

Ezra, Nehemiah, Esther (Daily Study Bible; Edinburgh: St Andrew Press/
Philadelphia: Westminster Press, 1985).

1993

Judgment and Promise: An Interpretation of the Book of Jeremiah (Leicester:
Apollos/Winona Lake: Eisenbrauns, 1993).
Grace in the End: A Study in Deuteronomic Theology (Carlisle: Paternoster/
Grand Rapids: Zondervan, 1993).

1994

Time and Place in Deuteronomy (Sheffield: JSOT Press, 1994). [co-authored
with J.G. Millar]

1996

The Old Testament (Teach Yourself World Faiths; London: Hodder, 1996).

2000

*Reconsidering Israel and Judah: Recent Studies on the Deuteronomistic
History* (Winona Lake: Eisenbrauns, 2000). [co-edited with
G. Knoppers]

2002

Deuteronomy (AOTC 5; Leicester: Apollos/Downer's Grove: IVP, 2002).
Exploring the Old Testament: The Prophets (London: SPCK/Downer's
Grove: IVP, 2002).

2006

God and Earthly Power: An Old Testament Political Theology (London: T & T Clark International, 2006).

2007

Reading the Law: Essays in Honour of Gordon J. Wenham (London: T & T Clark International, 2007). [co-edited with Karl Möller]

Exploring the Old Testament: The Historical Books (London: SPCK, 2007). [co-authored with Philip Satterthwaite]

2010

Joshua (Two Horizons Old Testament Commentary; Grand Rapids: Eerdmans, 2010). [co-authored with Stephen Williams]

Articles

1979

'God's "Name" and God's "Glory"', *Tyndale Bulletin* 30 (1979), 149–63.

1980

'Drafting Techniques in Some Deuteronomic Laws', *VT* 30 (1980), 248–52. [co-authored with G. J. Wenham]

1981

'The Place of Ritual in OT Religion', *Irish Biblical Studies* 3 (1981), 120–33.

1983

'Priests and Levites in Ezekiel: A Crux in the Interpretation of Israel's History', *Tyndale Bulletin* 34 (1983), 3–31.

1986

'1 Chronicles 28:9: Yahweh "seeks out" Solomon', *JTS* 37 (1986), 105–108.

'Statement of Assurance in Psalms of Lament', *Irish Biblical Studies* 8 (1986), 64–75.

'Diversity and Obscurity on Old Testament Books: A Hermeneutical Exercise Based on Some Later Old Testament Books', *Anvil* 3 (1986), 33–47.

'Ezra-Nehemiah and the Fulfilment of Prophecy', *VT* 36 (1986), 205–24.

1989

'Narrative and Meaning in the Books of Kings', *Biblica* 70 (1989), 31–49.

1991

'Jeremiah: Prophet and Book', *Tyndale Bulletin* 42 (1991), 80–95.

1992

'1 Kings viii 46–53 and the Deuteronomic Hope', *VT* 42 (1992), 67–79.

1993

'Abraham and Melchizedek: Horizons in Genesis 14', in R.S. Hess, *et al.* (eds.), *He Swore an Oath* (Cambridge: Tyndale House, 1993), 93–118.

'Yahweh and the Gods in the Old Testament', *European Journal of Theology* 2 (1993), 107–117.

1994

'Jerusalem in the Old Testament', in P.W.L. Walker (ed.), *Jerusalem Past and Present in the Purposes of God* (Carlisle: Paternoster, 2nd edn, 1994), 21–51.

1995

'Messianic Interpretation of the Old Testament in Modern Context', in Philip E. Satterthwaite, *et al.* (eds.), *The* Lord's *Anointed: Interpretation of Old Testament Messianic Texts* (Carlisle: Paternoster, 1995), 1–17.

1996

'Faces of Exile in Old Testament Historiography', in John Barton and David J. Reimer (eds.), *After the Exile: Essays in Honour of Rex Mason* (Macon: Mercer University Press, 1996), 27–44. [repr. in V.P. Long (ed.), *Israel's Past in Present Research: Essays on Ancient Israelite Historiography* (Winona Lake: Eisenbrauns, 1999), 519–34].

'Die Gerichtsorganisation Israels im deuteronomischen Gesetz', *Journal of Theological Studies* 47 (1996), 563. [co-authored with J.C. Gertz]

1997

'Time and the Millennium', *European Journal of Theology* 6 (1997), 95–99.

'Out of the Midst of the Fire. Divine Presence in Deuteronomy', *Journal of Theological Studies* 48 (1997), 150. [co-authored with I. Wilson]

1998

'King and Messiah in Deuteronomy and the Deuteronomistic History', in John Day (ed.), *King and Messiah in Israel and the Ancient Near East: Proceedings of the Oxford Old Testament Seminar* (JSOTSup 270; Sheffield: Sheffield Academic Press, 1998), 271–95.

1999
'Priesthood in Joshua to Kings', *VT* 49 (1999), 73–87.

2000
'The Old Testament and Enjoyment of Wealth', in C. Bartholomew and
T. Moritz, (eds.), *Christ and Consumerism* (Carlisle: Paternoster Press,
2000), 34–53.
'Deuteronomy: Torah for the Church of Christ', *European Journal of
Theology* 9 (2000), 33–47.
'Deuteronomy's Unification of Passover and Massot – A Response to
B. M. Levinson', *JBL* 119 (2000), 47–58.

2001
'Restoration in Deuteronomy and Deuteronomic Tradition', in James
M. Scott (ed.), *Restoration: Old Testament, Jewish, and Christian
Perspectives* (Journal for the Study of Judaism Supplement series;
Leiden: Brill, 2001), 11–40.
'Metaphor, Symbol and the Interpretation of Deuteronomy', in
C. Bartholomew, *et al.* (eds.), *After Pentecost: Language and Biblical
Interpretation* (Scripture and Hermeneutics Series, 2; Carlisle:
Paternoster/Grand Rapids: Zondervan, 2001), 329–51.
'Biblical Theology: Canon, Plurality and Plain Sense', *Scottish Bulletin of
Evangelical Theology* 19 (2001), 134–57.

2002
'Divine Speech and the Book of Jeremiah', in Paul Helm and Carl Trueman
(eds.), *The Trustworthiness of Our God* (Leicester: Apollos/Grand
Rapids: Eerdmans, 2002), 18–38.
'Singular Address in the Deuteronomic Law and the Politics of Legal
Administration', *JSOT* 97 (2002), 19–36.
'Law and Monarchy in the Old Testament', in C. Bartholomew, *et al.* (eds.),
A Royal Priesthood: The Use of the Bible Ethically and Politically
(Scripture and Hermeneutics Series, 3; Carlisle: Paternoster/Grand
Rapids: Zondervan, 2002), 69–88.

2003
'A Dialogue with Gordon McConville on Deuteronomy', *SJT* 56 (2003),
508–31 [with R.E. Clements and R.W.L. Moberly].

2004
'Pilgrimage and Place: an Old Testament View', in C. Bartholomew and

F. Hughes (eds.), *Explorations in a Christian Theology of Pilgrimage* (Aldershot: Ashgate, 2004), 17–28.

'The Judgment of God in the Old Testament', *Ex Auditu* 20 (2004), 25–42.

2006

'"How can Jacob Stand? He is So Small!" (Amos 7:2): The Prophetic Word and the Re-Imagining of Israel', in Brad E. Kelle and Megan Bishop Moore (eds.), *Israel's Prophets and Israel's Past: Essays on the Relationship of Prophetic Texts and Israelite History in Honor of John Hayes* (London: T & T Clark International, 2006), 132–51.

'Old Testament Laws and Canonical Intentionality', in C. Bartholomew, *et al.* (eds.), *Canon and Biblical Interpretation* (Scripture and Hermeneutics Series, 7; Carlisle: Paternoster/Grand Rapids: Zondervan, 2006), 259–81.

2007

'"Fellow-Citizens": Israel and Humanity in Leviticus', in J.G. McConville and Karl Möller (eds.), *Reading the Law: Studies in Honor of Gordon J. Wenham* (LHB/OTS; New York: Continuum, 2007), 10–32.

Forthcoming

'Righteousness and the Divine Presence in Psalm 17', in Jill Middlemas, *et al.* (eds.), *The Centre and Periphery: A European Tribute to Walter Brueggemann* (Hebrew Bible Monographs, 27; Sheffield: Sheffield Phoenix, 2010).

'Book of Hosea', in *Dictionary of the Old Testament* (vol. 4; Downers Grove: IVP, 2011).

Gordon has also written dozens of reviews of significant academic works that have been published in peer-reviewed journals.

Part I

PENTATEUCH AND HISTORY

Chapter 1

IMAGES OF GOD AND CREATION IN GENESIS 1–2

Karl Möller

University of Cumbria

In his recent book *God and World in the Old Testament*, Terence Fretheim has proposed a relational understanding of creation, maintaining that both God and the creatures have important roles to play in 'the creative enterprise'. Whereas God is traditionally understood as entirely independent and the creatures conversely as being absolutely dependent upon God,[1] Fretheim stresses that the Old Testament lays a strong emphasis upon God's resolve to establish an interdependent relationship with his creation and even be dependent upon his creatures regarding the accomplishment of his purposes in the world. And he argues for an understanding of creation as a continuing process over against the traditional emphasis on creation as a finished product.[2]

To be sure, Fretheim does not negate that 'Genesis 1 stresses the divine initiative, imagination, transcendence, and power'; and he is well aware that 'the placement of Genesis 1 suggests that these divine characteristics should stand at the beginning and in the foreground in any discussion of creation'.[3] Yet he maintains that creation is also presented in relational terms, as in Genesis 2, where the first human being is drawn into God's creative work. Fretheim therefore suggests that, if what is usually understood as the first creation account is read in the light of Genesis 2, the entire portrayal of creation is seen as highly relational in character. This means that the creatures are meant to be involved in God's creative work, as the creator moves over, as it were, in order to make room for the Other and to allow 'for genuine decisions on the part of human

---

1. Thus e.g. B.W. Anderson, *From Creation to New Creation* (Minneapolis: Fortress Press, 1994), 28.

2. T.E. Fretheim, *God and World in the Old Testament* (Nashville: Abingdon Press, 2005), 270–71.

3. Fretheim, *God*, 271.

beings as they exercise their God-given power'.[4]

This understanding of God's approach to creation is of fundamental importance for how we perceive humanity's role vis-à-vis God's creation, for

> the human vocation to be in God's image is modeled on the creative actions of God. If the God portrayed in [Genesis 1] is understood only or fundamentally in terms of overwhelming power, absolute control, and independent, unilateral activity, then human beings, created in the image of this God, rightfully understand their relationship to the nonhuman world as one of power over, absolute control, and independence.[5]

However, because God creates with great care, 'the human task of subduing the earth does not pit humanity against nature, but reflects a working *with* nature . . . through promoting and harnessing creation's integrity'.[6]

The significance of such an understanding of creation for contemporary reflection regarding our relationship with the created order does not require spelling out, but the relational theology of creation advocated by Fretheim stands in sharp contrast to some traditional perceptions of God's work of creation, which emphasize precisely his 'overwhelming power, absolute control, and independent, unilateral activity'. Given these different perceptions, the present essay seeks to re-examine the images of God and creation presented in Genesis 1–2 in order to ascertain whether Fretheim's relational understanding of creation is warranted by the text.

1. Hermeneutical Reflections on the Interpretation of the Genesis Creation Account

Scholarly discussions of creation have frequently been confined to Gen. 1.1–2.4a.[7] This goes against the traditional inclination of Jewish and Christian communities to read Genesis 1–2 (or better perhaps, 1–3) as an integrated whole, but it seemed a justifiable move given the source-critical conclusion that we are dealing with two separate accounts composed not only by different authors but also in different periods of Israel's history. More importantly, we are also

---

4. Fretheim, *God*, 272.

5. Fretheim, *God*, 276.

6. Thus W.P. Brown, *The Ethos of the Cosmos* (Grand Rapids: Eerdmans, 1999), 126.

7. See e.g. K. Löning and E. Zenger, *To Begin with, God Created . . .* (Collegeville: Liturgical Press, 2000), which features two chapters on Genesis 1 but has no corresponding reflections on Genesis 2.

dealing with two passages that could not be more different in their theological outlook.

The differences in style, terminology, idioms and theology have been well summed up by Habel.[8] Whereas P's account (Gen. 1.1–2.4a) features balanced structures and focuses on an ordered world, created by a transcendent, majestic and sovereign God, J's version in Gen. 2.4b-25 is characterized by its artistic, picturesque, story-form style, its portrayal of God as immanent, intimate and involved, and its bold use of anthropomorphisms.

Scholarly reflection on creation has typically preferred P's focus on the sovereignty of a transcendent God, while downplaying or ignoring J's alternative account. As Fretheim notes, the source-critical separation of sources 'has often been accompanied by a subtle or not-so-subtle conviction that Genesis 1 is a more mature theological statement about the Creator and the creation and Genesis 2 a more primitive account'.[9]

However, this approach has been called into question by redaction-critical conclusions that regard P as the redactor of Genesis 1 *and* 2, who purposely included the Yahwistic material in Genesis 2. This suggests that J's version of creation should not be ignored, because it forms an integral part of the picture of creation that the Priestly writer wanted us to see.[10] Quite apart from all the theories about the development of the biblical text, canonical critics have long argued not only that J's account has been absorbed into P's portrayal of creation, but also that the 'canonical text speaks with a single voice'.[11] Childs can even say that 'by continuing to speak of the "two creation accounts of Genesis" the interpreter disregards the canonical shaping and threatens its role both as literature and as scripture'.[12]

It seems right then for our focus to be on Genesis 1 *and* 2, because the canonical shaping implies that 'a theologically coherent perspective on creation . . . is to be found in these two chapters in interaction with each other'.[13] But the question still remains as to how this interaction is perceived. Fretheim adduces the distinctive portrayal of God and humans in Genesis 2 in his argument for

---

8. N.C. Habel, *Literary Criticism of the Old Testament* (Philadelphia: Fortress Press, 1971), 18–27.

9. Fretheim, *God*, 33.

10. Thus D. Patrick and A. Scult, *Rhetoric and Biblical Interpretation* (JSOTSup, 82; Sheffield: Almond Press, 1990), 105, 114; and Fretheim, *God*, 33.

11. M.C. Callaway, 'Canonical Criticism', in S.L. McKenzie and S.R. Haynes (eds.), *To Each Its Own Meaning* (Louisville: Westminster John Knox Press, 2nd edn, 1999), 142–55 (148).

12. B.S. Childs, *Introduction to the Old Testament as Scripture* (Philadelphia: Fortress Press, 1979), 150.

13. Thus Fretheim, *God*, 33.

a 'relational theology of creation', including the notion that the initial creation was good but not perfect, thus requiring further development and human
involvement. Patrick and Scult have come to different conclusions, maintaining
that 'human beings cannot engage the world presented to them as co-creators.
God's authorship provides the "true" construction of reality . . . God's original
creation must eventually circumscribe human action'.[14]

Like others before them, Patrick and Scult begin by contrasting the two
accounts. Regarding J's version, they note the use of anthropomorphisms and
that God is essentially portrayed like a parent: 'Nothing of what God does in
the story subsequent to the actual creation is peculiarly divine. They are the
actions of any parent in a similar situation.'[15] Moreover, Adam is invited by
God 'to participate in the completion of creation',[16] which stands in sharp contrast to P, where human beings are never the subject but are 'confined always
to grammatical objectivity'[17] and the innate excellence of the divine creation
God is celebrated.[18]

So how are we to understand the relationship of these two perspectives? Patrick
and Scult maintain that, having been utilized by P, J now serves 'as an argument
and an interpretation, a series of proofs which illuminate or amplify P's stating of
the case'.[19] This means that, although humans matter (as those created in God's
image, they are given dignity), because they always feature in the objective
case in P's account, they are not 'actors on the stage God occupies':[20]

> in P's mind, whatever J says should be read in the frame of realizing that free-
> dom of will in human beings exists only as the actor's craft in relation to an
> author's script. Human will, in other words, is a matter of style, nuance, bal-
> ance, and emphasis, not a matter of creativity or authorship . . . With regard
> to the nature of authorial power, P asserts that God-as-author possessed an
> absolutely unqualified capacity to create, constrained neither by the task of
> creation nor by need to take other similar powers into account.[21]

Moreover, the creation has been completed perfectly, and thus there is nothing
further to do. 'Humans have no creative potential of their own to serve as the

---

14. Patrick and Scult, *Rhetoric*, 119.
15. Patrick and Scult, *Rhetoric*, 109.
16. Patrick and Scult, *Rhetoric*, 110.
17. Patrick and Scult, *Rhetoric*, 113.
18. Patrick and Scult, *Rhetoric*, 112.
19. Patrick and Scult, *Rhetoric*, 114.
20. Patrick and Scult, *Rhetoric*, 116.
21. Patrick and Scult, *Rhetoric*, 116.

basis for more story', and 'P's vision of God's authorship . . . forecloses any significant story that might follow . . . Perfection has realized itself'.[22]

In this reading, P trumps J, to put it crudely. P is the interpreter of J, and we are to read J's version of creation through the lens supplied by the Priestly writer. This, it has to be said, is a possible interpretation.[23] If P is the redactor of J, it makes sense to conclude that the authorities behind P saw it as important that J's perspective be prefaced with (and thereby corrected by) their own version of creation.

However, redaction-critical scenarios like this one, which is still widely accepted in Old Testament scholarship, raise the question of how much specialist knowledge readers are expected to bring to the text.[24] Can these chapters only be rightly interpreted if their redaction-historical development is understood? For how else are we to recognize what P has done to J? Leaving aside these diachronic questions, different interpretative possibilities suggest themselves simply by the given sequentiality of the two chapters. Fish once described literature as a 'kinetic art', noting that during the reading process the book does not remain stationary but is moving (pages are turning and lines are receding into the past as we read), and *we* are moving with it.[25] Accordingly, Fish speaks of the '*temporal* flow of the reading experience'[26] and 'the developing responses of the reader in relation to the words as they succeed one another in time'.[27]

For Genesis 1–2 this means that the text's initial focus on the creation of an ordered world by a transcendent God eventually gives way to a more picturesque account that portrays God as immanent, intimate and involved. Human beings also now truly come to the fore, as they are allowed to participate in the completion of creation and are freed from the confines of grammatical objectivity. The temporal process of reading leads readers to revise their first impressions of God and humankind; and, far from trumping J's account, P's version now receives a corrective, as the reader finds out more about God, human beings and creation.

Even from a diachronic perspective, it is difficult to avoid the conclusion

22. Patrick and Scult, *Rhetoric*, 117.

23. Having said that, however, some further reflections on the theological import of Gen. 1.26-28 would seem to be in order, for when God addresses the humans in 1.28, they are clearly elevated out of their confinement to grammatical objectivity.

24. See K. Möller, 'Reconstructing and Interpreting Amos's Literary Prehistory', in C. Bartholomew, *et al.* (eds.), *'Behind' the Text* (Carlisle: Paternoster Press, 2003), 397–441 (esp. 424–26), for further discussion.

25. S. Fish, *Is There a Text in This Class?* (Cambridge, MA: Harvard University Press, 1980), 43.

26. Fish, *Text*, 27.

27. Fish, *Text*, 26.

that, by including J, P has not only allowed the Yahwist's perspective to stand but has thereby taken the chance that it might subvert his own. Patrick and Scult note the complementarity of the texts, but their redaction-critical assumptions lead them to construe the relationship of the two accounts in the way outlined above. This move may be driven partly by dogmatic concerns, as is suggested by statements such as that 'as human beings live through the story of their relationship with God, their participation in creation is circumscribed by God's authorship' and 'God's power as author circumscribes the power of human beings to transact with him as authority'.[28] There may be valid theological reasons for these conclusions, but literary and canonical considerations require that we take the perspective offered by Gen. 2.4b-25 more seriously than has sometimes been the case. But the Priestly account, too, warrants another look to determine the extent to which Patrick and Scult's analysis does justice to its theological thrust.

2. *Images of God and Creation in Genesis 1–2*

Biblical interpreters and theologians alike have often stressed that God's creative work is without analogy. Wellhausen, one of the most influential biblical interpreters in the modern era, may serve as an example of this trend. Commenting on Genesis 1, he maintained that 'the most important point is that a special word is employed, which stands for nothing else than the creative agency of God, and so dissociates it from all analogy with human making and shaping'.[29] More recently, writing as a systematic theologian, Moltmann has similarly suggested that our text portrays God's creative activity as being without analogy.[30]

As Wellhausen's comment indicates, one of the reasons why God's work as creator is thought to be dissimilar from any human creative efforts is the use of ברא ('create'), which, it has been claimed, is only ever used with God as subject and denotes the process of creating out of nothing (*creatio ex nihilo*). However, Arnold has pointed out that 'the assertion that Israel's God is always and only the subject of [ברא] is slightly misleading',[31] because the Hebrew lexicons list an identical root ברא[III], which always occurs in the piel, is used of human subjects (e.g. Josh. 17.15, 18; Ezek. 21.24; 23.47) and means something like 'shape or

---

28. Patrick and Scult, *Rhetoric*, 118.
29. J. Wellhausen, *Prolegomena to the History of Ancient Israel* (New York: Meridian Books, 1957), 305; see also recently B. Becking and M.C.A. Korpel, 'To Create, to Separate or to Construct', *JHS* 10.3 (2010), 2–21 (15).
30. J. Moltmann, *God in Creation* (London: SCM Press, 1985), 73.
31. B.T. Arnold, *Genesis* (Cambridge: Cambridge University Press, 2009), 36.

separate by cutting'. Arnold cautions us not to assume too quickly that ברא[III]
is a different root, suggesting that it would be more accurate to conclude that,
when used in the qal and niphal, ברא has God as subject, but that it is also used
of humans in the piel.

Even more significant than the fact that ברא piel is used of human subjects is
the underlying concept of 'cutting', which Hanson has argued to be the primary
meaning of the term even when employed in the qal.[32] His starting point is the
use of ברא qal in Num. 16.30 where, he suggests, the phrase ואם־בריאה יברא יהוה
is best translated 'if the LORD splits open a crevice'.[33] This is demanded by the
context and especially the 'prophecy–fulfilment scheme' in vv. 30–33.

'Prophecy' (v. 30)	'Fulfilment' (vv. 31–33)
ואם־בריאה יברא יהוה	ותבקע האדמה אשר תחתיהם
ופצתה האדמה את־פיה	ותפתח הארץ את־פיה
ובלעה אתם ואת־כל־אשר להם	ותבלע אתם ואת־בתיהם
	ואת כל־האדם אשר לקרח ואת כל־הרכוש
וירדו חיים שאלה	וירדו הם וכל־אשר להם חיים שאלה

The sequence in these corresponding lines is the same in both cases: there is a
splitting of the ground, which is described as the earth or the ground opening
its mouth. This leads to the rebels being swallowed up, so that they are finding themselves on their way towards Sheol. Although the first line in v. 30 is
frequently rendered along the lines of 'if the Lord creates something new' (see
NRSV, ESV, NIV), Hanson points out that the incident would never be construed
as involving creation were it not for preconceived ideas regarding the meaning
of ברא.[34] As already noted, he believes the notion of cutting to be the primary
meaning of the term, and he illustrates this with reference to Isa. 40.28; 42.5
and Ps. 148.5-6, where he finds an at least implicit polemic against the worship of Marduk. Thus, whereas in the *Enuma Eliš* epic Marduk is presented
as the one who created heaven and earth by splitting the slain Tiamat, the Old

32. H.E. Hanson, 'Num. XVI 30 and the Meaning of *Bārā*'', *VT* 22 (1972), 353–59.

33. Hanson, 'Num. XVI 30', 355. NEB reads similarly 'if the LORD makes a great chasm',
and this understanding has been adopted also by J. Milgrom, *Numbers* (Philadelphia:
Jewish Publication Society of America, 1990), 137.

34. Hanson, 'Num. XVI 30', 353. Becking and Korpel, 'To Create', 13, object that
'most modern dictionaries, translations and commentaries prefer to translate ברא בריאה as
"to create a creation, to create something totally new"', but, apart from the use of בריאה in
Qumran, they fail to offer any arguments in support of their preferred reading.

Testament writers insist that it was Israel's God who 'cut out the heavens and stretched them out'.[35]

As regards the meaning of ברא, it thus seems possible that an original sense of 'cutting' may have first led to the notion of 'creating by cutting', which then eventually gave way to the meaning 'creating' where the notion of 'cutting' was no longer understood. It is, of course, important to guard against the mistaken assumption that words always retain their original meaning,[36] but the concept of God creating by means of a series of 'cuts' or 'separations' clearly is particularly apt in Genesis 1, where the process of creation is perceived largely in terms of progressive acts of separation and distinction (see vv. 4, 6–7, 14, 18).[37] There are therefore good reasons for understanding ברא in Genesis 1 as denoting creating by cutting or separating, an interpretation that had already been suggested by Ibn Ezra[38] and has been adopted recently by Arnold.[39]

But if this is correct, would we not have to conclude that ברא cannot refer to a *creatio ex nihilo* in this context? To be sure, in recent years commentators have become less dogmatic about this issue. For instance, Wenham has noted that, because of the theological importance of the idea, traditional notions of creation are easily read into the Hebrew verb despite the fact that it is not 'exclusively reserved for creation out of nothing'.[40] Yet, others are reluctant to let go of the traditional understanding. Arnold, for example, maintains that the notion of *creatio ex nihilo* is 'not false to the intent of Gen 1' and that if we had 'an opportunity to pose the question to the author of this text, we may assume with Westermann and others that he would "certainly have decided in favor of *creatio ex nihilo*"'.[41]

But does the evidence really allow for such an assumption? While it is correct that ברא is never used with the accusative of the material out of which

---

35. This is Hanson's rendering of Isa. 42.5a ('Num. XVI 30', 356).

36. The classic critique of the etymological fallacy remains J. Barr, *The Semantics of Biblical Language* (London: Oxford University Press, 1961).

37. See D.J.A. Clines, *The Theme of the Pentateuch* (JSOTSup, 10; Sheffield: JSOT Press, 1978), 74–75.

38. See I. Husik, *A History of Mediaeval Jewish Philosophy* (Philadelphia: Jewish Publication Society of America, 1946), 190.

39. Arnold, *Genesis*, 37. E. van Wolde, 'Why the Verb ברא Does Not Mean "to Create" in Genesis 1.1–2.4a', *JSOT* 34 (2009), 3–23, has taken the argument a step further by suggesting that ברא does not mean 'create' at all but is best translated as 'separate'. For a critique of van Wolde's proposal, see Becking and Korpel, 'To Create'.

40. G.J. Wenham, *Genesis 1–15* (WBC, 1; Dallas: Word Books, 1987), 14; see also Schmidt, 'בָּרָא', *TLOT* 1 (1997), 253–56 (255).

41. Arnold, *Genesis*, 36; the reference is to C. Westermann, *Genesis 1–11* (London: SPCK, 1984), 108–109.

God creates, passages such as Isa. 43.15, which refers to God as the creator of Israel (בורא ישראל), indicate that *creatio ex nihilo* is not necessarily implied.[42] And if ברא in Genesis 1 is to be understood as signifying creation by cutting or separating, then this would imply the pre-existence of something to be cut or separated. We have already seen that such an understanding not only befits the portrayal of God's creative acts of separation and distinction in Genesis 1 but also ties in with ancient Near Eastern conceptions as exemplified by the *Enuma Eliš* epic. In addition, we should note that the concept of *creatio ex nihilo* only developed in response to Gnosticism[43] and 'was not yet a significant theological idea' in the ancient Near Eastern world.[44] It would thus not have been of particular concern to the authors of our Genesis passage.

While it may be important for Christian theology to retain the doctrine of *creatio ex nihilo* as a 'protection against any type of ultimate dualism',[45] Christian interpretation of Genesis 1 needs to recognize that this text originated in a different cultural context in which the key issue appears to have been God's sovereignty over anything that might have threatened his good creation rather than the origins of his raw material.

It therefore appears that the term ברא has frequently been overloaded with theological significance in ways that go beyond what it can bear.[46] The authors of Genesis 1 are adamant that the heavens and the earth have been created by Elohim rather than by any other Ancient Near Eastern deity and also that God's work of separating and setting boundaries was achieved with unmatched authority. But to suggest that God's creative acts are entirely without human analogy invests the term ברא with connotations that derive more from subsequent Jewish and Christian reflection upon creation than the thrust of the Genesis passage itself. As Gordon has suggested, 'the non-anthropomorphic nature of ברא ("create") may not have been so obvious to [the] biblical writers'.[47]

---

42. R.C. Van Leeuwen, 'ברא', in W.A. VanGemeren (ed.), *New International Dictionary of Old Testament Theology and Exegesis* (5 vols.; Grand Rapids: Zondervan, 1997), 1:728–35 (731), lists additional passages and adds that, although the term 'does not appear with mention of material out of which something is created, it is regularly collocated with vbs. that do'.

43. Thus e.g. A.E. McGrath, *The Science of God* (London: T & T Clark, 2004), 50, who notes that in order to counter Gnosticism 'Christian theologians *gradually* came to the conclusion that creation was best understood as an action *ex nihilo*' (my italics).

44. See J.E. Atwell, *The Sources of the Old Testament* (London: T & T Clark, 2004), 4.

45. Thus P. Tillich, *Systematic Theology*, vol. 1 (Chicago: University of Chicago Press, 1951), 253.

46. For this conclusion, see Van Leeuwen, 'ברא', 731; and Arnold, *Genesis*, 36.

47. R.P. Gordon, 'The Week That Made the World', in J.G. McConville and K. Möller

We also must not overlook that ברא is not the only term used to describe God's creative activity. In Gen. 2.7-8, 19, the use of יצר ('form') evokes the image of God as a potter, while in 2.22 Eve is built (בנה) by God. More importantly, the Priestly account too features 'an everyday verb . . . commonly used for human activity'[48] when it repeatedly employs עשה ('make') to speak of God making things (Gen. 1.7, 16, 25–26, 31; 2.2-4, 18). That עשה and ברא can be used interchangeably (1.26-27) suggests that there is no desire to portray God's work of creation as incomparable to human creation. If that had been the intention of the biblical writers, one would expect that perspective to have been maintained more consistently.[49] Instead, the picture that emerges is more complex in that God's work is presented both as unique (creation by his word comes to mind, but see below for further discussion) and as comparable to humanity's creative endeavours.

Van Leeuwen aptly concludes that, 'while cosmic creation is a unique and ultimately incomprehensible divine activity, the OT expresses this in a humanly comprehensible, highly metaphorical vocabulary'.[50] And Fretheim notes that this use of metaphorical language is of great significance, because 'given the fact that metaphors drawn from human work and life processes can be used for God's creative activity, continuities with human creativity are genuine; God's creative work is not absolutely unparalleled among the creatures'.[51]

A related issue concerns the question of whether God's creating can be understood as a continuous creative activity (*creatio continua*). It has often been argued that the creative process expressed by ברא refers exclusively to the 'absolute beginning of our world'.[52] Patrick and Scult's conclusions that 'P's vision of God's authorship . . . forecloses any significant story that might follow' and that in this account 'perfection has realized itself'[53] illustrate this trend. Childs similarly argues that after 'God pronounced his workmanship good and blessed it [. . .] the creation rested in its perfection; no further work

(eds.), *Reading the Law* (LHBOTS, 461; New York: T & T Clark International, 2007), 228–41 (233).

48. Fretheim, *God*, 37. Gordon, 'Week', 233, speaks of the 'workman character of the creator'.

49. Against Becking and Korpel, 'To Create', 20, who understand ברא as a neologism coined in order to avoid 'anthropomorphic confusion'. S. Paas, *Creation and Judgement* (OTS, 47; Leiden: Brill, 2003), 64, more appropriately refers to ברא as a 'theological umbrella term' that is capable of expressing diverse forms of creation.

50. Van Leeuwen, 'ברא', 732.

51. Fretheim, *God*, 2.

52. See D.J. McCarthy, '"Creation" Motifs in Ancient Hebrew Poetry', in B.W. Anderson (ed.), *Creation in the Old Testament* (London: SPCK, 1984), 74–89 (79).

53. Patrick and Scult, *Rhetoric*, 117.

was needed'.[54] And Goldingay concludes that 'the portrait of God completing a week's work and then stopping assures its readers that the work of creation is over [. . .] Genesis allows us to think in terms of continuity of creation, but not of continuous creation'.[55]

However, Ollenburger maintains that 'to demand of "creation" that it refer only to absolute beginnings . . . is virtually to deny the possibility of speaking of creation with respect to the Bible'.[56] Again, we may be in danger here of reading a traditional Christian conception back into texts that in and of themselves have a different emphasis.

Fretheim helpfully distinguishes between three types of creation, i.e. originating, continuing and completing creation.[57] Genesis 1 exemplifies origination, but we must note that creation language does not necessarily refer to the origins of the physical universe but is also used with respect to the beginnings of the social, cultural and national orders. This is a common feature in Ancient Near Eastern cosmogonies, which were interested not so much in the beginnings of the physical universe as the emergence of a particular society and thus the 'world' of human beings as perceived by the writers.[58]

An example of Fretheim's category of continuing creation[59] is found in the use of ברא in Ps. 104.30, which speaks of the new creation in connection with God renewing the earth with life.[60] But the best example of creation language being used in this way comes from Isaiah 40–55, where God's salvific action of enabling his people to return from exile is presented as his ongoing creative work. Far from creation being confined to the days of old, in Isa. 48.6-7, verses that 'develop the aspect of . . . total newness in a far more radical form than anything before',[61] God creates 'new things' (חדשות). Regardless of his claim that Genesis does not allow us to speak of continuous creation, Goldingay notes that

54. B.S. Childs, *Biblical Theology of the Old and New Testaments* (London: SCM Press, 1992), 385.

55. J. Goldingay, *Old Testament Theology*, vol. 1 (Downers Grove: InterVarsity Press, 2003), 127–28.

56. B.C. Ollenburger, 'Isaiah's Creation Theology', *Ex Auditu* 3 (1987), 54–71 (60).

57. See Fretheim, *God*, 5–9.

58. R.J. Clifford and J.J. Collins, 'Introduction', in idem (eds.), *Creation in the Biblical Traditions* (CBQMS, 24; Washington: Catholic Biblical Association of America, 1992), 1–15 (8).

59. Fretheim's third category of 'completing creation' cannot concern us here.

60. Thus J.L. Mays, *Psalms* (Interpretation; Louisville: John Knox Press, 1994), 335.

61. B.S. Childs, *Isaiah* (OTL; Louisville: Westminster John Knox Press, 2001), 375.

the new events envisaged in this passage 'embody the marvellous sovereignty of the original and ongoing creation';[62] and Childs, again despite his insistence that a perfect creation needed no further work, similarly recognizes that God 'is engaged in constant creative activity'.[63]

Fretheim accordingly stresses God's ongoing involvement in the creation, which he finds expressed already in Genesis 1–2 in God evaluating his works. God experiences and is affected by what he has created.[64] Surprisingly though, the seven pronouncements that creation 'was good' (Gen. 1.4, 10, 12, 18, 21, 25 and the climactic 'it was very good', טוב מאד, in 1.31) are followed by the judgment that 'it is *not* good that the man should be alone' (2.18). For Fretheim, 'this negative *divine* evaluation of God's own work suggests that creation is conceived . . . in terms of a process wherein the divine response to what has been created leads to further development of the creation'.[65] With Steck he maintains that the Yahwist regards the world as an event or process;[66] and it is for this reason that he rejects Childs's assessment that the creation 'rested in its perfection'.[67]

Yet Fretheim's line of argument is open to criticism at this point, for Gen. 2.4b-25 does not talk about further developments of the creation after it had received God's approving comment that it was very good. However the precise redaction-critical development of the two-part creation account is construed, in the text as it now stands, Genesis 2 offers a flashback that takes a closer look at the creation of humankind. It is concerned with matters that pre-date the verdict found in 1.31. Of course, the fact that at some stage in the creative process things were declared not to be good suggests that God's creation is not conceived in static terms, as Fretheim maintains, yet Childs could nonetheless be right that, regardless of what had happened up to that point, the completed creation from then on 'rested in its perfection'.

That does not appear to be the case, however, because Gen. 1.28 indicates that God's creation, even prior to the events in Genesis 3, needs to be 'subdued' by humankind, who are commanded to have 'dominion over' their fellow creatures (thus NRSV's translation of וכבשה ורדו). That this should be necessary is sometimes explained by the *Chaoskampf* theory,[68] the view that creation was

62. J. Goldingay, *The Message of Isaiah 40–55* (London: T & T Clark International, 2005), 348.

63. Childs, *Biblical Theology*, 397.

64. Fretheim, *God*, 40.

65. Fretheim, *God*, 40.

66. See O.H. Steck, *World and Environment* (Nashville: Abingdon Press, 1980), 67.

67. Fretheim, *God*, 41.

68. See e.g. A. Schüle, *Der Prolog the hebräischen Bibel* (ATANT, 86; Zurich: TVZ,

the result of God's battle with and victory over the forces of chaos represented by the 'deep' (תהום) in 1.2. It was Gunkel who suggested that תהום be identified with Tiamat, the Babylonian goddess in the Mesopotamian creation myths, whose carcass was used by Marduk to create heaven and earth.[69] Gunkel's theory has found many followers,[70] but others have rejected his conclusions,[71] arguing that תהום derives from the Proto-Semitic term *tihām-* ('ocean'), which usually refers to the underground waters, and that the phrase תהו ובהו, another bone of contention, signifies not chaos but merely a desolate and empty earth.[72]

It will not be possible to engage in a full discussion of the issues surrounding the terms תהום and תהו ובהו, but it is in any case evident that Genesis 1 does not develop the notion of primordial combat. In contrast to poetic passages, such as Job 26.7-14; Pss. 74.12-17 and 89.10-15, the emphasis is on God's unchallenged mastery during the process of creation. In this respect, Genesis differs significantly from other Ancient Near Eastern creation texts. Yet, the conclusion that it features absolutely no notion of *creatio ex tumulto* (creation out of chaos) again appears to reflect prior commitments on the part of Christian and Jewish interpreters.[73] While such commitments are perfectly acceptable in principle,[74]

2006), who speaks of the *dominium terrae* in connection with the primordial chaos, arguing that creation in Genesis 1 is best characterized as *creatio ex tumulto*.

69. H. Gunkel, *Creation and Chaos in the Primeval Era and the Eschaton* (Grand Rapids: Eerdmans, 2006), originally published as *Schöpfung und Chaos in Urzeit und Endzeit* in 1895.

70. See e.g. J. Day, *God's Conflict with the Dragon and the Sea* (Cambridge: Cambridge University Press, 1985) and B.F. Batto, *Slaying the Dragon* (Louisville: Westminster John Knox Press, 1992).

71. See A. Heidel, *The Babylonian Genesis* (Chicago: University of Chicago Press, 2nd edn, 1951), 98–101; and J.R. Middleton, 'Creation Founded in Love', in L.J. Greenspoon and B.F. LeBeau (eds.), *Sacred Text, Secular Times* (Omaha: Creighton University Press, 2000), 47–85.

72. Thus D.T. Tsumura, *Creation and Destruction* (Winona Lake: Eisenbrauns, 2005).

73. An example of this is J.R. Middleton's interpretation of Genesis 1 in *The Liberating Image* (Grand Rapids: Brazos Press, 2005). Wishing to articulate 'an alternative to the violent cosmogony of the chaos-cosmos scheme', Middleton is keen to detect this alternative in the Bible's opening chapter. With P. Trigo, *Creation and History* (Maryknoll: Orbis, 1991), he maintains that the goodness of God 'is more primordial than either evil or the struggle against evil'; and he needs Genesis 1 to make that point so that readers of scripture, having been inoculated, as it were, by that text, are enabled to then 'face squarely the presence of cosmogonic conflict' in other texts that may be experienced 'as difficult, even repugnant' (see Middleton, *Liberating Image*, 266–69).

74. The recognition that interpreters inevitably read from a specific perspective is now commonplace, and many would maintain that we have every right to be an 'interested

it is important that our contemporary perspective (Christian or otherwise) does not eclipse the voice of the textual 'Other'.[75]

Christian interpretation has frequently understood Genesis 1 as depicting a perfect creation. However, following the lead of Irenaeus, who argued that although creation was unqualifiedly good it was not perfect,[76] Fretheim maintains: 'that the divine command, "subdue the earth," is needed at all means that the evaluative word *good* does not mean perfect; the creation is not a static reality, forever fixed just as God initially created it.'[77] Yet, although Fretheim does not regard the creation as perfect, he is nonetheless adamant that the notion of creation as a victory over chaos is 'represented only on the edges of the Hebrew Bible' and 'only in poetry'.[78] We may note in passing that he thus admits to these traces being present, but it is more imperative to observe that his reasons for downplaying the notion of *creatio ex tumulto* are primarily of a theological nature. According to Fretheim,

> if evil is a precreation reality, then (unless one opts for certain forms of dualism) it has its origins in God . . . To opt for an eternal dualism is to claim that something comes into being without God, and the claim that God is the Creator of all is a compromised confession.[79]

While I appreciate Fretheim's concerns about an eternal dualism, the decisive question regarding Genesis 1 is whether these concerns were shared and therefore addressed by the biblical writers. Levenson's remarks on *Gen. Rab.* 1.5 are instructive here. This text illustrates that the notion that God created out of a malignant substratum represented by the phrase תהו ובהו had already been entertained by ancient Jewish Midrash:

> Rav said: . . . In human practice, when a king builds a palace in a place of sewers, dung, and garbage, if anyone comes and says, 'This palace is built on

party', to put it in the words of D.J.A. Clines (see his *Interested Parties* [JSOTSup, 205; Sheffield: Sheffield Academic Press, 1995]). One of the consequences of the rise of ideological approaches in the postmodern context has been the development of a fresh opportunity for the pursuit of theological interpretation of scripture as exemplified, for instance, by the recently established *Journal of Theological Interpretation*.

75. See A.C. Thiselton, *Interpreting God and the Postmodern Self* (Edinburgh: T & T Clark, 1995), 51, who calls for 'attentive respect', arguing that a text deserves 'respect for the otherness of the Other as Other'.

76. Irenaeus, *Adversus Haereses* iv, 38; see R.E. Brown, 'On the Necessary Imperfection of Creation', *SJT* 28 (1975), 17–25.

77. Fretheim, *God*, 276.

78. See the discussion in Fretheim, *God*, 12–13.

79. Fretheim, *God*, 13 and 298, n. 59.

sewers, dung, and garbage,' does he not pronounce it defective? Therefore, if anyone comes and says, 'This world was created out of chaos [*tōhû wābōhû*],' does he not pronounce it defective? Rabbi Huna said in the name of Bar Qappara: If the thing were not in Scripture, it would be impossible to say it! 'In the beginning God created heaven and earth.' Out of what? 'The earth was chaos [*tōhû wābōhû*].'[80]

This discussion between the early Jewish Amora Abba Arika, known as Rav, and his disciple Huna is pertinent to the modern debate not only because it reflects the same 'dilemma' that the biblical text's theology is deemed problematic because of its qualification of the goodness of God's creation but, more importantly, because it leads to the conclusion that theological doctrine must not trump the Torah.[81]

Fretheim somewhat grudgingly accepts that some biblical texts talk about creation in terms of a victory over chaos, but his desire to confine those texts to 'the edges of the Hebrew Bible' exemplifies a widespread struggle with the fact that the thing, i.e. *creatio ex tumulto*, is in scripture. As Levenson notes, 'the language of combat, victory, and enthronement that is prominent in so many biblical creation texts is not [always] given its due'.[82] And pointing out that Gen. 1.1–2.3 'deals in large part with the question of how to neutralize the powerful and ongoing threat of chaos',[83] he worries about a 'false finality or definitiveness' being ascribed to God's creation, which leads to 'the fragility of the created order and its vulnerability to chaos' being downplayed.[84]

Who then is right? Does the Genesis creation account talk about or assume a *creatio ex tumulto* or does it not? There is, to be sure, no actual *Chaoskampf* in Genesis 1. The passage does not talk about primordial combat, and it emphasizes the complete and unchallenged mastery of Israel's God in creation. However, that notwithstanding, there are several textual hints that suggest that the notion of *creatio ex tumulto* features in the background as something that is taken for granted by the biblical writers.[85] All too often, the discussion has

---

80. *Gen. Rab.* 1.5, as quoted (and translated) by J.D. Levenson, *Creation and the Persistence of Evil* (Princeton: Princeton University Press, 1994), xx.

81. See Levenson, *Creation*, xx.

82. Levenson, *Creation*, xxv.

83. Levenson, *Creation*, xxx.

84. Levenson, *Creation*, xxix.

85. Goldingay, *Old Testament Theology*, vol. 1, 73–74, aptly comments that 'whatever conflict Yhwh had been involved in did not imply that Yhwh experienced any insuperable difficulty in achieving or asserting sovereignty over primeval elements of the universe. But their needing to be confined implies they have the capacity to work in negative ways'.

focused on Gunkel's theory regarding the link between the Hebrew term תהום and the Babylonian goddess Tiamat[86] while failing to pay proper attention to the logic of the story as a whole.

Even if we were to disregard the terms תהום and תהו ובהו altogether, the conclusion that the notion of *creatio ex tumulto* lies in the background of Genesis 1 would still be warranted. To begin with, the waters are not identified as God's creation, unless we understand Gen. 1.1 as depicting a comprehensive creative act on the first day that embraces everything. Our interpretation depends upon the question whether v. 1 is a temporal clause that is dependent upon a main clause in v. 2 ('In the beginning when God created . . . the earth was a formless void')[87] or in v. 3, in which case v. 2 would be a parenthetical comment ('When God began to create heaven and earth – the earth being unformed and void . . . – God said'),[88] or whether it is to be construed as an independent sentence ('In the beginning God created the heavens and the earth').[89] Taking v. 1 as an independent clause entails two further possibilities in that it could be regarded as a title or superscription that stands outside the six-day pattern of creation or as the first act of creation.

Because the grammatical construction is open to different construals, theological convictions about the subject impinge upon the decisions made by translators and commentators alike. However, given the wider intellectual context in which our text originated and the logic of the story, there are good reasons for taking v. 1 as a dependent temporal clause.[90]

If it thus appears that the waters may be pre-creational, they certainly are presented as something that needs to be contained (1.6-7, 9–10).[91] As we noted earlier, the process of creation is presented as a series of separations, which are about containment and the setting of boundaries. Levenson is right to complain that 'the creation and maintenance of boundaries, which . . . is essential to the Priestly (P) conception of creation, [tends to be] downplayed and ignored'.[92]

---

86. See e.g. Tsumura, *Creation*.

87. Thus NRSV, NAB.

88. TNK.

89. ESV, NIV, NJB.

90. R.D. Holmstedt, 'The Restrictive Syntax of Genesis i 1', *VT* 58 (2008), 56–67, seeking to do justice to the fact that the opening word of Gen. 1.1 is בְּרֵאשִׁית rather than בָּרֵאשִׁית, has argued that v. 1 is an unmarked, restrictive relative clause, translating it 'In the initial period that/in which God created the heavens and the earth . . .' (65). For further discussion, see W.P. Brown, *Structure, Role, and Ideology in the Hebrew and Greek Texts of Genesis 1:1–2:3* (SBLDS, 132; Atlanta: Scholars Press, 1993), 62–73; and M. Bauks, *Die Welt am Anfang* (WMANT, 74; Neukirchen-Vluyn: Neukirchener Verlag, 1997), 65–92.

91. This 'negative' assessment of the sea is still reflected in Rev. 21.1.

92. Levenson, *Creation*, xxv.

However, it is not only the waters that appear to be pre-creational, for the same can be said of the darkness,[93] which needs to be contained as well (1.4). Since there is no mention of the darkness being created by God, Levenson criticizes Niebuhr's definition of 'radical monotheism', which is expressed as 'the confidence that whatever is, is good, because it exists as one thing, among the many which all have their origin and their being in the One – the principle of being which is also the principle of value'.[94] As Levenson points out, 'the effect of Niebuhr's "radical monotheism" . . . is to remove that crucial separation, that crucial boundary, between light and darkness, as if the scripture had actually read:

> God said, "Let there be darkness and light"; and there were darkness and light, and God saw that both darkness and light were good.'[95]

To be sure, in order to underline God's total control over his creation it can also be said of him, 'I form light and create darkness' (ובורא חשך) (Isa. 45.7). Here, as in Amos 3.6, Israel's God is affirmed as 'the sole source of good and evil, of light and darkness, of life and death'.[96] However, this is not the vision of Genesis 1, just as it is evident that in some biblical traditions, most notably in the apocalyptic literature, rival powers are depicted as posing a challenge to Yhwh, a challenge that will need to be overcome.

It thus appears that the Old Testament contains both the roots of a 'radical monotheism' (although not in the definition of Niebuhr, according to which everything that exists is good), which avoids any hint of dualism, and of an at least implicit dualistic understanding that regards the forces of evil as pre-creational yet under the control of Israel's God.[97] It is the latter notion that underlies Genesis 1, which presents a God who is in supreme control throughout and succeeds quite effortlessly in setting the boundaries that are meant to keep all destructive elements at bay.

Another narrative clue that supports an underlying notion of *creatio ex tumulto*

---

93. Löning and Zenger, *To Begin with*, 18, list four pre-creational elements: 'the *tohu-wabohu* earth', the darkness, the primeval ocean and the waters.

94. Thus H.R. Niebuhr, *Radical Monotheism and Western Culture* (New York: Harper & Row, 1943), 32, as quoted in Levenson, *Creation*, xxiii.

95. Levenson, *Creation*, xxiv.

96. B.W. Anderson, *Creation versus Chaos* (Philadelphia: Fortress Press, 1987), 151.

97. Goldingay, *Old Testament Theology*, vol. 1, 75, notes that the Old Testament features three perspectives on the origin of evil in that it can be located within the godhead, attributed to human rebellion against God or regarded as a supernatural force that asserts itself against God.

is God's command to humankind to subdue the earth and have dominion over it (1.28). The second verb, רדה, essentially means 'rule'. It features prominently in royal language in the Old Testament and is frequently used with the preposition ב to refer to the subjects of that rule. There are implications of violence in some passages, but the dominion envisaged by this term does not inherently require force.[98] Regarding its use in Gen. 1.28, Zobel concludes that human dominion 'derives from being made in the image of God and is understood as an aspect of God's blessing'. Hence, 'human rule must have positive consequences for the ruled; in ruling, humans must preserve their humanity and remain humane'.[99]

The other term, כבש, is even stronger in force. Its principal meaning is 'subdue', and it is used, for instance, with reference to the land (Num. 32.22; Josh. 18.1; 1 Chron. 22.18). According to Wagner, 'to "subdue" [the land] means primarily to conquer and subdue its previous population, but also to make use of all [its] economic and cultural potential'.[100] As Hamilton notes, the population's military subjection is clearly included in this[101] (see 2 Sam. 8.11). Apart from this, כבש can also refer to the subjection of individuals to slavery (2 Chron. 28.10; Neh. 5.5; Jer. 34.11, 16)[102] and to sexual assault (Est. 7.8).[103]

Commentators on Genesis 1 appropriately stress that the terms כבש and רדה ב need to be understood in the light of the context in which they appear. This speaks of humankind's creation in the image of God and of God's blessing, thus providing important pointers as to how humanity's rule over creation is to be understood. However, von Rad correctly saw that the expressions used in Gen. 1.28 for humankind's dominion are 'remarkably strong',[104] and Davis cautions against a perceived tendency to downplay the force of כבש in particular.[105] Such a tendency is evident in Hamilton's claim that 'it appears unlikely that we need to transfer the nuance of force . . . into the use of *kābaš* in Gen. 1:28'.[106] While the human rule envisaged here is clearly meant to be a channel of God's blessing, it is less obvious that this necessarily excludes any aspect of force. We need to be careful not to sanitize the text to make it conform to our modern sensibilities regarding issues such as force and violence.

98. See H.-J. Zobel, 'רָדָה *rādâ*; רָדָה *rādâ* II; רָדַד *rādad*', in *TDOT* 13 (2004), 330–36.
99. Zobel, 'רָדָה', 335.
100. S. Wagner, 'כָּבַשׁ *kābaš*; כֶּבֶשׁ *kebeš*; כִּבְשָׁן *kibšān*', in *TDOT* 7 (1995), 52–57 (54).
101. V.P. Hamilton, *The Book of Genesis: Chapters 1–17* (NICOT; Grand Rapids: Eerdmans, 1990), 139.
102. See Hamilton, *Genesis*, 139; and Wagner, 'כָּבַשׁ', 54–55.
103. See J.D. Levenson, *Esther* (OTL; London: SCM Press, 1997), 104.
104. G. von Rad, *Genesis* (OTL; Philadelphia: Westminster Press, rev. edn, 1972), 60.
105. E.F. Davis, *Scripture, Culture, and Agriculture* (Cambridge: Cambridge University Press, 2009), 59.
106. Hamilton, *Genesis*, 139.

Perhaps Davis is correct to suggest that the authors of Genesis 1 intended their audience to be startled by the command to 'conquer' the earth, as she puts it, and to puzzle over its meaning.[107] She also aptly highlights the agrarian dimensions of the text, but I am not convinced that she has truly made a case for the conclusion that there is 'no awareness of a primordial struggle' and that humans are 'the source of most if not all threats to the integrity of the created order'.[108] In Genesis, humans are indeed the source of most threats to the created order, but that is precisely the irony which the story seeks to convey. Having been enlisted by God to maintain his good creation by keeping the forces of evil permanently at bay, humanity turns out to be the biggest problem. This becomes more and more evident as the story progresses (see below). But to return to Genesis 1, the harshness implied in the terms כבש and רדה ב should not be explained away. Yes, human rule is intended to be a channel of the divine blessing, and yet our writers are implying that some kind of force will be required because of what Levenson has called the 'persistence of evil' in God's good creation.[109]

This understanding of Genesis 1 in terms of creation out of chaos and the concomitant view that the human task of ruling over the earth requires force has been criticized by Middleton, who seeks to offer a paradigm for non-violent human agency in a world filled with violence. Middleton argues against Levenson that the notion of primordial combat is ethically problematic because of its inherent ethnocentric perspective,[110] as is confirmed by the use of *Enuma Eliš*'s combat myth to support Neo-Babylonian imperial aspirations. Indeed, Middleton notes that 'in the contemporary world . . . a democratized *imago Dei* combined with the us/them framework of the chaos-cosmos scheme may harbor significant potential for the legitimation of human violence at numerous levels'.[111]

He is therefore particularly worried by the idea, suggested by Batto, that Genesis 1 'was intended to address Israel's sense of injustice and disenfranchisement during the Babylonian exile',[112] because this would merely 'turn Israel into a mirror image of its enemy'.[113] What Middleton is looking for in Genesis 1 is 'a genuine alternative worldview', because 'if Genesis 1 did utilize some version of the chaos-cosmos scheme to articulate God's creation of

---

107. Davis, *Scripture*, 60.
108. Davis, *Scripture*, 63.
109. Levenson, *Creation*.
110. Middleton, *Liberating Image*, 251.
111. Middleton, *Liberating Image*, 254.
112. These are Middleton's words (*Liberating Image*, 260), with reference to B. F. Batto, 'Creation Theology in Genesis', in Clifford and Collins (eds.), *Creation*, 16–38.
113. Middleton, *Liberating Image*, 261.

the world, this would seal the ideological triumph of Mesopotamia'.[114] Several comments are in order in response to Middleton's reading of Genesis.

1. As already noted, our passage does not dwell upon the concept of primordial conflict; there is no description of combat that resembles *Enuma Eliš*. And yet the notion of *creatio ex tumulto* is assumed by the biblical writers, who are, however, adamant that the forces that in *Enuma Eliš* can only be overcome by excessive violence pose no threat to Israel's God. It is in that sense that Genesis speaks about 'creation without opposition'.[115] Israel's God is of such stature that there cannot be any genuine opposition. Thus, rather than to lead to 'profound anxiety and a sense of constant threat', as Middleton worries,[116] the theology of creation expressed in Genesis 1 offers an 'answer to anxiety and resignation in the face of catastrophic experiences of the world and of life'.[117]

2. Middleton's unease regarding the dangers of ethnocentrism and nationalism is understandable, given the case of the *Enuma Eliš* epic. Indeed, further examples could be cited, including biblical texts like Psalm 89 where the connection of the cosmic battle with the monarchy has led Clifford to suggest that 'the psalm regards the founding of the house of David as part of the foundation of the world just as several Mesopotamian cosmogonies list the king and the temple as things created at the beginning'.[118] As Levenson notes, 'it is now the Davidic throne that guarantees cosmic stability, the continuation of the order established through primeval combat. In Psalm 89, as in the *Enuma elish*, the bond between the exaltation of the deity and the imperial politics of his earthly seat of power is patent'.[119] Middleton thus concludes that 'even in the Bible, the combat myth – particularly when connected to creation – could serve to ground Israel's historical exercise of cultic and

---

114. Middleton, *Liberating Image*, 262.
115. Thus Levenson, *Creation*, 127.
116. Middleton, *Liberating Image*, 256.
117. Thus Löning and Zenger, *To Begin with*, 25; similarly Goldingay, *Old Testament Theology*, vol. 1, 74. Another positive reception of Levenson's reading of Genesis 1 is found in R.W.L. Moberly, *The Theology of the Book of Genesis* (Cambridge: Cambridge University Press, 2009), 57, who picks up on Levenson's comments regarding the role of the cult in 'build[ing] and maintain[ing] order, transform[ing] chaos into creation, ennobl[ing] humanity, and realiz[ing] the kingship of . . . God' (*Creation*, 127), noting that Levenson 'leaves the reader with a sense of the role of human obedience and worship in maintaining Genesis 1's vision of the world, which one would not have otherwise'.
118. R.J. Clifford, 'Creation in the Psalms', in idem and Collins (eds.), *Creation*, 57–69 (63).
119. Levenson, *Creation*, 22–23.

political/military power (by which the human world is ordered) in God's primordial (violent) ordering of the cosmos'.[120]

This is not the place to comment on Psalm 89, but it bears pointing out that Genesis 1 features no obvious ethnocentric or nationalistic tendencies. Middleton is of course aware of its universalist mould but worries that this might be a 'false universalism'[121] in that the seemingly universal language may not have been thus understood. But whether Priestly or not,[122] the creation account in Genesis 1 functions, as Middleton himself rightly maintains, as an aetiology of all nations (see Genesis 10),[123] not just Israel, as von Rad had argued.[124] There is thus no evidence in these chapters that the concept of *creatio ex tumulto*, which anyway only exists in the form of an undercurrent and is not developed in the same gory details known from Mesopotamian texts, necessarily goes hand in glove with ethnocentric or nationalistic predispositions.

3. Finally, in response to Middleton's concerns about the combat myth leading to and justifying violence, we should note that Gen. 1.28 does not envisage intra-human strife but the rule of *all* of humanity over God's creation. We have already seen that this rule is meant to be a blessing for the rest of creation; and it is indeed of great significance that Genesis 1 does not present a scenario of violent combat so that the God who emerges from these lines can serve as a paradigm for responsible human agency and the human exercise of power. However, the force of the verbs used in Gen. 1.28 does suggest that the human task envisaged here may involve some kind of struggle.

In order to understand the nature of this struggle, we must return to the logic of the Genesis story, which will also allow us to appreciate that an underlying notion of *creatio ex tumulto* and the persistence of evil helps to explain the development of the plot. Without prejudging the question of how the Garden of Eden story is best understood, it is clear that, when we get to the Cain and Abel story in Genesis 4, sin (חטאת), personified in the form of a wild beast or some other malevolent being (many commentators think of a demon here),[125]

120. Middleton, *Liberating Image*, 250.

121. Middleton, *Liberating Image*, 205.

122. Middleton is not convinced of the text's Priestly provenance (*Liberating Image*, 205).

123. Middleton, *Liberating Image*, 252 n. 48.

124. G. von Rad, *Old Testament Theology*, vol. 1 (Edinburgh: Oliver & Boyd, 1962), 138.

125. For discussions of the portrayal of sin in this verse see e.g. von Rad, *Genesis*, 105; and Wenham, *Genesis 1–15*, 105–106. That sin may be spoken of as a demon is particularly interesting in the light of Trigo's suggestion that the conception of creation as the

has appeared on the scene. Whence did it come, and how did it get introduced into the world? What role did the serpent of Genesis 3 play, and how could any of this have happened in God's good creation? These and similar questions have exercised many a reader in the reception history of our passage.

The theological and philosophical questions regarding the origins of evil are important, but in the context of the plot of the Bible's opening chapters there is no need for an explanation. God's creation was good, very good even (טוב מאד; 1.31), and yet the continued presence of evil does not come as a surprise to the attentive reader. Although God had succeeded in curtailing the realm of evil by setting the requisite boundaries, there is a sense of evil's persistence.

However, to aid him in his endeavour to keep evil permanently at bay God had entrusted humanity with the task of subduing the earth. But rather than to master (משל) sin, as Cain is told to do in 4.7, humanity proves susceptible to the advances of the forces of evil and chaos, thus making it necessary for God to intervene repeatedly in the course of the story in order to keep his project on track. A particularly striking example of God's continuing involvement with his creation in Genesis 1–11 is the Flood story, which is often understood in terms of de-creation and re-creation. Together with the Cain and Abel story and, for instance, the Lamech episode (Gen. 4.19-24), it serves to condemn human violence (see the reference to חמס in 6.11), which confirms that traces of the combat myth do not necessarily 'serve to ground human violence', as Middleton worries.[126]

What has been here described as God's continuing creation in the context of the persistence of evil has often been understood as God's redemptive work.[127] But, as Fretheim points out, it is equally possible to understand redemption in terms of creation, as in Isa. 43.1-2; 45.11; 54.5, 14, where several of the words used for creation (e.g. ברא, יצר and עשה) are employed to refer to God's salvific intervention in his people's history.[128] Isaiah thus invites us to conceptualize God's redemptive and salvific work, which is expressly understood with reference to Genesis 1–2, as his continuing work of creation. Rather than to drive a wedge between God's work of creation and his redemptive and salvific

conquest of chaos serves to demonize one's opponents (see Trigo, *Creation*). It is highly significant that our text does not demonize human opponents but חטאת as a personified representation of the evil that still persists in God's good creation.

126. Middleton, *Liberating Image*, 236.

127. See G. von Rad, 'The Theological Problem of the Old Testament Doctrine of Creation', in idem, *From Genesis to Chronicles* (Minneapolis: Fortress Press, 2005), 177–86, according to whom Israel's faith is 'primarily concerned with redemption' (177).

128. Fretheim, *God*, 10.

activities,[129] it therefore seems preferable, in certain cases, to speak with Fretheim of God's *originating* creation in Genesis 1–2 vis-à-vis his *continuing* creation elsewhere.[130]

It might justifiably be argued that it is preferable to make a clear conceptual distinction between the categories of creation, redemption/salvation and sustenance. And yet, it is important that we do not reject the biblical witness's invitation to conceptualize the latter two categories as God's creation. Not only would this prevent us from perceiving the particular thrust of the Old Testament's conceptuality of creation; it would also exacerbate the tendency of erecting a barrier between God's original creation and his ongoing creational engagement with it. I should perhaps add, however, that I am not suggesting that the notions of creation and redemption be generally collapsed into one another. Even in Deutero-Isaiah where creation and redemption are 'very closely connected' the two do not generally merge.[131] The point rather is that some passages compel us to think of God's redemption in terms of his continuous creation, and this is an insight worth having.

The thrust of my argument thus far has been to suggest that the portrayal of God as Creator in Genesis 1–2 is far more nuanced than is often allowed for. Thus, while the biblical writers celebrate[132] the supremacy and sovereignty of the Creator God, it would appear to be a dogmatically inspired overstatement to claim that their aim was to portray his activity as Creator as being entirely without analogy.

The God we meet in Genesis 1–2 is depicted as unique in some respects, and yet the language chosen by the biblical writers in other important ways relates him to his creatures, who have been created in order to participate in God's ongoing work of creation. This is evident not only in the command to subdue the earth in 1.28, but also in the task given to האדם of naming and thus assessing the animals in terms of their potential suitability as a partner (2.18-20). This, in turn, not only leads God to engage in further creational activity but also in itself continues the creative process in that naming involves 'a discernment of the place of the creature in relationship to other creatures'.[133] In naming his fellow

---

129. As Löning and Zenger, *To Begin with*, 189, have stressed, in the biblical understanding 'the theology of creation and soteriology are . . . inextricably linked'. See also Levenson, *Creation*, xxi.

130. In addition to redemption, this also includes God's sustaining of his creation (see Anderson, *From Creation*, 89; and Van Leeuwen, 'ברא', 730).

131. See C. Westermann, *Isaiah 40–66* (OTL; Philadelphia: Westminster Press, 1969), 25.

132. For a 'liturgical reading' of Genesis 1–2, see S.E. Balentine, *The Torah's Vision of Worship* (Minneapolis: Fortress Press, 1999), ch. 4.

133. Thus Fretheim, *God*, p. 41.

creatures, האדם thus contributes to the ordering of God's creation, a process that is at the heart of the account in Genesis 1.

Having thus underlined the correspondences between God and his creatures in terms of their respective creative potential, some comments are required regarding the mode of creation by means of God's word, which is frequently taken as an indication of the biblical writers' intention to portray God and his creative work as 'wholly other'.[134] The undue stress that is sometimes put on this concept to the neglect of any textual signs that suggest a more complex picture is due to the fact that in the later development of Christian doctrine the notion of creation by God's word was used to reject Gnostic conceptions of creation as a divine emanation. Von Rad's reading illustrates this when he notes that 'the idea of creation by the word preserves first of all the most radical essential distinction between Creator and creature. Creation cannot be even remotely considered an emanation from God'.[135]

There is an undeniable focus in Genesis 1 on God speaking and on his word being 'powerful and of the highest creative potency'.[136] Both the announcement formula 'and God said' and the concomitant fulfilment formula 'and it was so' emphasize God's transcendence and his ability to create in ways that are unmatched by anyone else. But we must not overlook that God's creating in Genesis 1–2 also involves deeds of separation (e.g. 1.6-7); his speaking with others, which invites their participation in the process of creation (1.11); his use of 'raw materials' in the creation of still other creatures, leading to a portrayal of God as a potter (2.7-8, 19), a surgeon and a builder (2.21-22); and his ordering of creation, partly by means of naming that which has been created (1.5, 8, 10), a process that human beings are invited to participate in (2.19-20).[137] Commenting in particular upon God's tactile engagement with his creation, as in the moulding of the animals and the first human being and the construction of the woman, Fretheim points out that the creator here 'comes into the closest possible contact with material reality' and that to stress God's transcendence in such a way that this very tangible involvement is spiritualized, discounted or denigrated runs the risk of resulting in a deistic understanding of God vis-à-vis his creation.[138]

---

134. Egyptian texts have shown that the concept of creation by the divine word is not unique to Israel (see R.J. Clifford, *Creation Accounts in the Ancient Near East and in the Bible* [CBQMS, 26; Washington: Catholic Biblical Association, 1994], 106–107, 110–12, 114).

135. Von Rad, *Genesis*, 51; see also Fretheim, *God*, 37.

136. Thus again Von Rad, *Genesis*, 52.

137. See Fretheim, *God*, 34–35.

138. Fretheim, *God*, 39.

Sometimes, the two modes of creation, i.e. by word and/or deed, have given rise to redaction-critical speculations that two originally different accounts, a 'deed account' and a 'word account', have been combined in our passage.[139] This is not the place to discuss the plausibility of this proposal, but it is instructive to note that the canonical text alternates between the two modes more or less throughout, thus suggesting that this expresses precisely how our writers understood God's creative work. Both God's word and his deeds were needed, as is evident in 1.6-7 where the words 'And God said, "Let there be a dome"' give way to the statement 'So God made the dome'. Fretheim rightly concludes that 'God does not create so much by "word events" [or "deed events", one might add] as by "word-deed events"'.[140]

3. *Summary and Concluding Reflections*

Where then does this discussion of the images of God and creation in Genesis 1–2 leave us? To conclude, I would like to summarize and briefly reflect on some of the main points, touching upon three areas in particular: (1) the portrayal of God as transcendent and immanent; (2) the relational theology detected by Fretheim (and others); and (3) the theological assumptions and commitments of the interpreter vis-à-vis the voice of the ancient text.

1. It has long been noted that God is portrayed in Genesis 1–2 as both transcendent and immanent. As we saw above, however, there has been a tendency in Christian exegetical and theological engagement with our passage to elevate the notion of God's transcendence and neglect or downplay his immanence. This trend appears to have weakened in recent years, and it should be pointed out anyway that my aim has not been to reverse it. Both concepts have to be held together. The portrayal of the deity in Genesis 1–2 is complex: God is transcendent, but he is also immanent; he is without analogy in some respects (who among us could have created the heavens and the earth?), and yet he corresponds to and is comparable to us (or rather we to him) in other ways.

    Fretheim rightly stresses that, because the biblical account opens with Genesis 1, the divine characteristics highlighted in that chapter, including God's incomparable power and transcendence, should stand in the foreground

---

139. See e.g. C. Levin, 'Tatbericht und Wortbericht in der priesterschriftlichen Schöpfungserzählung', in idem, *Fortschreibungen* (BZAW, 316; Berlin: de Gruyter, 2003), 23–39; and M. Arneth, *Durch Adams Fall ist ganz verderbt . . .* (FRLANT, 217; Göttingen: Vandenhoeck & Ruprecht, 2007), 22–32.

140. Fretheim, *God*, 38.

of our thinking about creation.[141] And yet it is equally important to note not only that this initial portrayal of the Creator gives way to the picture of an immanent, intimate and involved deity in Genesis 2, but also that the depiction of God even in Genesis 1 is more complex than is often allowed for. As we saw above, notions such as that ברא is used only with God as subject, that it denotes a *creatio ex nihilo*, and that there are no concepts either of a *creatio continua* or of a *creatio ex tumulto* seek to curtail the picture presented by the biblical writers in ways that appear to be shaped more by the theology of the interpreter than by what is demanded by the biblical text itself.

2. The images of God and creation presented in Genesis 1–2 invite the concept of a relational theology of creation. When Patrick and Scult maintain that 'human beings cannot engage the world presented to them as co-creators',[142] they are correct in the sense that our text speaks of God's initial acts of creation as being prior to any human action and as having been performed without the involvement of any other creatures (or deities). However, when they then argue that 'P's vision of God's authorship . . . forecloses any significant story that might follow' and that 'humans have no creative potential of their own to serve as the basis for more story',[143] they close down the possibility for the creative interplay between the two accounts in Genesis 1 and 2 that their canonical pairing demands. Although the placement of P's version does invite us to keep God's transcendence in the foreground, it is equally clear that, canonically speaking, this is not the last word.

The gist of the canonical text has been captured more aptly by Fretheim, who notes that 'God's sovereignty is understood, not in terms of absolute divine control, but as a sovereignty that gives power over to the created for the sake of a relationship of integrity'.[144] Welker similarly maintains that

> the classical creation accounts emphasize the connectedness and cooperation of creator and that which is creaturely. In no way do the creation accounts of Genesis offer only a gloomy picture of sheer dependence. God's creative action does not confront that which is created with completely finished facts. The creature's own activity as a constitutive element in the process of creation is seen in harmony with God's action.[145]

---

141. Fretheim, *God*, 271. Von Rad, 'Theological Problem', 178, by contrast, regarded the placement of Genesis 1 at the beginning of the Bible as a mere 'circumstance'.

142. Patrick and Scult, *Rhetoric*, 119.

143. Patrick and Scult, *Rhetoric*, 117.

144. Fretheim, *God*, 272.

145. M. Welker, 'What Is Creation?', *Theology Today* 47 (1991), 56–71 (64).

The involvement of the creatures in the project of creation has not been within the purview of the present discussion (and may need to be explored elsewhere), but the portrayal of God in Genesis 1–2 clearly warrants a relational understanding of creation.

3. Another important issue for reflection concerns the theological commitments of the interpreter vis-à-vis the voice of the ancient text, especially given the strong revival of interest in theological interpretation of the Bible that we have been witnessing in recent years. I welcome this trend, but it will be important to guard against the danger of the interpreter's theological commitments eclipsing the textual voice. This is not a new danger, however, as we saw with reference to modern scholarship and ancient Jewish Midrash. Interpreters ancient and modern, Christian and Jewish, have always struggled to hear the voice of the text over against their own theological commitments and traditions. It is a struggle we all face.

But there is a bigger issue here, which is perhaps best outlined in the form of a question: Does theological interpretation, i.e. reading the Bible as the Church's scripture, require a 'dogmatic reading' of Genesis 1–2? In other words, is it important, in order to guard against dualistic and Gnostic ideas of creation, to find the notion of *creatio ex nihilo* in Genesis 1? And would similar reasons require us to be able to exclude an underlying concept of *creatio ex tumulto* in the Bible's opening chapter? I think not. Jewish and Christian theology have evolved over the course of many centuries and even millennia, and there are reasons as to why the development has taken the forms that it has. The theology of Genesis 1–2, with its focus upon the one creator God, has been a significant milestone en route as far as the advancements of Jewish and Christian reflection upon creation are concerned, but we must also recognize the limitations of our passage's contribution to this reflection. Some developments in our thinking about creation clearly post-date the Genesis creation account, but that in no way diminishes the beauty and profundity of the Bible's opening chapters.[146]

It is an honour and a great pleasure to have the opportunity to offer this contribution to Professor Gordon McConville, a friend, mentor and former colleague of mine, whose prolific work in the areas of Old Testament exegesis and theology has been an inspiration for me for many years.

146. Parts of the research presented in this essay have been funded by Research and Creative Enterprise Services, Faculty of the Arts, University of Cumbria.

Chapter 2

THE PASSOVER IN EXODUS AND DEUTERONOMY: AN INTRODUCTORY EXAMINATION

Peter T. Vogt

Bethel Seminary

Introduction

The presentation of Passover in Exodus and Deuteronomy is a subject that has long been discussed, particularly in connection with the interpretation of Deuteronomy.[1] Recently, the topic has been explored by Gordon McConville and Bernard Levinson in a dialogue in the *Journal of Biblical Literature*.[2]

The purpose of this essay is not to repeat the arguments presented by McConville and Levinson, but rather to seek to build off their discussion and present a preliminary understanding of the differences between Exodus and Deuteronomy. I will in this essay seek to identify the problems and to offer some possibilities and trajectories towards resolving them.

1. *The Nature of the Problem*

The problem of Passover in Exodus and Deuteronomy is the fact that the festival appears to be treated very differently in the two books. First, there is a question as to whether or not the two festivals, Passover and Unleavened Bread (Massot), are intended to be understood as a single festival, or two separate ones. They are often seen as separate festivals in the book of Exodus. Regulations concerning Massot are found in Exod. 23.14-17, and this festival is presented there as

---

1. The presentation of Passover in Deuteronomy was discussed already in S.R. Driver, *Deuteronomy* (ICC, Edinburgh: T & T Clark, 1895), 190–95.

2. J.G. McConville, 'Deuteronomy's Unification of Passover and Massot: A Response to Bernard M. Levinson', *JBL* 119,1 (2000), 47–58; B.M. Levinson, 'The Hermeneutics of Tradition in Deuteronomy: A Reply to J.G. McConville', *JBL* 119, 2 (2000), 269–86.

one taking place אֶל־פְּנֵי הָאָדֹן יְהוָה ('before the Lord Yahweh'), clearly not in
the home. Passover, on the other hand, is described in Exodus 12–13. Unlike
Massot, Passover was to be eaten in the home. In addition, Exod. 12.5 limits
the Passover sacrifice to animals from the flock (i.e. sheep or goats), and Exod.
12.9 specifies that the Passover sacrifice is to be roasted, not boiled.

In Deuteronomy, on the other hand, the two festivals are combined, as may
be seen in Deut. 16.1-8. The legislation there opens with a command to שָׁמוֹר
אֶת־חֹדֶשׁ הָאָבִיב וְעָשִׂיתָ פֶּסַח לַיהוָה אֱלֹהֶיךָ ('Observe the month of Abib and carry out
Passover to Yahweh your God'[3]). This is similar to the command concerning
Massot in Exod. 23.15, but in Deuteronomy it is followed by a discussion of
Passover, not Massot. Moreover, the regulations concerning Passover include
the elimination of leaven, as seen by v. 3, which notes לֹא־תֹאכַל עָלָיו חָמֵץ ('You
shall not eat leaven with it'). In addition, Deuteronomy apparently alters the legislation from Exodus by allowing for the boiling of the sacrifice (Deut. 16.9), as
well as permitting animals from both flock and herd to be used for the Passover
sacrifice (Deut. 16.2).

Most striking, perhaps, is the fact that Deuteronomy specifically forbids the
celebration of Passover in the towns, demanding instead that it be carried out at
'The Place' that Yahweh would choose (Deut. 16.5). This stands in marked contrast to the presentation in Exodus, which demands that Passover be celebrated
in the homes (Exod. 12.7, 22, 46), and further states that the requirements are
to be kept 'as a statute for you and your children forever' (Exod. 12.24).

The differing presentations of Passover-Massot in Deuteronomy and Exodus
thus raise two issues. The first is whether the two festivals were understood as
separate celebrations in Exodus and were then combined in Deuteronomy. The
second issue is the significance of Deuteronomy's emphasis on 'The Place' in
connection with Passover-Massot. We will address these issues in turn.

2. *The Unification of Passover and Unleavened Bread*

Not surprisingly, many scholars have seen in Deuteronomy the combination of
various strata that originally related to either Passover or Massot.[4] Levinson,
on the other hand, has advanced the view that Deuteronomy's legislation
of Passover-Massot reflects a unique development in the history of Israel's

---

3. Biblical translations in this essay are mine unless otherwise indicated.
4. See e.g. R.E. Clements, *The Book of Deuteronomy* (Epworth Commentaries,
Peterborough, UK: Epworth, 2001), 71; A.D.H. Mayes, *Deuteronomy* (NCB, London:
Oliphants, 1979), 254–55; I. Cairns, *Word and Presence: A Commentary on the Book of
Deuteronomy* (International Theological Commentary, Grand Rapids: Eerdmans, 1992),
152–54.

religion. He maintains that Deuteronomy has revolutionized the festival, but has done so using the very lexemes of the earlier legislation. In his view, this serves to give the new legislation legitimacy as it appears to be congruent with the earlier material, while in fact it represents a radical innovation.[5]

In response, we should note first that it is far from certain that the two festivals are united for the first time in Deuteronomy. Indeed, Exod. 34.25 appears to see the two celebrations as united when, in the context of a series of commandments related to Massot, it refers explicitly to the sacrifice of Passover. The close connection between 'blood of my sacrifice' and 'sacrifice of the Feast of Passover' suggest that they are seen as related. Moreover, this verse uniquely makes specific reference to a 'feast' (חַג) of Passover, something that was applied only to Massot earlier. This verse, at least, appears to support the idea that the two festivals were combined, as Passover derives its status as a 'feast' through its connection to Massot.[6]

In addition, we should note that the material of Exod. 34.18-26 deals with the three pilgrimage festivals, as noted in vv. 22–24. The explicit reference to Passover in v. 25 in the context of the pilgrimage festivals further suggests that the author envisioned a combined pilgrimage festival of Passover-Massot.

Similarly, the legislation in Exodus 12 and 13 sits comfortably with the idea that the two festivals were conceived of as a single celebration. For example, Exod. 12.1-13 deals with Passover, and provides detailed instructions for its proper observation. Verse 14 then says, וְהָיָה הַיּוֹם הַזֶּה לָכֶם לְזִכָּרוֹן וְחַגֹּתֶם אֹתוֹ חַג לַיהוָה לְדֹרֹתֵיכֶם חֻקַּת עוֹלָם תְּחָגֻּהוּ ('This day will be a memorial for you, and you shall celebrate it as a feast to Yahweh. Throughout your generations, as an everlasting statute, you shall celebrate the feast'). Interestingly, the text goes on to provide instructions describing Massot in vv. 15–20. Then, v. 21 reverts to a discussion of Passover once again. If the author of Exodus is envisioning two separate feasts, he has not seemed constrained to delineate them clearly, as the regulations appear to blend, all describing a celebration referred to as הַיּוֹם הַזֶּה ('this day').[7]

Some scholars have attempted to solve the problem by maintaining that the

5. B.M. Levinson, *Deuteronomy and the Hermeneutics of Legal Innovation* (Oxford: Oxford University Press, 1997), 56.

6. D.K. Stuart, *Exodus* (New American Commentary, 2; Nashville: Broadman, 2006), 732, sees the use of 'Passover Feast' here as a synecdoche for the three festivals (Passover-Massot, Pentecost, and Ingathering/Booths) commanded to be carried out at the central sanctuary.

7. Note that Lev. 23.5-8 describes the two festivals sequentially. The passing reference to Passover and the more detailed discussion of Massot may point to their being seen as related, if not combined.

various texts in Exodus 12–13 represent different literary strata.[8] The challenges to this approach are well known, so there is no need to detail them here.[9] What I will add is that the attempt to identify and separate out literary strata in this section presupposes that the hypothetical final redactor of Exodus working in the seventh century BC was unaware of the difficulties he was creating in stitching together the sources in this manner. Yet it seems to me to be highly unlikely that a redactor would fail to see that his final product appears to envision a unified festival consisting of two separate, but intimately related, parts. It seems more likely that even such a redactor would have noted the presentation of the final form, and, therefore, that the final form of the text reflects the intentionality of the redactor.

A similar criticism can be levelled against Levinson's solution to the problem as well. Levinson maintains that, as part of a programme of radical reform in the Josianic period, Deuteronomy has combined the two festivals using the very terminology of the older sources in an attempt to demonstrate continuity with them. This is necessitated, in his view, by the reality of centralization carried out by Josiah.

In carrying out its reforms, Deuteronomy effectuates what Levinson calls a 'double transformation' of the previously separate festivals.[10] It transforms Passover from a private celebration in the home into a sacrifice that is all but completely 'assimilated to the standard sacrificial protocol'.[11] Passover thus becomes a pilgrimage festival, whereas it earlier was not. At the same time, Massot is denied its status as a pilgrimage festival.

McConville has noted that the terminology of Deuteronomy does not actually support such a view, as Deut. 16.16 explicitly refers to the 'festival' (חַג) of Unleavened Bread.[12] If the author of Deuteronomy were really trying to boldly reform religious practice in support of centralization, as Levinson argues, it seems likely that he would have had no concerns about referring to a 'festival

---

8. See, for example, W.H.C. Propp, *Exodus 1–18: A New Translation with Introduction and Commentary* (AB, 2; New York: Doubleday, 1999), 380–82; B.S. Childs, *Exodus* (OTL, London: SCM, 1974), 184–87.

9. In addition to the seminal work by R.N. Whybray, *The Making of the Pentateuch: A Methodological Study* (JSOTSup, 53; Sheffield: Sheffield Academic Press, 1987), see the recent discussion in J.H. Sailhamer, *The Meaning of the Pentateuch: Revelation, Composition, and Interpretation* (Downers Grove: InterVarsity, 2009), 283–415. See also G.J. Wenham, 'Pondering the Pentateuch: The Search for a New Paradigm', in Baker and Arnold (eds.), *The Face of Old Testament Studies: A Survey of Contemporary Approaches* (Grand Rapids: Baker, 1999), 116–44.

10. Levinson, *Legal Innovation*, 72–74.

11. Levinson, *Legal Innovation*, 72.

12. McConville, 'Passover and Massot', 50–51.

of Passover'. As we have seen, the author of Exodus referred to Passover as a 'festival' (חַג) in Exod. 34.25. Given Levinson's thesis that the Deuteronomic author used the lexemes from earlier texts to support his radical innovations, it seems surprising that the author of Deuteronomy does not refer to Passover as a 'festival' (חַג) and instead uses that language in connection with Massot.

As we have seen, Levinson's argument is based on the perceived reuse of vocabulary and syntax of the earlier law. He sees in the use of the words of the earlier law a radical hermeneutical 'transformation', such that the 'lemma is viewed atomistically: legal or textual authority operates at the level of individual words that, even when recontextualized, retain their operative force'.[13] But serious concerns may be raised as to whether or not language functions in this way, and, more importantly, whether the authors of Deuteronomy had such a theory of language. Levinson's contention that legal authority rests in individual words and phrases that retain their 'operative force' even when recontextualized is that it does not seem to do justice to the significance of the recontextualization that he himself envisions. From the insights of speech-act theory we recognize that when words from another context are used in a new one, this constitutes a new speech-act.[14] How the speaker/author of the later speech-act intends the 'operative force' of the words used to be understood is a matter of interpretation based on the circumstances of the new speech-act. Lohfink rightly notes that the meaning of each speech-act is determined through contextual, situational, and textual considerations, not simply through words and syntax.[15] It cannot be assumed that the operative force of words from a different speech-act applies in the new one. Rather, it must be shown that this is the case, and reuse of certain words is insufficient proof, since the reuse of terminology may be explained on other grounds (contextual, rhetorical, etc.).

This, in turn, raises a more general objection to Levinson's programme. Largely unaddressed in Levinson's work is the question of who, specifically, is the audience of Deuteronomy and therefore the 'target' of these transformations. Or, to put it another way, to whom is this lemmatic 'sleight of hand'[16] directed? If his thesis is correct, then Deuteronomy has radically revised religious practice for the Israelites (or at least was intended to do so). But this dramatic transformation was sure to be noticed, if Deuteronomy in fact centralizes Passover after

---

13. Levinson, *Legal Innovation*, 46.

14. See, e.g. J.R. Searle, *Speech Acts: An Essay on the Philosophy of Language* (Cambridge: Cambridge University Press, 1969), esp. 22–53.

15. N. Lohfink, 'Bund als Vertrag im Deuteronomium', *ZAW* 107, 2 (1995), 215–39 (221).

16. J. Barton, 'Review of *Deuteronomy and the Hermeneutics of Legal Innovation* by B.M. Levinson', *JR* 79 (1999), 650–51 (651).

centuries of its being celebrated in the home and in towns. A general or popular audience is still going to notice the radical shift, notwithstanding the reuse of lemmas from the earlier laws. Moreover, a general audience is unlikely to be so intimately familiar with the earlier texts that such a tendentious reuse of the earlier lexemes is necessary. If, on the other hand, the audience is a scribal school well versed in the texts being reworked and reworded, the familiarity of that audience with the original texts would ensure that they, too, would notice the radical nature of the transformation.[17] In either case, Levinson's view of transformation based on reuse of particular lemmas seems unlikely.

I conclude, then, that since the final forms of both Exodus and Deuteronomy appear to reflect the idea of a combined festival of Passover-Massot, it is reasonable to conclude that the two festivals were conceived of as a combined celebration, and may have always been celebrated together. Though technically separate celebrations, with Passover celebrated on the 14th of Abib and Unleavened Bread celebrated on the 15th through the 23rd, their close proximity most likely led to their being viewed as a single entity. We can now turn our attention to the differences between the celebration envisioned by Exodus and Deuteronomy.

3. *The Differences between Exodus and Deuteronomy*

Even if we accept the premise that Passover-Massot was largely seen as a single celebration, we still must account for the differences between the portrayal of the celebration in Exodus and Deuteronomy. Clearly, there are significant and important differences between the two books that must be addressed.

In my estimation, some attempts to account for the differences between the presentation of Passover in Exodus and Deuteronomy have not adequately taken into consideration the historical contexts of the texts in question or the particular theological and rhetorical priorities reflected in the texts. Yet these considerations help explain the obvious dissimilarities between the texts.

In the narrative world presented in the Pentateuch, we must assume that both Exodus and Deuteronomy were intended to be understood as having been written at some point after the last event described in the texts, but prior to Moses' death on the plains of Moab.[18] Deuteronomy is most explicit in noting that the

---

17. See the more detailed treatment of Levinson's approach in P.T. Vogt, *Deuteronomic Theology and the Significance of Torah: A Reappraisal* (Winona Lake: Eisenbrauns, 2006), 51–66.

18. Understanding the perspective of the implied author and audience and the narrative world being established does not necessarily determine when the texts were actually written. Though many (myself included) are convinced that the Pentateuch is substantially

text covers the words 'that Moses spoke to all Israel beyond the Jordan in the wilderness . . .' (Deut. 1.1). Thus, the implied audience of Deuteronomy is unambiguously the second generation of Israelites who left Egypt in the Exodus.[19]

With Exodus, however, the situation is more complex. As part of the Pentateuch, which is best understood as a coherent whole, the final form of the book almost certainly dates to – or is intended to be understood as dating to – the end of Moses' life (as the implied author). At the same time, it is likely that the final form of Exodus preserves material written by Moses at an earlier time period.[20] Exodus records that Moses wrote certain things down at the times at which they occurred:

1. Exodus 17.14 notes that Yahweh commanded Moses to write the account of the defeat of Amalek.
2. Exodus 24.4 says that Moses wrote כָּל־דִּבְרֵי יְהוָה ('all the words of Yahweh'). With respect to Passover-Unleavened Bread, this presumably includes at a minimum Exod. 23.15, but may include the instructions in chs. 12 and 13 as well.
3. Exodus 34.27-28 describes the writing of the Decalogue.

Each of these texts, written at various times following the exodus, was available for use in the composition of the Pentateuch as a whole.

Mosaic, the interpretation of the text does not rely solely on the identification and dating of the empirical author. Rather, the construct of the implied author allows for interpretation of the text based on the projection of the narrative world and the point of view of the implied author. For more on the construct of the implied reader, see J.K. Brown, *Scripture as Communication: Introducing Biblical Hermeneutics* (Grand Rapids: Baker, 2006), 26–27. A fuller treatment of this issue is available in J.K. Brown, *The Disciples in Narrative Perspective: The Portrayal and Function of the Matthean Disciples*, (SBL Academia Biblica, 9; Atlanta: SBL, 2002), 123–28. See also the treatment of W.C. Booth, *The Rhetoric of Fiction* (Chicago: University of Chicago Press, 1961), 71–77 *et passim*. For a discussion of the relationship between empirical author, implied author, and narrator, see P.T. Vogt, *Interpreting the Pentateuch: An Exegetical Handbook* (Handbooks to Old Testament Exegesis, Grand Rapids: Kregel, 2009), 58–60.

19. Indeed, the tendency of Deuteronomy to blur the lines between generations is due in large measure to the fact that the generation addressed in Deuteronomy did not, in fact, experience Yahweh at Horeb firsthand. For more on Deuteronomy's tendency to blur the generational lines, see J.G. Millar, 'Living at the Place of Decision: Time and Place in the Framework of Deuteronomy', in Millar and McConville, *Time and Place in Deuteronomy* (JSOTSup, 179; Sheffield: Sheffield Academic Press, 1994), 15–88 (41–49).

20. See Stuart, *Exodus*, 28–29. On the unity of the Pentateuch and its nature as a coherent whole, see J.H. Sailhamer, *The Pentateuch as Narrative: A Biblical Theological Commentary* (Grand Rapids: Zondervan, 1992), 1–25.

It is my contention that Exodus preserves material from an earlier time period.[21] As a result, some of the material dealing with Passover-Massot in Exodus is directed towards the exodus generation itself. For example, Exod. 12.7 commands the daubing of blood on the doorposts of the houses of the people in Egypt, something that was not part of later Passover commemoration. In addition, Exod. 12.11 mandates that the meal be eaten מָתְנֵיכֶם חֲגֻרִים נַעֲלֵיכֶם בְּרַגְלֵיכֶם וּמַקֶּלְכֶם בְּיֶדְכֶם וַאֲכַלְתֶּם אֹתוֹ בְּחִפָּזוֹן ('with your loins girded, your shoes on your feet, and your staff in your hand; you shall eat it in haste'). This, too, apparently deals with the original Passover, as it fits that situation neatly and there is no evidence to suggest that this was carried out in subsequent Passover celebrations.[22] Finally, Exod. 12.3 states that the Passover sacrifice is to be taken on the tenth day of the month. Maimonides notes that, like the other two elements, this requirement was for the exodus generation, not subsequent ones.[23]

The treatment of Passover in Exodus does include instructions for its observance by future generations, most notably in Exod. 12.43-49. It is important to note, however, that those instructions do not conflict with the commands in Deuteronomy except for v. 46, which instructs that the Passover was to be eaten בְּבַיִת אֶחָד ('in one house'). It is impossible to know for certain whether or not the general instructions for Passover in Exod. 12.43-49 were originally recorded at the time of its institution and preserved by Moses and/or later editors in the composition of the Pentateuch, or whether they represent what Sailhamer calls a 'contemporization' of the earlier material towards the end of Moses' life.[24] If they are a preservation of earlier material (as is the case with the general instructions for the celebration of Passover in Egypt), it is possible that the more general instructions are intended to describe how the Passover is to be celebrated prior to entry into the land.

We should further note that even the commands in Exodus that are explicitly described as 'everlasting' are not in genuine conflict with the commands in Deuteronomy. Exodus 12.14 says 'This day will be a memorial for you, and

---

21. This is not unlike the view of the composition of Genesis proposed by D. Garrett, *Rethinking Genesis: The Sources and Authorship of the First Book of the Pentateuch* (Fearn by Tain, Scotland: Mentor, 2003).

22. Sailhamer, *Pentateuch as Narrative*, 262, notes that this accounts for why Jesus and the disciples could celebrate the Passover reclined at table, rather than hastily eating the meal standing up.

23. Maimonides, *Qorbenot*, 10.15, cited in Sailhamer, *Pentateuch as Narrative*, 262.

24. Sailhamer, *Pentateuch as Narrative*, 31. I prefer the term 'contextualization,' as it more aptly notes the contextual nature of *all* texts, and highlights the broader issues affected by later reflection on earlier events. For more on this, see Brown, *Scripture as Communication*, 232–51.

you shall celebrate it as a feast to Yahweh. Throughout your generations, as an everlasting statute, you shall celebrate the feast'. The specifics of the Passover celebration that precede this statement are clearly descriptive of the celebration of the first Passover in Egypt, a point demonstrated, again, by the fact that subsequent generations did not feel constrained to celebrate Passover in the way described in the preceding verses. The subsequent verses describe the way in which the Feast of Unleavened Bread was to be celebrated, and are not at odds with the commands in Deuteronomy. The same can be said for Exod. 12.17 as well.

Exodus 12.24 presents more of a problem, as it says וּשְׁמַרְתֶּם אֶת־הַדָּבָר הַזֶּה לְחָק־לְךָ וּלְבָנֶיךָ עַד־עוֹלָם ('You shall keep this word as a statute for you and your sons forever'). Here, the 'word' referred to involves the Passover ritual, including the daubing of the blood on the doorposts. The next verse explicitly notes that this is to be carried out when the Israelites come to the land Yahweh is giving them. This could suggest that Deuteronomy is altering the practice described in Exodus, despite the fact that the instructions in Exodus are said to constitute an 'everlasting' statute. After all, there is no mention of daubing blood in the Deuteronomic law concerning Passover, and elimination of such a ritual would be consistent with what is sometimes seen as a trend in Deuteronomy towards 'demythologization'.[25] This is more likely if, as has been argued, the daubing of the blood reflects an earlier practice with pagan connotations.[26]

In response, we should note that nothing in Deuteronomy actually contradicts this command. It is true, of course, that Deuteronomy does not repeat the command to place blood on the doorposts. But it does not forbid it either. It is possible, as we will discuss below, that Deuteronomy envisions the people as living in tents at the central sanctuary for the feast of Passover-מַצּוֹת. If that is the case they could carry out the command of Exod. 12.24 just as the earlier wilderness generation who are described as keeping the Passover in Numbers 9 presumably did. On the other hand, it is possible that Deuteronomy envisions that the command of Exod. 12.24 would be carried out in the houses throughout the land, even as the sacrifices of Passover are carried out at the central sanctuary. We will discuss this possibility further below. The point is that Deuteronomy need not be seen as abrogating this command, even if it is not repeated there.

---

25. See, for example, the discussion in M. Weinfeld, *Deuteronomy and the Deuteronomic School* (repr., Winona Lake, IN: Eisenbrauns, 1992), 190–224.
26. Cairns, *Word and Presence*, 153.

4. *Deuteronomy's Conception of Passover*

We have examined the differences between Deuteronomy and Exodus in terms of how Passover is presented, and I have suggested that the differences between them are not of the sort posited by Levinson and others. Nevertheless, the differences cannot be denied, and so we must now turn our attention to addressing why Deuteronomy's presentation of Passover-Massot differs from its portrayal in Exodus.

Key to understanding Deuteronomy's portrayal of Passover-Massot is the importance of Yahweh's sovereignty in determining how and where he is to be worshipped. The altar law in Deuteronomy 12 is insistent that legitimate worship take place 'before Yahweh' and at the place he chooses. I have argued elsewhere that this absolute requirement that sacrifice take place *only* at 'The Place' (הַמָּקוֹם) chosen by Yahweh functions to highlight his supremacy and uniqueness when contrasted with the worship of Canaanite gods.[27] The emphasis in Deuteronomy 12 is on the contrast between the false worship of Canaanite religion and the proper worship of Yahweh. Worship of Yahweh may be considered proper, according to Deuteronomy 12, only when it is carried out in accordance with his instructions and at the place of his choosing.

We see this in the clear rhetorical emphasis in these verses on the contrast between the worship of the gods of the nations and the worship of Yahweh. Thus, there is a contrast between the 'places' (הַמְּקֹמוֹת) in which the nations serve their gods (v. 2) and the 'place' (מָקוֹם) which Yahweh would choose (v. 5). We should note, as well, the way in which the author has referred to the 'names' of the gods at their holy sites, and the 'name' of Yahweh at his chosen site. The Israelites are commanded to eliminate every last vestige of the worship of the gods of the nations (vv. 2–3), and are commanded to obliterate the names of the gods from the places of worship. The Israelites are then told (v. 5) that they shall 'seek the place Yahweh your God will choose . . . to set his name'. The emphasis of this passage is on the way Yahweh is to be worshipped by his people. The text makes clear that the Israelites are not to worship Yahweh in the same manner as the nations. So the destruction of the 'names' of the gods of the nations implies elimination of all their claims to legitimacy over the people of the land (including the Israelites). Similarly, the establishment of Yahweh's 'name' at the place of his choosing demonstrates that he has the right to establish his place, by virtue of his sovereignty and his ownership of the land. As Wright notes, 'To remove the names of Canaan's gods was to remove *their*

---

27. Vogt, *Deuteronomic Theology*, 160–203.

presence and *their* power, just as the putting of Yahweh's name in a place was to fill it with *his* availability and *his* nearness'.[28]

Though scholars have long debated the question of how many worship sites are in view in this chapter,[29] the wording of the text and the emphasis on Yahweh's sovereignty in choosing suggests that the primary issue is not the number of worship sites. Rather, the emphasis is on the contrast between the false worship of Canaanite religion and the proper worship of Yahweh. Miller correctly notes that the emphasis in Deuteronomy 12

> is not upon *one* place so much as it is upon the place *the Lord chooses* . . . The central activity of Israel's life, the worship of the Lord, is fully shaped and determined by the Lord . . . The point is that there is an appropriate place where the Lord may be found and worshiped, but that place is not arbitrary and anywhere. In the Lord's order, the Lord will choose and reveal the locus of dwelling and encounter with human life and with God's people.[30]

Unity of Israel's worship is achieved through the exclusive veneration of him as sovereign Lord as opposed to any other gods.[31]

In light of this, Deuteronomy's insistence that the Passover sacrifice take place at 'The Place' is much more comprehensible. From the perspective of

---

28. C.J.H. Wright, *Deuteronomy* (New International Biblical Commentary, Peabody, MA: Hendrickson; 1996), 159, emphasis in original.

29. Some recent studies have argued that Deuteronomy 12 itself does not necessarily limit all worship to one sanctuary. G.J. Wenham, 'Deuteronomy and the Central Sanctuary', *Tyndale Bulletin* 22 (1971), 103–18, esp. 109–16, has argued that Deuteronomy envisions a central, but not sole, sanctuary for Israel. That is, the legislation in Deuteronomy provides for a central sanctuary, but this does not preclude the possibility of other legitimate Yahweh sanctuaries elsewhere. Evidence for this view is found in the fact that Deuteronomy 27 explicitly commands the construction of an altar on Mount Ebal, and that burnt offerings and peace offerings are to be offered there. Furthermore, Wenham notes, Deuteronomy 27 calls for the inscription of the law at the site on Mount Ebal, which is appropriate for a sanctuary. E.H. Merrill, *Deuteronomy* (New American Commentary, 4; Nashville: Broadman & Holman, 1994), 223–24, follows Wenham in seeing this distinction. A similar view is advocated in J.G. McConville, *Law and Theology in Deuteronomy* (JSOTSup, 33; Sheffield: JSOT Press, 1984), 28–29. Later, however, McConville (McConville and Millar, *Time and Place in Deuteronomy*, 117–23) altered his views in favour of seeing the legislation in Deuteronomy as demanding a sole sanctuary, but one which could be met in a succession of places.

30. P.D. Miller, Jr., *Deuteronomy* (Int., Louisville: John Knox, 1990), 131–32.

31. For more on the significance of the altar law in Deuteronomy and its development of the idea of Yahweh's sovereignty and supremacy, see Vogt, *Deuteronomic Theology*, 167–79.

Deuteronomy, localized sacrifice of the Passover when in the land could per-haps undermine the Israelites' awareness of Yahweh's uniqueness and lead to the infiltration of pagan conceptions of the gods and their worship into Yahweh worship. This would have devastating effects on the ability of the people to properly be the people of Yahweh as a light to the nations.

We should note, however, that though *sacrifice* is limited to 'The Place', *worship* is not. Deuteronomy is radical in its insistence that all Israel participate in proper worship in the festivals, whether at the central sanctuary or elsewhere in the land.[32] Deuteronomy 16.4 mandates that leaven is to be removed from the entire territory (גְּבוּל), that is, from the whole land. This suggests that while the focal point of the festival is the central sanctuary, where sacrifices are carried out (Deut. 16.2), the whole land is somehow understood as being within the realm of the feast, and accordingly must be cleansed of leaven.

This is in keeping with how Deuteronomy conceives of the holiness of the land as a whole. We find, first of all, the command in Deut. 12.1-2 to destroy *all* pagan worship sites throughout the whole land. This implies that the entire land is to be considered the realm of Yahweh. Moreover, Deuteronomy 7 as a whole makes the case for the incompatibility of pagan worship with Yahweh worship, and explicitly notes that the vestiges of pagan worship throughout the land must be destroyed due to the fact that the Israelites are a holy people (Deut. 7.6). The presence of pagan worship anywhere in the land is incompat-ible with the presence of the holy people of Yahweh.

Also relevant are the laws of warfare in Deuteronomy. In Deuteronomy 20 there is a difference in treatment of cities far off and those nearby. Deuteronomy 20.13-15 says that when cities far away (presumably those outside the land) are conquered, the Israelites may allow the women to live and may take them as wives and take the conquered people's property as their spoils. But in the case of cities nearby, within the land, the חֵרֶם ('ban') is to apply. The rationale provided (Deut. 20.18) is so that the captives may not corrupt Israelite wor-ship with their abominable practices. However, it may be the case that the war envisioned in Deut. 20.10 is a war of conquest outside of the land of Canaan. Therefore, the women and children taken as captives would be subject to the Israelites, and also in a position to entice them to follow other gods. There is no apparent significant difference between the people far away (who could, perhaps, entice the Israelites to follow after other gods but are not subject to the ban) and those nearby (who are subject to the ban) except that the latter reside in the land while the former do not. It could be countered that women and children are not in a position to entice the Israelites to follow after other gods, and therefore the captured women from far away are not a threat to the purity

---

32. Vogt, *Deuteronomic Theology*, 183–89.

of Yahweh worship. But the same could be argued with respect to the women and children captured within the land, yet they are commanded to be destroyed with the men. The most likely conclusion is that Deuteronomy considers the land itself to be holy.

We also find more explicit statements of the holiness of the land itself in a number of other places in Deuteronomy. Deuteronomy 21.23 mandates that the body of an executed criminal be taken down so as not to defile the land. Deuteronomy 24.4 describes the remarriage of a divorced woman by her first husband as an abomination before Yahweh; tellingly, the practice is forbidden lest it bring sin upon the *land*, not the people involved.[33] Finally, Deut. 21.1-9 commands that the ceremony of the broken-necked heifer be carried out in the case of an unsolved murder. Weinfeld rightly argues that in that text, expiation is for the people, not the land.[34] But according to Deut. 21.1 the law becomes operative only when the people are in the land.[35] Furthermore, Milgrom notes that the ceremony is 'incomprehensible without the assumption that blood does contaminate the land on which it is spilt and that this ritual transfers the contamination to untillable land'.[36] Given this evidence, it is likely that Deuteronomy seeks to expand the realm of the holy.[37]

In addition, there is some ambiguity as to what is intended by the use of the word אֹהֶל ('tent') in Deut. 16.7. It may be used in the sense of 'to go home', implying that following the Passover sacrifice, the people were to return home (cf. Josh. 22.4, 6; 1 Kgs 8.66).[38] A problem with this understanding is that Deuteronomy consistently envisions the people as living in houses, and uses the term אֹהֶל to refer to their temporary dwellings in the desert (Deut. 1.27; 5.30; 11.6). So, others have concluded that אֹהֶל refers to temporary dwellings constructed near the central sanctuary for use during the week of the festival. Both

---

33. N. Lohfink, 'Opfer und Säkularisierung im Deuteronomium', in A. Schenker (ed.), *Studien zu Opfer und Kult im Alten Testament: mit einer Bibliographie 1969–1991 zum Opfer in der Bibel* (Tübingen: Mohr Siebeck, 1992), 15–43 (37); J. Milgrom, 'The Alleged "Demythologization and Secularization" in Deuteronomy (Review Article)', *IEJ* 23, 3 (1973), 156–61 (157).

34. Weinfeld, *Deuteronomic School*, 210–11.

35. Lohfink, 'Säkularisierung', 37. Note, as well, how the expression 'the land' frames the entire chapter (vv. 1, 23).

36. Milgrom, 'Alleged "Demythologization and Secularization"', 157.

37. Milgrom, 'Alleged "Demythologization and Secularization"', 157. See also Vogt, *Deuteronomic Theology*, 183–85, for a more detailed treatment of the way in which the holiness of the land is envisioned in Deuteronomy.

38. This is the view of J.H. Tigay, *Deuteronomy* דברים: *The Traditional Hebrew Text with the New JPS Translation* (Jewish Publication Society Torah Commentary, Philadelphia: Jewish Publication Society, 1996), 120.

interpretations are possible. The key point is that the celebration of the festival is not limited to the boundaries of the central sanctuary, but rather extends (as demonstrated by v. 4) into the whole of the land. In this way the festival includes the women and children who were not required to make the pilgrimage to the central sanctuary according to Deut. 16.16, as well as those men who may not have made the journey.[39] The ambiguity surrounding the sense of אֹהֶל is seen by McConville as a deliberate effort to convey the 'extension of the worship life of Israel into the land'.[40]

Further evidence for this comes in Deut. 16.8, which commands that on the seventh day there is to be an עֲצֶרֶת ('sacred assembly') to Yahweh. But there is a question as to the location of this assembly. If the tents in v. 7 are understood as being the homes of the people throughout the land, then the law apparently would require the people to return to the מָקוֹם at the end of the week for this assembly.[41] This seems rather implausible in practical terms, as for some the journey could be quite long. This may point towards the view that the pilgrims live in tents at the central sanctuary for the week, participate in the assembly, and then return home. I would suggest an alternative possibility.

It is possible that this section seeks to extend the worship of Israel into the land itself. If the term אֹהֶל in Deut. 16.7 is understood to refer to the people's homes, it is unlikely that they would be required to return to the מָקוֹם later in the week, as we noted above. It is possible, therefore, that the text envisions the holding of an assembly in the towns throughout the land.[42] If so, the celebration of the festival would be carried out in the whole of the land, though clearly sacrifice would be carried out only at the central sanctuary. This is potentially problematic, however, as the term עֲצֶרֶת is usually used in connection with the

---

39. Although Deut. 16.16 makes clear that only males are required to attend the three annual pilgrimage festivals, the heavy emphasis in Deuteronomy on the inclusion of women in the religious life of the nation (cf. Deut. 12.12, 15; 15.12, 17; 16.11, 14) suggests that that women may have done so in any event.

40. McConville, 'Unification', 56. Levinson, 'Reply', 276–77, argues that this suggestion is unlikely due to the fact that sacrificial worship is restricted to the temple, according to Deut. 16.5-6. But this seems to miss the point of McConville's argument, since what he (rightly, in my estimation) argues is not that sacrifice is intended here to be carried out throughout the land, but rather that the worship is not limited to the central sanctuary and therefore may be seen as extending into the land as a whole. This is similar to the arguments of Tigay, *Deuteronomy*, 156, and W.S. Morrow, *Scribing the Center: Organization and Redaction in Deuteronomy 14:1–17:13* (SBLMS, 49; Atlanta: Scholars, 1995), 145, n. 44.

41. Levinson, *Legal Innovation*, 79–80.

42. Tigay, *Deuteronomy*, 156.

central sanctuary.[43] The end of v. 8, however, sheds light on this issue. That clause commands that no work is to be done on the day of the assembly. While this can, of course, apply to pilgrims 'dwelling' temporarily at the sanctuary, it has greater relevance for people who either did not go to the sanctuary in the first place or who have returned home prior to the seventh day.[44] Those who have made the journey to the sanctuary are, more or less by definition, unable to carry out their normal work.[45] Those in the towns, however, could conduct normal work throughout the week (while abstaining from leaven, as required by v. 4), but they would observe the conclusion of the festival by not working on the seventh day.

I conclude, then, that regardless of whether or not the tents are envisioned as homes or as actual tents at the sanctuary or whether the assembly is local or centralized, the celebration of the feast is not limited to the confines of the מָקוֹם. Instead, the celebration is extended into the whole of the land, at least through the cessation from work on the seventh day and through the removal of leaven from the entire land. If the tents are thought of as homes and the assembly is carried out locally, the extension of holiness to the entire land is even more pronounced. In any event, the religious celebration at the מָקוֹם extends into and is paralleled by actions taken throughout the land.

If this is the case, then it is possible that Deuteronomy envisions that even certain practices from Exodus be carried out throughout the land. As we have seen, Exod. 12.21-24 commands certain rituals (such as daubing blood on the doorposts) be carried out that are said to be a statute for the Israelites 'forever'. We have noted that Deuteronomy does not repeat these commands, but it is possible that the people were expected to carry them out throughout the land. If the people were dwelling in tents at the central sanctuary, they could have daubed blood on their tents. On the other hand, if the people are in their homes, they could have carried out these rituals at their homes, as a means of participating in the festival whose focus is located at the sanctuary, but whose effects were intended to be manifest throughout the whole of the land.

---

43. Lev. 23.26; Num. 29.35; 2 Chron. 7.9; Neh. 8.18; Joel 1.14; 2.15-17.

44. In terms of who would have remained behind to participate in this extended celebration, it is quite likely that there were a number of people who did not journey to the sanctuary. Women and children, as we noted, are not required to attend, but may have done so (Deut. 16.16). In addition, it is probable that an assembly consisted of representatives of the entire nation in practice, given the problems associated with all the men journeying to a potentially distant sanctuary and remaining for seven days. See Tigay, *Deuteronomy*, 372, n. 24, and B. Halpern, *The Constitution of the Monarchy in Israel* (HSM, 25; Chico, CA: Scholars, 1981), 190. In this way the requirement for cessation of labour on that day would allow for non-pilgrims to nevertheless participate in the end of the festival.

45. Morrow, *Scribing the Center*, 145.

In light of this, the unique presentation of Passover-Massot in Deuteronomy may have more to do with Deuteronomy's intention to foster a sense of participation in the festivals throughout the land than with an intentional abrogation of the legislation of Exodus.

Chapter 3

THE UNDERSTANDING OF THE NAZIRITE VOW

Christine Hahn
Université de Genève

Introduction

It is with pleasure I dedicate this essay to Gordon for his sixtieth birthday. His scholarship and knowledge in Deuteronomy and the Hebrew Bible have shaped my study and understanding of the Scriptures.

In asking the question 'What type of judge is Samson?', we quickly discover he is a Nazirite. But what does this status represent? We shall try in the course of this essay to understand more about the Nazirite vow and see how the different texts of the Hebrew Bible inform each other on this subject. The basic meaning of the root נזר in Hebrew is 'to take away from normal usage', 'to separate'. Further the term is related to 'consecration', 'dedication', 'crown' and 'diadem'.[1] This essay seeks to examine what this separation looks like in the texts of Numbers 6, Judges 13–16, 1 Samuel 1 and Amos 2.11-12.

We shall first examine the text of Numbers 6 and then proceed to examine Judges 13–16, 1 Samuel 1 and Amos 2.11-12 in light of the narrative of Genesis-Kings. Although we are aware of the composition history of the text over a period of time, the method used here is of a more synchronic nature. This study is interested in understanding the narratives themselves as they stand and the theological connections between these texts.

In the text of Numbers we shall examine in particular the restrictions of the vow and try to draw out the theological meaning of the text. We then turn to the text of Judges 13–16 and study how the vow is presented in a different way. We shall investigate the text in itself by looking at the implications of breaking the vow in particular. When the restrictions of the Nazirite in the book of

---

1. G.J. Botterweck (ed.), *Theologisches Wörterbuch zum Alten Testament* (vol. 5; Stuttgart: Verlag W. Kohlhammer, 1984), 329–33.

Numbers are applied to the text of Judges, we can see a different understanding of the text. In the last part of this study we shall look at the text of 1 Samuel 1 and the narrative links with the text of Judges. We shall try to demonstrate that the text of Judges 13–16 shows the failure of the Nazirite vow, then proceed to show that the text of 1 Samuel and the character of Samuel, in a certain sense, give an example of a successful living out of the vow.

1. *Numbers 6.1-21*

Numbers 6.1-21 is the first occurrence of the Nazirite vow in the Hebrew Bible. This passage is found in the first major section of Numbers (chs. 1–10) and, more specifically, in the section from 5.1 to 6.27 which encompasses 'various laws concerned with the purity of the camp and priestly responsibilities'.[2] It is an elaborate passage beginning with Yahweh speaking to Moses about those who want to undertake a Nazirite vow as an introduction (vv. 1–2), followed by three restrictions imposed on the Nazirite (vv. 3–8). First, he shall not drink any wine or strong drink; he has to refrain from anything that comes from the vine. Second, he shall not cut his hair for the whole of his consecration. Third, he shall not touch any corpse, even that of a dead close family member. The next section refers to the sacrifice to be offered in case of defilement through a dead body (vv. 9–12). If someone dies suddenly beside the Nazirite, the vow becomes void. After a rite of purification, the Nazirite has to rededicate himself. The last main section (vv. 13–21) gives instructions for the sacrifices offered at the end of the Nazirite's vow. At the end of this period, the Nazirite is allowed to drink wine again (v. 20) and the text's conclusion is found in v. 21 which emphasizes the personal decision of the vow maker.[3]

We shall focus on vv. 1–8 in particular as they give instructions about the vow and at least a partial understanding of its meaning. Verses 9–21 refer to the sacrifices related to the vow and shall only be referred to in order to clarify our understanding of vv. 1–8. According to most exegetes the law of the Nazirite in Numbers 6 is a law that regulates an already existing institution.[4] As we shall see, the instructions regarding the Nazirite in Numbers have clear echoes with the priesthood, particularly in the restrictions imposed on the priest and the Nazirite.

The introductory formula of divine speech in vv. 1–2 is similar to that found

2. J. Milgrom, 'Encroaching on the sacred: Purity and Polity in Numbers 1–10', *Interpretation* 51 (1997), 241–53 (241).

3. See E. Zuckschwert, 'Zur literarischen Vorgeschichte des priesterlichen Nazir-Gesetzes (Num. 6.1-8)', *ZAW* 88 (1976), 191–205.

4. G.B. Gray, *Numbers* (ICC; Edinburgh: T & T Clark, 1903), 57.

in Num. 5.1-2a, 5-6a and 11-12a. The vow of the Nazirite is first addressed to 'a man or a woman' (v. 2). There seems to be no restriction in Numbers as to who is allowed to take this vow. The next interesting feature is the use of the term פלא, indicating something outstanding and unusual. This same word also occurs in similar circumstances and in the same verbal form in Judg. 13.17, with the general meaning 'to do something wonderful',[5] describing what is beyond normal human activity.[6] At the outset we can see this text setting out a special vow taken freely by a person. At this stage there is no mention of time limit; the emphasis resides in the specificity of the vow of the Nazirite.

In Num. 6.3-8, three rules of abstinence are mentioned: first, abstinence from wine, strong drink and anything that comes from the vine (vv. 3–4); second, abstinence from cutting one's hair during the time of the vow (v. 5); and third, abstinence from touching and approaching a dead body (vv. 6–8). The regulations concerning the wine and the touching of the dead bodies show similarities to the restrictions placed upon the priests (cf. Leviticus 10 and 21). Further, these restrictions are to some degree more severe than the ones for the priest (see below). This enhances the idea of the Nazirite being set apart and being 'holy' for Yahweh.[7] The cutting of the hair most distinguishes the Nazirite from the priest.[8]

The first restriction about wine mentions that the Nazirite has to renounce everything relating to grapes, from the fruit to the finished product. First, the Nazirite has to separate himself from wine and 'strong drink'.[9] Further, he has to abstain from the vinegar made from wine and other intoxicating drinks. Drinking the 'juice' of the wine or anything that is produced by the grapevine including seeds or unripe grapes is also prohibited. This long list of words and expressions shows the scope of the restriction, which is found nowhere else in the Hebrew Bible. Restriction regarding drinking wine is present in the priestly legislation (Lev. 10.8-11) but this is limited to the time of service in the tent of meeting only. There is no such restriction for the priest when he is off duty. For the Nazirite, the restriction is limited to the duration of the vow. Parallels are found in Judg. 13.5-7, 9 and Amos 2.11-12, and a similar theme is also

5. L. Koehler, Walter Baumgartner, and J.J. Stamm, *The Hebrew and Aramaic Lexicon of the Old Testament* (trans. and ed. M.E.J. Richardson; 2 vols.; Leiden: Brill, 2001), 927.

6. R.D. Cole, *Numbers* (New American Commentary, 3B; Nashville: Broadman & Holman, 2000), 121.

7. M. Noth, *Numbers* (trans. J.D. Martin; OTL; Philadelphia: SCM Press, 1968), 55.

8. Gray, *Numbers*, 63.

9. R.G. Boling, *Judges* (AB, 8; New York: Doubleday, 1975), 219. Strong drink can be used to express the generic term for all intoxicating drink including beer.

found in 1 Sam. 1.15, although in a different context, as Hannah is wrongly accused of drinking wine. The restriction for the Nazirite in Amos 2.11-12 is only about drink. Amos does not mention the cutting of the hair or separation from dead bodies. It has been suggested that the abstinence of wine was common in nomadic symbolism as opposed to an urban way of life.[10]

The second restriction in v. 5 concerns the cutting of hair. It is also taken up in Judg. 13.5; 16.16 (17) and 1 Sam. 1.11. The text of Numbers specifies two things in this verse. First, the hair shall not be cut 'all the days of his vow of separation' and 'no razor shall touch his head'. Second, 'he shall be holy to Yahweh'. This shows that, in the understanding of Numbers, the vow is limited to a certain period of time even though this time is never specified. The texts of Judges 13–16 and 1 Samuel 1 both suggest a lifelong Naziriteship, whereas the text of Amos 2.11-12 is silent on the subject.

A word has to be said about the razor. In Numbers 6 the word used is תער, but in Judg. 13.5 and 1 Sam. 1.11 it is מורה. We find the word תער in Num. 8.7 relating to the priests who have to shave their bodies in a normal cleansing ritual for service. The term מורה is used as the oath formula for the Nazirite only found in Judg. 13.5, 16.17 and 1 Sam. 1.11.[11] This connection of the word תער further links the Nazirite to the priestly legislation.

The third restriction in vv. 6–8 concerns contact with the dead. Our text is the only reference where a Nazirite has to abstain from touching dead bodies. In v. 6 the Nazirite should not even approach a dead body, including the closest family members like father, mother, brother and sister (v. 7). A similar restriction concerns the high priest in Lev. 21.10-11. The priests are also restricted in this regard but they are allowed to take care of the burial of their close kin (Lev. 21.1-3). Here again our text shows a link with the priesthood. Some scholars have even argued that the function of the restrictions is to consecrate the Nazirite and thus endow him with a status equivalent to the priesthood.[12] In Numbers this is certainly the case. However, in examining other narratives about the Nazirite vow, the situation is far more complex.

Two sacrifices are mentioned in this text. The first sacrifice is offered in the case of defilement (vv. 9–12), thus rededicating the Nazirite. The rite of purification here is similar to the purification of the parturient, the gonorrhoeaic individual, and the leper (Lev. 12.6-8; 14.10; 15.14, 29). The second sacrifice marks the end of the time of consecration (vv. 13–17) and involves the cutting of the hair (vv. 18–20). At the end of the offering the Nazirite will shave his

10. Baruch A. Levine, *Numbers* (AB, 4; Garden City: Doubleday, 1993), 232.

11. Koehler, Baumgartner and Stamm, *The Hebrew and Aramaic Lexicon*, vol.1, 561.

12. J. Milgrom, *Numbers: The Traditional Hebrew Text with the New JPS Translation: Commentary* (New York: The Jewish Publication Society, 1990), 46.

head at the entrance of the tent of meeting. Once the whole ritual is completed he is allowed to drink wine (vv. 19–20). Two main interpretations have been offered with regard to the disposal of the hair. Gray, for example, suggests that the burning of the hair was an offering.[13] Noth rejects this idea, arguing that the burning of the hair represents the annihilation of a sacred thing once it has fulfilled its function.[14]

As we have seen above, the Nazirite in Numbers 6 shows several characteristics. First of all, the text suggests that a person (man or woman) is undertaking a vow to separate himself/herself voluntarily to fulfil some purpose for Yahweh. The person undertaking the vow does so for a limited period of time although the period is not defined. There is no suggestion in Numbers 6 of a lifelong consecration as a Nazirite. A sacrifice signals the end of the Nazirite vow.

Secondly, three restrictions are imposed on the Nazirite: abstinence from wine and all products from the vineyard, not cutting the hair and finally not touching any dead body. All these restrictions point toward a dedication and separation of a person or thing (vine). These restrictions are also linked in one way or another to the expectations imposed on the priests who are not allowed to drink wine or alcoholic beverages during their service nor to touch dead bodies. Vocabulary referring to them shaving their bodies as they enter the tent of meeting also echoes the Nazirite vow in terms of the razor used. It is chiefly in letting the hair grow that the Nazirite differs significantly from the priest, although it should also be noted that the Nazirite has no cultic function. The priest is part of a professional group set apart for the service to Yahweh. In our text, the Nazirite sets himself a given time, but no specific function is linked to his vow. In the text of Numbers 6, the specificity of the Nazirite is to be holy for Yahweh. The visible aspect of this position is linked to the hair (v. 5), which is truly the most obviously significant feature of the Nazirite and symbolizes their separation for Yahweh. With all these elements we can argue that the Nazirite, in his setting himself apart, demonstrates his holiness towards God. He shows that a non-priest can also take part in the separation for Yahweh.

2. *The Nazirite in Judges 13–16*

After the Nazirite Law in the book of Numbers, we next encounter a Nazirite in the character of the judge, Samson (Judges 13–16). One of the main themes in the book of Judges is relevant here, namely, obedience to Yahweh. The leaders in the book of Judges, called by Yahweh are meant to deliver the people and bring them back to obedience to their God. The Samson narrative relates

---

13. Gray, *Numbers*, 68.
14. Noth, *Numbers*, 57.

the adventures of the last-named judge in the book of Judges. In this section we shall look at the meaning of the vow and how it shapes the role of Samson as judge in the narrative of Judges 13–16. We shall look at the narrative in itself without referring too much to the parallels passages, which we consider below. The narrative begins (ch. 13) with a birth announcement for a deliverer revealing that the child to be born shall be a Nazirite. In the next two chapters (chs. 14–16), different episodes of Samson's life are told without mentioning the Nazirite vow. The theme of the Nazirite appears again at the end of the narrative with the breaking of the vow and a tragic end to Samson's life.

'The people of Israel again did what was evil in the sight of the Lord, so the Lord gave them into the hand of the Philistines' (Judg. 13.1); thus begins the Samson narrative. Instead of continuing with the usual framework found in Judges – namely that the people cry out to Yahweh and he sends a deliverer – the text begins with a birth narrative. An angel appears to an unnamed barren woman, Manoah's wife (13.3). He announces that she shall bear a son and gives her instruction concerning the child and herself. First, she has to abstain from wine and alcoholic beverages and unclean food (13.4, 7, 14; cf. Num. 5.3-4 and Lev. 21). Second, no razor shall touch the head of the child (13.5; cf. Judg. 16.17 and 1 Sam. 1.11), as he shall be a Nazirite from birth. After the visitation the woman recounts the story to her husband.

Manoah asks for a second visitation. As the angel reappears the instructions about the restriction given to the woman are repeated but not the restriction for the child (13.8-14). The text continues with an offering to Yahweh and the angel going up in the flame of the altar (13.15-23) and the narrative ends with the birth of a son, named Samson (13.24-25).

In this chapter the Nazirite vow imposed on the child is mainly associated with a restriction on the cutting of his hair (v. 5).[15] It is the only restriction formally imposed on the Nazirite. The mother receives instruction to refrain from drinking wine, alcohol, and from eating anything unclean similar to the one in Numbers 6. Here the common restriction imposed on all Israelites concerning consumption of unclean food is specified for the woman. At the second appearance of the angel the restriction on wine is enhanced: 'she may not eat from anything that comes from the vine' in addition to anything that is unclean (v. 14). Here we have a direct parallel with Num. 6.4 and the restriction imposed on the priests.

15. 'The fact that Samson had no say in the matter of becoming a Nazirite is central to the overall theme of lack of freedom. The decision has been made for him by the divine, and perpetuated by the acceptance of the vow by his mother who performs the requirements of the Nazirite vow until his birth' (Victor H. Matthews, 'Freedom and Entrapment in the Samson Narrative', *Perspectives in Religious Studies* 16 [1989], 245–57 [247]).

After this birth narrative, the text relates some of Samson's heroic deeds without referring to the Nazirite vow. He is involved in a constant brawl with the Philistines as they take vengeance on each other. The link between the text and our theme of the Nazirite is explained in Judg. 16.17 by Samson himself. He argues that the source of his strength comes from his Nazirite vow. The biblical text mentions that the spirit of Yahweh rushes upon Samson and each time it is to accomplish a form of killing. In all the episodes of Samson's life he is involved in a personal conflict with the Philistines. First, he wants to marry one of their women. In the course of the marriage transactions, going down to Timnah to meet his Philistine wife, he tears apart a lion (14.6). During the marriage feast, his 30 companions succeed in explaining Samson's riddle. This is the end of peace. Samson, empowered by the spirit, kills 30 men of Ashkelon to provide for their price (14.19). After the episode where Samson burns the Philistines' fields, he is betrayed by his own people and given to the Philistines. Again he is invested by the spirit and kills 1,000 of them with the jawbone of an ass (15.14). The conflict with the Philistines is real but instead of Samson raising an army, he 'seeks personal revenge, not freedom from oppression for his people'.[16]

The theme of the Nazirite vow is taken up again in Judg. 16.4-31. Samson falls in love with a Philistine woman, Delilah, who entices him to tell her the secret of his strength in order to sell him into the hands of the Philistines. Three times Samson misleads her deliberately. At the fourth time, Delilah pulls all the emotional stops to get his confession.[17] Samson falls into the trap, telling her that his strength comes from his hair. Consequently when his hair is shorn, he is captured, blinded and made to tread the mill by the Philistines. The last twist of the story shows Samson's hair grow again and as the Philistines want him to perform for them, Samson kills 3,000 of them at the feast for their god. Although he dies during this event, it fulfils the announcement of the angel made in 13.5: 'he will begin to deliver Israel from the hand of the Philistines'. Even in this very last episode Samson's previous attitude of taking personal revenge is still seen. He asks God to give him strength in order to be avenged for the loss of his eyes.

If we try to understand the Nazirite vow only from the point of view of the references made in the narrative, we can reach the following conclusions: (1) Yahweh imposes the vow of the Nazirite to an unborn child; (2) the child is not to shave his head; (3) the vow appears to be lifelong; (4) superhuman strength is given Samson, as Nazirite, through the vow; (5) a restriction on

---

16. L.R. Klein, *The Triumph of Irony in the Book of Judges* (JSOTSup, 68; Sheffield: Almond Press, 1989), 135.

17. Matthews, 'Freedom and Entrapment', 256.

drinking wine and other alcoholic beverages and also on eating any unclean food which is imposed on the mother during her pregnancy. From this last restriction we may infer that this is also imposed on the Nazirite himself.[18]

The purpose of being a Nazirite is never explained in the text itself and leaves the protagonist as well as the reader puzzled. As we have seen above, Samson explains that the source of his strength is found in his Nazirite vow which is the only explanation given in the whole narrative. It does not give any further comment on the role of the Nazirite. Comparing the episode of the angel in the birth narrative with its parallel text in the Gideon account of Judges 6, we could suppose a link between the Nazirite and a deliverer figure. If this was the purpose, then the result is much less impressive than that which came before in the book of Judges. Here, contrary to the Gideon narrative no army is raised, no great victory obtained; only a broken vow. There is the possibility this text wants to show Israel's failure and desolation even though the spirit of Yahweh is still in action. In this case Samson becomes a symbol of the whole people, having no purpose and no guidance. Although the narrative mentions he is a judge in Israel for 20 years (15.20; 15.25), the events of his life show failings, not only in character but also in the lack of a goal to deliver the people from their enemies. The lack of guidance shown here is picked up again in the last four chapters of the book in the expression 'In those days there was no king in Israel' (17.6; 18.1; 19.1; 21.25) which introduces two disastrous narratives where desolation ultimately culminates in civil war. However, the ending of the Samson narrative, where the protagonist seems nevertheless to fulfil the announcement of a beginning of deliverance (as with the inheritance of Benjamin at the end of Judges [Judg. 21.16-25]) leaves hope for the future. Will this future also contain a new beginning for the Nazirite vow?

Before we answer this question we shall look at the interpretation of the text in light of Numbers 6. Scholarship has correctly linked Judges 13–16 with Numbers 6. We shall see that the understanding of Judges 13–16 slightly changes when one makes a comparison between the two texts. The Samson narrative in itself does not give enough clues about the nature of the Nazirite, which automatically leads the reader to look for an explanation elsewhere in the Hebrew Bible.

---

18. See J. Blenkinsopp, 'Structure and Style in Judges 13–16', *JBL* 82 (1963), 65–76. However, several scholars note rightly that the restriction of wine and unclean food has been imposed on the woman only. See for example V.H. Matthews, *Judges and Ruth* (NCBC; Cambridge: Cambridge University Press, 2004), 140.

3. *Judges 13–16 and Numbers 6*

In comparison with Numbers 6, scholars have demonstrated Samson's breaches of the vow, but in the broader perspective of this narrative in Judges references to those failures are subdued. It has been argued that Samson broke his vow on all three levels of the restrictions imposed in Numbers.[19] Samson broke his vow on several occasions by failing with regard to the restriction not to touch dead bodies. First, Samson takes apart a lion and then takes honey from its carcass (Judg. 14.6, 9). Second, Samson goes down to Askalon to kill 30 men in order to take their garments as presents for the young men of his wedding (Judg. 14.19). Third, he takes the jawbone of an ass to kill 1,000 men (Judg. 15.14-15).

Concerning the drinking of wine, the references are not explicit but it is implied that during the seven days' feast of his marriage Samson drank wine (Judg. 14.10-18). To a lesser degree, some scholars mention that Samson had to cross a vineyard to go to Timnah (14.5).[20] They understand this as a temptation to consume fruit of the vineyard.

The Samson narrative most explicitly shows the breaking of the Nazirite vow when Samson's hair is cut off (16.19). This is where the narrative of Numbers is closest to Judges. In taking all the above instances as components of the breaking of the vow, scholars have shown different possible links between Numbers 6 and Judges 13–16. They have also shown that the function of Judges 14.1–16.3 is a prelude to what will happen in Judges 16.4-31, where the cutting of the hair ends the stories about the Nazirite vow in Judges. This interpretation highlights not only Samson's failure to keep his vow but also his failure to bring deliverance to the people. In the text itself, however, we have seen that in the breaking of the vow Samson becomes a type of the whole people: lacking purpose and guidance.

There are differences between the narratives of Numbers 6 and Judges 13–16. There is no explicit mention of the touching of the dead body in the text of Judges. Further, in the Samson narrative the vow is considered lifelong whereas Numbers 6 considers the vow limited in time. An important difference is that the Nazirite in Judges 13–16 is chosen by Yahweh and he does not set himself apart. Numbers 6 suggests that one can make a vow and set oneself apart for a certain period of time. Judges suggests that God himself sets apart a person for his or her whole life. Numbers gives us no clues as to how life is when one is set apart. Judges gives us an example and one could readily then go back to

---

19. See for example: K.F.D. Römheld, 'Von den Quellen der Kraft (Jdc 13)', *ZAW* 104, 1 (1992), 28–52, and also J.C. McCann, *Judges* (Int.; Louisville: John Knox Press, 2002), 110–15.

20. McCann, *Judges*, 103.

Numbers and apply lessons from the Samson narrative to that text. The main connecting point between the narratives is the hair. A person is set apart with the visible sign of not cutting his hair. Numbers 6 enhances the importance of the hair, as it is the only permanent visible sign unique to the Nazirite. The abstaining from touching dead bodies and the restriction about the wine are not specific to the Nazirite as they are linked with the priests.

After reading Numbers 6 and reaching Judges 16, the reader understands clearly that the cutting of the hair is a breaking of the vow, which would then require a sacrifice to restart the whole procedure. The breaking of the vow however, is not linked to the defiling through a dead body as is the breaking of the vow in Numbers 6, but it is related to the betraying of a secret. The vow is broken and the question that can be asked now is: is Samson still a Nazirite? The text of Judges 16 suggests he is because Samson's strength comes back. In the text of Numbers the defiling implies that the maker of the vow must start over but it does not prevent him from being a Nazirite. Both texts imply that the cutting of the hair in irregular circumstances is not the end of the vow. It is a new beginning. In Numbers 6, the vow starts over again and in Judges Samson regains his strength for one last victory over his enemies.

McCann suggests that Samson fails in his calling as he fails to deliver Israel.[21] His argument is based on the fact that Samson shows no faith in Yahweh and consistently makes decisions going against God's purpose to deliver Israel. Although I agree with this general understanding, the situation is not that simple because the author of the text somewhat blurs the issue. In Samson's death he mentions that 'the dead whom he killed at his death were more than those he killed during his life' (Judg. 16.30). This sentence is highly ambiguous. It can be understood that Samson, in a sense, fulfilled his purpose of beginning to deliver Israel. On the other hand, it can be understood as a tragic note: 'This man, with his unprecedentedly high calling and with his extraordinary divine gifts, has wasted his life.'[22]

In Numbers, the Nazirite role has connections with the priesthood. In the text of Judges, it is connected to the deliverer. Refraining from cutting hair elsewhere in the Hebrew Bible might further link the Nazirite vow to the figure of the deliverer.[23] The biblical reference for this argument is Judg. 5.2, which

---

21. McCann, *Judges*, 92–115.

22. D.I. Block, *Judges, Ruth* (New American Commentary, 6; Nashville: Broadman & Holman, 1999), 469.

23. See for example F. Parente, 'Die Ursprünge des Naziräats', in A. Vivian (ed.), *Biblische und Judaistische Studien* (Festschrift Paolo Sacchi; Judentum und Umwelt, 29; Frankfurt am Main: Peter Lang, 1990), 65–83; J. Gray, *Joshua, Judges, Ruth* (New Century Bible; London: Thomas Nelson and Sons Ltd, 1967), 276.

could be translated: 'when the flowing hair was let loose'.[24] The presupposition is that this refers to a collective Naziriteship in early times with the following function: the Nazirites were warriors in permanent status of holiness.[25] This relationship is however tenuous as other references concerning warfare and abstinence like 1 Sam. 21.5-6 and 2 Sam. 11.11, which refer to abstinence from sexual relationships by fighting men. Failure to keep this would be considered a violation of the terms of their enlistment.[26] Even with a military link between the Nazirite and warriors, Samson hardly fits the profile as he does not raise an army but fights out his personal grudges with the Philistines.

In this short study, we have seen that Numbers 6 does inform Judges 13–16, specifically with reference to the breaking of the vow by Samson. It also highlights some clear differences. As Numbers 6 is linked with the figure of the priest, so the Samson narrative is linked to the deliverer figure. These different connections both imply a dedication to Yahweh which can take a variety forms.

In reading the biblical text in sequence we can see a development of the Nazirite vow. First, the law about the vow is given with its restrictions closely linked to the priestly restrictions. However there is no specific purpose for a person who has taken this vow. In the text of Judges, the vow is imposed and again there is no purpose given to the Nazirite. The echo of Numbers in Judges is present in the restrictions of the vow and highlights the breaking of the vow by Samson. However, it fails to let the text speak of Samson's inadequacy. It fails to show that not only Samson but also the whole people of Israel are at a loss and hopeless. In the Samuel narrative a child is dedicated to Yahweh by his mother before his birth (1 Sam. 1.11). This young man experiences a calling from Yahweh (1 Sam. 3.1-14). The different episodes of Samuel's life show the reader an example of what a Nazirite may look like: a person dedicated to Yahweh and fulfilling Yahweh's will. It has to be added that the narrative of Samuel offers much more than simply a reference to the Nazirite, but the reading of Samuel as a successful Nazirite is clearly implied by the text.

4. *The Nazirite in Amos 2.11-12 and 1 Samuel 1–7*

In this section we shall discuss how Amos 2.11-12 and 1 Samuel 1–7 are linked with the Nazirite vow. We shall also compare them with Numbers 6 and Judges 13–16.

24. Gray, *Joshua, Judges and Ruth*, 276.
25. F. Parente, 'Die Ursprünge des Naziräats', 65–83 (77) (translation is mine).
26. Levine, *Numbers 1–20*, 232. For a discussion see also B. Lindars, *Judges 1–5* (Edinburgh: T & T Clark, 1995), 225–27.

Amos 2.11-12 mentions the Nazirite alongside the prophets. In this text there is no mention of the cutting of the hair but the abstinence from drinking wine is highlighted. In Amos the close link between the Nazirites and prophets shows the complete dedication of the prophets to Yahweh.[27] The interesting point is that the Nazirites are not prophets but they are close to prophets in Amos, whereas the Nazirites are close to priests in Numbers and close to judges/deliverers in Judges.

The MT of 1 Samuel 1.11, 'no razor shall touch his head', is the only direct echo we have with the Nazirite in Judges 13–16. The LXX and 4QSam[a] mention explicitly the term נזר. As has been persuasively suggested, these are additions to the MT which reinforce the image of Samuel as Nazirite.[28] The author of the MT seems to favour discretion in linking Samuel to the Nazirite vow. The echoes between the Samson and the Samuel narratives, however, are not confined to that sentence. Actually, the two narratives bear considerable similarities. For example, the birth narrative[29] and the theme of the barren woman (Judges 13 and 1 Samuel 1) show a strong degree of similarity. This motif occurs several times in the Hebrew Bible (Gen. 18.1-15; 25.21; 29.31; Judges 13; 1 Samuel 1; 2 Kgs 4.8-17). Ackerman has shown that most of these texts associate a near-death experience of the son with the motif. The only sons who did not experience a near-death experience were Samuel and Samson as they were dedicated to Yahweh. She concludes that the promise of a son to a barren woman implies that her son belongs to Yahweh with a dedication of some sort.[30]

The second similarity, which we have already mentioned, is the expression, 'no razor shall touch his head'. As we have seen above, Judges 13 and 16 and 1 Samuel 1 are the only texts in the Hebrew Bible where this expression occurs. We can argue that these two narratives are deliberately linked in order to draw out the differences between the two protagonists.

Another echo is the fight against the Philistines, which concerns both Samson and Samuel. Here, again, the narratives are linked by a same theme but the outcome is different. Samson fights against the Philistines in personal matters

27. For further discussion see F.I. Anderson and D.N. Freedman, *Amos* (AB, 24A; New York: Doubleday, 1989), 331.

28. S.S.J. Pisano, *Additions or Omissions in the Books of Samuel* (OBO, 57; Fribourg: Universitätsverlag, Göttingen: Vandenhoeck und Ruprecht, 1984), 19–22.

29. For the discussion on the links between the Samuel birth narrative and Saul see S.S. Brooks, 'Saul and the Samson Narrative', *JSOT* 71 (1996), 19–25. See also P.K. McCarter, Jr., *1 Samuel* (AB, 8; Garden City: Doubleday, 1980).

30. S. Ackerman, *Warrior, Dancer, Seductress, Queen: Women in Judges and Biblical Israel* (The Anchor Bible Reference Library; New York: Doubleday, 1996), 186.

whereas Samuel sends the people to fight with the result of victory (1 Sam. 4–7, particularly 1 Sam. 7.3-14).

The comparison between the Samson and the Samuel narratives demonstrates a sharp contrast between the two. Where Samson fails, Samuel succeeds. Samuel truly delivers Israel from the hands of the Philistines, who are then subdued (1 Sam. 7.13). Samuel plays an important public role in his different functions whereas Samson is engrossed in his personal conflicts. The Samuel narrative is much more complex than the Samson narrative and it gives some important clues to Samuel's actions. After the birth narrative the readers are informed of Samuel's call, which is an important narrative[31] for the future development of the character. Samuel becomes a prophet (1 Sam. 3.20; 9.9) and a judge (1 Sam. 7.3-17).[32] He also occupies a priestly position (1 Sam. 7.8-11). Indirectly, Samuel is a deliverer. Although he does not raise up an army and lead it into battle he does intercede for the people as they fight against the Philistines (1 Sam. 7.3-14). Further he anoints the first two kings of Israel (1 Sam. 10.1; 16.13).

This comparison proceeds to reaffirm the link between these two narratives and show that the contrast between the two characters comes from a different application of the Nazirite vow. As said above, the text of Judges leaves Samson puzzled at his role as a Nazirite. He seems to only understand that he is not allowed to cut his hair and that his Nazirite status gives him supernatural strength. But despite that strength, even the spirit of Yahweh does not bring the success desired. Even though Samson is called a judge, there is no indication of his role being successful. Rather, the people of Judah bind him and give him over to the Philistines! In the Samuel narrative, the Nazirite vow is only hinted at in the birth narrative and never taken up again in the remainder of the Samuel story. However, Samuel seems to know his role and function among the people of Israel. He successfully fights against the Philistines with the help of the people. He also successfully exercises the role of the judge, leading the people back to Yahweh. Samuel's dedication seems flawless whereas Samson fails miserably in letting his hair be shorn. The success of Samuel is enhanced by the comparison with the failure of Samson. This text has demonstrated an example of true dedication, which will lead to the institution of kingship, a new hope after the troubled times of the judges.

---

31. Some scholars have mentioned that Samuel's call narrative does not give the mission for the hero. For further discussion see A. Caquot and P. de Robert, *Les Livres de Samuel* (Commentaire de l'Ancien Testament, 6; Genève: Labor et Fides, 1994), 65–71.

32. See for example R.P. Gordon, *1 & 2 Samuel: A Commentary* (Exeter: Paternoster, 1986), 106.

Conclusion

In this study we have been looking closely at the meaning of the Nazirite vow through the texts of Numbers 6, Judges 13–16 and 1 Samuel 1. We have shown that the restrictions for the Nazirite in Numbers 6 are linked with different restrictions imposed on the priest or high priest. However, those restrictions do not imply a cultic function for the Nazirite. It is the Nazirite who sets himself apart to Yahweh for a certain period of time. A theological understanding of the Nazirite vow in Numbers shows that the Nazirite is holy to Yahweh in taking upon himself some restrictions imposed on the priest.

In Judges 13–16, we have seen that the main restriction imposed on the Nazirite is the abstinence from shaving his head and indirectly a restriction about drinking wine. The text of Judges taken on its own leaves the reader rather puzzled about the role of the Nazirite. The vow is imposed on a deliverer/judge figure close to other characters in the book of Judges. Contrary to other judges in the book, Samson does not deliver the people – he lives life according to his own interests. The actions which one would expect to be deliverance are, in fact, personal acts of vengeance. Even after his vow has been broken, Samson remains focused on personal vengeance and the tone of the author leaves a sense of utter despair towards Israel's situation. In the narrative of Judges, this text shows, through the character of Samson, the disobedience of the people towards their God and their lack of purpose and goal.

Amos 2.11-12 links the Nazirite to the role of the prophet. This brief mention does not give many clues about the Nazirite vow. Its only connection with Numbers 6 is that of abstinence from drinking alcohol.

1 Samuel does not mention explicitly the Nazirite vow. However, the character of Samuel encompasses the function of priest, judge and prophet. The story begins in a similar fashion to the Samson narrative, with the statement that 'no razor shall touch his head' (1 Sam. 1.11). As the narrative unfolds, a successful character emerges. Samuel is leading the people back to Yahweh and giving again a sense of relationship with Yahweh and hope of a brighter future. Even here, the text does not refer to a specific function of the Nazirite. The role of Samuel is complex. Although it cannot be wholly linked to the Nazirite vow, it nevertheless gives an understanding of the vow, which can be understood in a much broader sense than the priestly connection or the deliverer connection. At the end of Samuel's life the reader has the impression of what a Nazirite might have been like, even though he is never called a Nazirite.

All the texts we have examined show the Nazirite vow from different angles which elaborate upon each other. We have seen that the vow can take different orientations. The similarity between all the texts, including Amos 2, is the idea of being set apart for Yahweh. We have also shown that the Nazirite is linked to different offices, like those of priest, judge and prophet. None of these links are exclusive, nor are they necessary in order to take the vow. The partial understanding from the passages of Numbers 6, Judges 13–16 and Amos 2 seems to lead to a fulfilment in the Samuel narrative.

The Nazirite vow in the examined texts can take different shapes and orientations. The visible sign of the long hair and the abstinence from alcoholic beverages seem to be the prerequisite of the vow. Possible orientations are: closeness to the priest (Numbers 6) but not a priest; closeness to the judge/deliverer (Judges 13–16) but not a judge or deliverer; closeness to a prophet (Amos 2.11-12) but not a prophet. Samuel, who encompasses all these connections, is never called a Nazirite. The forms of the Nazirite vow suggested in the Hebrew Bible, which does not specify a precise meaning of the vow, leave space for other forms of dedication.

Chapter 4

RHETORICAL, THEOLOGICAL AND CHRONOLOGICAL
FEATURES OF EZRA-NEHEMIAH

Herbert H. Klement

Staatsunabhängige Theologische Hochschule Basel

1. *Features Peculiar to Ezra-Nehemiah*

The book Ezra-Nehemiah is of considerable historical interest, containing as it does the ultimate biblical account of Israel's history prior to the events related in the New Testament.[1] Some familiarity with the period of Persian rule in which Ezra-Nehemiah originated is essential for a full grasp of the book, chronologically the last in the Old Testament canon. Ezra-Nehemiah is moreover of inestimable value as a source of information about the province of Judah in the Persian period, for which there is little extra-biblical testimony.[2] A historical enquiry into Ezra-Nehemiah reveals a number of unusual features.

1.1 *Quotations from Other Documents*
Even a cursory reading reveals that Ezra-Nehemiah makes reference to a

---

1. I follow here the Masoretic tradition of reading Ezra and Nehemiah as one book. For a discussion of their literary unity see the commentaries, e.g. D.J.A. Clines, *Ezra, Nehemiah, Esther* (New Century Bible; Grand Rapids: Eerdmans, 1984); H.G.M. Williamson, *Ezra, Nehemiah* (WBC, 16; Waco: Word, 1985); J. Blenkinsopp, *Ezra-Nehemiah* (OTL; London: SCM, 1988). For the long-standing question of their relationship to Chronicles, see H.J. Koorevaar, 'Die Chronik als intendierter Abschluss des alttestamentlichen Kanons', *JETh* 11 (1997), 42–76; idem, 'De afsluiting van de canon van het Oude Testament', in P. Nullens (ed.), *Dicht bij de Bijbel* (Heverlee: Bijbelinstitut België,1997), 63–90; J. Steinberg, *Die Ketuvim: Ihr Aufbau und ihre Botschaft* (Bonner Biblische Beiträge, 152; Hamburg: Philo, 2006), 197–206.

2. An extensive treatment can be found in E.M. Yamauchi, *Persia and the Bible* (Grand Rapids: Baker, 1996).

number of documents in the form of direct quotations, accounts or summaries, whereby it is not always possible to distinguish between these categories. Some of the most important are:

> Cyrus' *edict* (Ezra 1.2-4)
> *List* of the temple items returned by Cyrus (Ezra 1.9-11a)
> *List* of the returning exiles (according to Cyrus' *edict*) (Ezra 2.3-70; as Neh. 7.5-72)
> *Letter* to Xerxes, unnamed accusation against the Jews (Ezra 4.6)
> Rehum and Schimshai's *letter* to Artaxerxes (Ezra 4.9-16)
> Artaxerxes' *letter* in reply (Ezra 4.17-22)
> The satrap Tattenai and Shethar-bozenai's *letter* to Darius (Ezra 5.8-17)
> *Copy in Aramaic* of Cyrus' edict (Ezra 6.3-5)
> Artaxerxes' *letter* in reply to Tattenai and Shethar-bozenai (Ezra 6.6-12)
> Artaxerxes' *letter of safe-conduct* to Ezra (Ezra 7.11-26)
> *List* of the exiles returning with Ezra (Ezra 8.1-14)
> *List* of the sacrifices (Ezra 8.35)
> *List* of those who had married non-Jews (Ezra 10.18-44)
> *Penitential Psalm* (Neh. 9.5-37)
> *Affirmation* of popular commitment (Neh. 10.1-40)
> *List* of the citizens of Jerusalem (Neh. 11.1-23)
> *List* of families from Judah and Benjamin (Neh. 11.25-36)
> *List* of priests and Levites (Neh. 12.1-26; from Zerubbabel's time 1–11;
>   from Joiakim's time 12–21; further lists up to the time of Darius II
>   22–25).

In addition to these directly or indirectly cited documents there are two important passages containing first-person accounts by Ezra and Nehemiah. Since the traditional classification of their genre as *memoirs* or *memoranda* seems inadequte, they are here referred to as *personal accounts*. Ezra's personal accounts are found in Ezra 7.27–8.34; 9.1-15, including a list (8.26-27) and a prayer (9.6-15). Nehemiah's personal accounts are found in Neh. 1.1b–7.5; 12.27-43; 13.4-31.

1.2 *Exact Dating of Documents and Events*
In addition to the many documents referred to above, the book's authenticity as a historical source is further enhanced by the exact dating of the events reported in the table following.

The dating format varies. The year of the king's reign is given only in the first of a series of dates, sometimes followed by the month as an ordinal number and sometimes the day. Only in Neh. 1.1; 2.1; 6.15 and Ezra 6.15 are the

Verse		Day	Month	Year
Ezra 1.1	וּבִשְׁנַת אַחַת לְכוֹרֶשׁ			1 Cyrus
3.1	וַיִּגַּע הַחֹדֶשׁ הַשְּׁבִיעִי		07	
3.6	מִיּוֹם אֶחָד לַחֹדֶשׁ הַשְּׁבִיעִי	01	07	
3.8	וּבַשָּׁנָה הַשֵּׁנִית לְבוֹאָם		02	2 Cyrus
6.15	עַד יוֹם תְּלָתָה לִירַח אֲדָר	03	Adar (12)	6 Darius
6.19	בְּאַרְבָּעָה עָשָׂר לַחֹדֶשׁ הָרִאשׁוֹן:	14	01	
7.7	בִּשְׁנַת־שֶׁבַע לְאַרְתַּחְשַׁסְתְּא הַמֶּלֶךְ			7 Artaxerxes
7.8	בַּחֹדֶשׁ הַחֲמִישִׁי הִיא שְׁנַת הַשְּׁבִיעִית לַמֶּלֶךְ		05	7 Artaxerxes
7.9	כִּי בְּאֶחָד לַחֹדֶשׁ הָרִאשׁוֹן	01	01	
7.9	וּבְאֶחָד לַחֹדֶשׁ הַחֲמִישִׁי	01	05	
8.31	בִּשְׁנֵים עָשָׂר לַחֹדֶשׁ הָרִאשׁוֹן	12	01	
10.9	חֹדֶשׁ הַתְּשִׁיעִי בְּעֶשְׂרִים בַּחֹדֶשׁ	20	09	
10.16	בְּיוֹם אֶחָד לַחֹדֶשׁ הָעֲשִׂירִי	01	10	
10.17	עַד יוֹם אֶחָד לַחֹדֶשׁ הָרִאשׁוֹן	01	01	
Neh. 1.1	בְחֹדֶשׁ־(כְּסְלֵו) [כִּסְלֵיו] שְׁנַת עֶשְׂרִים		Kislev (9)	20 Artaxerxes
2.1	בְּחֹדֶשׁ נִיסָן שְׁנַת עֶשְׂרִים לְאַרְתַּחְשַׁסְתְּא		Nisan (1)	20 Artaxerxes
5.14	מִשְּׁנַת עֶשְׂרִים			20 Artaxerxes
5.14	וְעַד שְׁנַת שְׁלֹשִׁים וּשְׁתַּיִם לְאַרְתַּחְשַׁסְתְּא			32 Artaxerxes
6.15	בְּעֶשְׂרִים וַחֲמִשָּׁה לֶאֱלוּל	25	Elul (12)	
7.72	וַיִּגַּע הַחֹדֶשׁ הַשְּׁבִיעִי		07	
8.2	בְּיוֹם אֶחָד לַחֹדֶשׁ הַשְּׁבִיעִי:	01	07	
8.14	בַּחֹדֶשׁ הַשְּׁבִיעִי		07	
9.1	וּבְיוֹם עֶשְׂרִים וְאַרְבָּעָה לַחֹדֶשׁ הַזֶּה	24	(07)	
13.6	כִּי בִּשְׁנַת שְׁלֹשִׁים וּשְׁתַּיִם לְאַרְתַּחְשַׁסְתְּא			32 Artaxerxes

months referred to by name (Elul, Adar, Kislev and Nisan) in connection with the year of the Persian king's reign.[3]

3. The fact that these names occur only in Nehemiah's personal accounts, not in Ezra's, has led Juha Pakkala to conclude from a literary point of view that the dates in Neh. 7.72-9.1 correspond to Ezra's personal account and belong to an early version of this text (*Ezra the Scribe – The Development of Ezra 7–10 and Nehemiah 8* (Berlin: Walter de Gruyter, 2004, 170–73).

Combining these dates with those of Persian history a rough chronology of the narrated events can be established as follows:

Cyrus II.	Edict – First return of exiles under	538	Ezra 1.1–2.70;
539–530	Sheshbazzar = governor of Judah. *Altar built*	537	3.1-13; Dan.
			1.1; 6.29; 10.1
539–	Daniel personal assistant to Darius the Mede		
	(= Cyrus?, Dan. 6.28; or = Gubaru?, King/		Dan. 5.31–6.2,
	Satrap of Babylon and Trans-Euphrates)		28; 9.1; 11.1
	Temple construction ceased		Ezra 4.4-5, 24
Kambyses II.			
530–522			
Darius I.	*Temple built and consecrated* – Passover	521	Ezra 5.1–6.22;
522–486	Zerubbabel governor of Judah	516	Hag. 1.1; 2.1,
	Joshua high-priest		11, 20;
			Zech. 1.1, 7; 7.1
	Tattenai, Official of Satrap of	522?–	Ezra 5.3, 13
	Trans-Euphrates		
Xerxes =	Letter accusing the Jews	?	Ezra 4.6
Ahasueros	Queen Vashti repudiated	482	Est. 1.3
485–465	*Persian defeats* (at Sea at Salamis, on land	480	
	at Platea)	479	
	Esther becomes queen	478	Est. 2.16;
	Pogrom against the Jews/Purim	472	Est. 3.7; 9.1-10
Artaxerxes I.	Attempted construction of the wall?		Ezra 4.7-22, 23
= Artahsasta	Jerusalem again destroyed	458	
13.4.464-424	Ezra: Priestly legislator under Persian		Ezra 7–10
	suzerainty, return of exiles		Neh. 8–10
	Nehemiah – governor of Judah –1st journey.	445	Neh. 1.1–7.3
	Construction and dedication of the wall.	444	Neh. 12.27-43
	Nehemiah's return to Babylon	433	
	Nehemiah's 2nd visit to Jerusalem, reform	n.432	Neh. 13
Darius II			Neh. 12.26
423–405			

1.3 *Discrepancies in the Chronological Order*

As noted in the commentaries, contrary to the normal expectation of modern Western readers, events in Ezra-Nehemiah are not always related in strict chronological order because the narrator evidently has other priorities.[4] Earlier commentaries tended to view this very critically as 'chaotic', 'very badly arranged'[5] or 'trivial'. In the light of modern readers' expectations, one encounters terms such as 'anachronism' or 'anomaly'.[6]

For example:

a. Ezra 4.1-5 refers to difficulties the returned exiles experienced with the local population from the reign of Cyrus to the reign of Darius. A letter is then referred to which was written during the reign of Xerxes (4.6), and correspondence between Rehum and Shimshai and the Persian overlord Artaxerxes (4.7-23).

   Ezra 4.24 then picks up the narrative thread from 4.5 and relates the completion of the temple under Darius. The reign of the Persian rulers Xerxes and Artaxerxes was subsequent to Darius, not between Cyrus and Darius, which was the reign of Cambyses, a figure who does not feature in the biblical record. Nevertheless, for the reader unfamiliar with the dates concerned, the conclusion in 4.24 gives the impression that it was the antagonism under Xerxes and Artaxerxes which was responsible for work on the temple stopping in the reign of Cyrus.

   Conservative commentators earlier sought to amend the chronology to make the correspondence fit into a time window between Cyrus and Darius. This involved reinterpreting Xerxes (Ahasueros) as Cambyses and Artaxerxes (Artasasta) as an usurper who seized power in Persia a few

---

4. This is the case in many biblical books, cf. H.H. Klement, 'David und Hiram von Tyrus – Zum Unterschied von literarischer und chronologischer Sequenz in biblischer Historiographie', *Jahrbuch für evangelikale Theologie* 14 (2000), 5–33.

5. e.g. C.C. Torrey, *The Composition and Historical Value of Chronicles – Ezra – Nehemiah* (Giessen: J. Richer'sche, 1896): 'No fact of Old Testament criticism is more firmly established than this; that the Chronicler, as a historian, is thoroughly untrustworthy. He distorts facts deliberately and habitually; invents chapter after chapter with the greatest freedom; and, what is most dangerous of all, his history is not written for its own sake, but in the interest of an extremely one-sided theory' (pp. 51–52). Leslie McFall, 'Was Nehemiah Contemporary with Ezra in 458 BC?', *WTJ* 53/2 (1991), 262–93 (266, n. 14) says of Torrey: 'He makes similar disparaging remarks regarding the Chronicler's "slovenly style" (pp. 27–28), and "his capacity to invent" events, such as the Return (pp. 52, 60, 62) and persons, such as Ezra (pp. 29, 61).'

6. K. Grünwaldt, 'Nehemiah', in *Biographisch-Bibliographisches Kirchenlexikon* (vol. 6; Verlag Traugott Bautz, 1993), Cols. 564–73.

months before Darius. Such conjectures remained unconfirmed and are no longer put forward today.[7]

b. Ezra 6.14 gives a summary of those responsible for the completion of the Second Temple. Construction recommenced at the instigation of the prophets Haggai and Zechariah according to the God of Israel's command and the decree of the Persian kings Cyrus, Darius and Artaxerxes. The following verse (6.15) gives the date of completion as the third of the month Adar in the sixth year of Darius' reign, i.e. long before Artaxerxes came to the throne. Anyone ignorant of the chronology might be forgiven for assuming Artaxerxes' support preceded the consecration of the temple, which was simply not the case. The author, fully familiar with the dates of the Persian kings and assuming similar familiarity in his readers, cites the names of the three kings because his concern is to show how they all legitimized and supported the temple. Later readers unfamiliar with Persian chronology might find this irritating and judge it erroneous or abnormal, which is hardly fair to the authorial intention.

c. According to Ezra 7.1 'after these things' Ezra went to Jerusalem in the seventh year of Artaxerxes. It is not clear whether this refers to events related in the immediately preceding co-text or, as Philip Brown thinks,[8] also a reference to the previous mention of Artaxerxes in Ezra 4. Rehum and Shimshai's letter to Artaxerxes refers to a group of Jews who had come up from him (4.12). The group which came with Artaxerxes' permission were the returning exiles under Ezra. Although they had been sent with full royal support, they did not enjoy full official protection (cf. Ezra 8.22). This makes it likely the group referred to in the accusing letter was identical with the exiles returning with Ezra. This letter is the only extant reference to their attempt to rebuild the walls of Jerusalem, which is not mentioned in later depictions of Ezra's activities.

d. Nehemiah also confronts one with chronological puzzles. Nehemiah 5 refers to social unrest among the population caused by the burdensome taxation of the Persian Empire, forcing some people to mortgage property or even sell their children into slavery. The tensions resulted in a popular assembly agreeing to a debt moratorium. The chapter makes no reference to any financial burden due to the cost of rebuilding the city wall, but as it constitutes a retrospect on the first 12 years of Nehemiah's office (5.14) it would have hardly been appropriate to insert the episode

---

7. See A.P. Brown II, 'Nehemiah and Narrative Order in the Book of Ezra', *BibSac* 162 (2005), 175–94 (183).

8. A.P. Brown II, 'Chronological Anomalies in the Book of Ezra', *BibSac* 162 (2005), 33–49 (43–47).

of the assembly into the narrative of the rebuilding the wall covering a period of only 52 days. It can easily be imagined that the reconstruction of the wall entailed an enormous financial burden, yet the narration of such tensions does not necessarily have to be placed in chronological sequence.

2. *Rhetorical and Theological Aims of the Work*

2.1 *Date and Authorship*
The question of the book's authorship continues to occupy commentators. Lack of precise information as to how the work originated means its traditional Jewish ascription to Ezra cannot be entirely ruled out but seems hardly plausible.

The book cannot have originated earlier than the dates referred to it already noted above. The last Persian overlord referred to is Darius II (Nothus, 423–405). After Jeshua, who officiated in Zerubbabel's day, the high priest's genealogy (Neh. 12.10-11) refers to Joiakim, Eliashib, Joiada, Jonathan and Jaddua. Eliashib and his family took part in rebuilding the wall (Neh. 3.1).[9] The sons of Joiada are referred to in Neh. 13.28 but whether they had succeeded as high priest is not mentioned. This would give a date before 400 BC.[10]

In a recent publication Kyung-jin Min has now also argued for an early dating closer to the events recorded.[11] Min moreover detects in Ezra-Nehemiah a Levitical apologetic, which is supported by the fact that the Levites play a crucial role in the interpretation of the Torah and that the book sees obedience to the Torah as constitutive for Israel's post-exilic identity.

9. The Eliashib named in Ezra 10.6 was not high priest, the one in Neh. 13.4 may not have been.

10. See Koorevaar, 'Die Chronik', 71: 'The close of Ezra's and Nehemiah's activity may be regarded as the *terminus ad quem* [for the dating of Chronicles], i.e. 411 BC or a little later, based on the names of the high priests in Ezra 10.6 and Neh. 12.10f, 22.' According to J.R. Shavers, *Torah and the Chronicler's History Work: An Inquiry into the Chronicles' References to Laws, Festivals, and Cultic Institutions in Relationship to Pentateuchal Legislation* (Brown Judaic Studies, 196; Atlanta: Scholars,1989), Neh. 12.23 'up to the days of Johanan' seems to imply Johanan was the last officiating high priest. C.F. Keil, *The Postexilic History: Chronicles, Ezra, Nehemiah and Esther* (Old Testament Biblical Commentary; Leipzig: Dörffling & Franke, 1870), 492–99 (496), concluded that Nehemiah was composed towards the end of Nehemiah's life and postulated a possible date of 415 BC, although Nehemiah may have survived until 405 BC.

11. K.-j. Min, *The Levitical Authorship of Ezra-Nehemiah* (JSOTSup, 409; London: T & T Clark, 2004).

2.2 *Content*

The book's content makes its intention clear and can be summarized in six main points:

1. Ezra-Nehemiah relates the *constitution of a new Israel* in continuity with the pre-exilic people. The book covers a period of some 140 years with several waves of returning exiles of which two are reported in some detail. The first group of more than 42,000 people connected with Sheshbazzar and Zerubbabel returned shortly after Cyrus' edict of 538 BC (Ezra 1–2; Neh. 7). A second important group connected with Ezra (Ezra 7.6-9) returned 80 years later (458 BC) and formed together with the exiles already in the land a spiritual and political community. Other individuals and groups joined them, as is clear from Nehemiah, whose family resided in Jerusalem although they are not referred to in either of the aforementioned groups. This community is portrayed in the narrative as the new Israel gathered round the temple.
2. The community of repatriated exiles finds cohesion and identity in gathering as Yahweh's people in their ancient homeland with the aim of *rebuilding Yahweh's Temple in Jerusalem*. This is central to the narrative, whereas other social, psychological, economic and political factors implied by the repatriation of such a numerous population are mentioned only in passing or have to be read between the lines. As a first step the altar is rebuilt on the site of the old temple as the spiritual focus of the community, and regular sacrificial services are instituted. Then work on rebuilding the temple begins and after some difficulties is completed in the sixth year of Darius' reign (516 BC). When the temple had been consecrated, 16 years after the departure from Babylon as a result of Cyrus' edict, the people celebrated a great Passover feast (Ezra 6.19-22) and thereby identified themselves with the first generation of Israel's Exodus under Moses, celebrating liturgically the Second Exodus from Mesopotamia predicted by the prophets (e.g. Jer. 16.14-15; 23.7-8). The reference to the date of Ezra's departure with his companions from the river Ahava as the 12th Nisan (Ezra 8.31) also establishes a parallel to the Exodus: just as Moses led the people out of Egypt, so under Yahweh's protection Ezra leads the exiles back to the land of their forefathers.
3. The completion of the temple as liturgical centre is then followed by a *fresh proclamation of the Torah*. This is closely connected with the figure of Ezra, whose high-priestly genealogy is traced back to Moses' brother Aaron, and who is portrayed as intercessor for his people and teacher of the law. Membership of the people of God is now defined not only in terms of genealogical descent but also as a commitment to observe the provisions of the Torah. An acid test of loyalty to the Torah is the controversial annulment of mixed marriages between repatriated exiles and the previous inhabitants,

reported in Ezra 10. Membership of Yahweh's community is determined by a written commitment of loyalty to Yahweh, and failure to comply results in exclusion from the community (Ezra 10.8; Neh. 10.1, 29–30).[12]

4. Nehemiah is closely linked with the account of the third concrete measure, the *rebuilding of the city wall of Jerusalem*. Although the idea originated much earlier (cf. Zech. 2.4-5; Ezra 4.12-13), the task was only completed in 444 BC, 93 years after the arrival of the first exiles following Cyrus' edict and 70 years after the consecration of the Second Temple. The reconstruction of Jerusalem constituted an important stage in the renewal of the people.

5. Only after the completion of the city wall round Jerusalem does Ezra-Nehemiah refer to it as '*îr haqqōdeš* 'sacred city' or 'city of holiness' (Neh. 11.1). Jerusalem is sacred because of the temple, although the description of its consecration in just three verses (Ezra 6.16-18) is modest in comparison with the narrative of the consecration of Solomon's temple in 1 Kgs 8.1-66 or the expanded account in 2 Chron. 5.2–7.2. Tamara Cohn Eskenazi[13] has urged that the temple reconstruction ordered by Cyrus should only be considered as accomplished once the city wall was completed, but her definition of the temple has rightly been criticized as too broad. The city of Jerusalem is neither designated a sanctuary nor confused with the temple. Ezra-Nehemiah regards them as distinct entities. The temple reconstruction is nevertheless of the greatest importance for the identity of the post-exilic community, for which a rebuilt and intact city of Jerusalem was vitally necessary. Jerusalem is denoted *a holy city* in the context of Nehemiah 10 because its inhabitants have been allotted as a 'tithe' of the total population. Just as the 'first-fruits' and 'tithes' sanctify the entire harvest by being devoted to Yahweh, so it is the implied theological function of the inhabitants of Jerusalem to constitute a 'tithe gift' which sanctifies the entire population of returning exiles. The emphasis is on the holiness and purity of the whole population.

6. The population's gift of the tithe to the holy city fulfilling this new destiny of Jerusalem is preceded by the consecration of the whole people through the proclamation of the Torah (Nehemiah 8), repentance (Nehemiah 9), and their commitment signed by the elders to observe the Torah and to guarantee provisions for the temple ministry. The consecration of the rebuilt wall is related only after Jerusalem being re-designated 'Holy City' (Neh. 12.27-34).

12. Stefan Stiegler has referred to this confessional discipline in the post-exilic community as a 'primitive form of free-church piety'; see S. Stiegler, 'Vorformen freikirchlicher Frömmigkeit im Alten Testament: die nachexilische Gemeinde in Jerusalem', *Theologisches Gespräch* 15/2 (1991), 16–24.

13. T. Cohn Eskenazi, *In an Age of Prose: A Literary Approach to Ezra-Nehemiah* (SBLDS, 36; Atlanta: Scholars, 1988).

The account of this outstanding national feast is bracketed by lists of the priestly families (Neh. 12.1-26) and provisions for the temple personnel (Neh. 12.44-47).

2.3 *Rhetorical Intent and Emphases*
The rhetorical intention and emphases of Ezra-Nehemiah are summed up in the following seven points:

1. Summarizing her literary-critical study of the themes of Ezra-Nehemiah, Eskenazi lists as the primary topic the people who constitute the new community rather than salient participants such as Sheshbazzar, Joshua, Zerubbabel, Ezra or Nehemiah.[14] Rather than being individually emphasized or characterized, they feature because of their contribution to the building up the people as a whole, resulting not in a series of separate biographies but the one story of the people. The numerous lists of names emphasize the actions of individuals. Cyrus' edict appealed to individuals among the people to return to Jerusalem (Ezra 1.3). 'The people gathered as one man to Jerusalem' to build the altar (Ezra 3.1). The temple was built and consecrated by the elders (Ezra 6.14-18), and it was by those 'who had returned from exile' (Ezra 6.19, 21), who celebrated the subsequent great Passover.

   It was not Ezra who took the initiative against mixed marriages but leaders of the people (Ezra 9.1,4; 10.1-4, 10, 14). It was 'some men of Judah' (Neh. 1.2) who stirred Nehemiah into action to rebuild the wall. He was overall in charge of the project, but Neh. 3.1-32 lists the names of the teams of workers. The initiative for public reading of the law also came from the people. 'All the people assembled as one man in the square before the Water Gate. They told Ezra the scribe to bring out the Book of the Law of Moses, which the LORD had commanded for Israel' (Neh. 8.1). The Torah is read and explained in the hearing of men, women and even young people – literally 'all who could understand it'. The subsequent repentance is an act of the entire people under the leadership of the Levites (Neh. 9.1, 5). The commitment to observe the law was decided and signed by the people's leaders (Neh. 10.1). It was the 'rest of the people' who decided by lot to send every tenth inhabitant to reside in Jerusalem (Neh. 11.1-2). It was the elders of the entire people who took part with the liturgical choirs in the two processions round the city walls. The entire population, including women and children explicitly, joined in the great joy of this feast (Neh. 12.43).

   This continuous emphasis on the people's responsible participation in building up the post-exilic community is rhetorically striking, suggesting

---

14. Eskenazi, *In an Age of Prose*, 185.

the book was written to involve the reader as a member of the community and as heir of the renewal movement.

2. The author's overarching perspective portrays a *new beginning* as a unified and cohesive period in which the events narrated lead step by step to the point reached by the completion of the Jerusalem city wall in the author's day. Looking back, the author perceives this period 'from Zerubbabel to Nehemiah' (Neh. 12.47) as coherent and concluded. The existence of other provincial governors is recognized (Neh. 5.15) but only referred to in passing. Some dates can be deduced from archaeological finds.[15]

Name	Source	Date (BC)
Sheshbazzar	Ezra 1.8; 5.14	538
Zerubbabel	Hag. 1.1, 14	515
Elnathan	Bull with seal	Late sixth century
Jehoezer	Jug inscription	Early fifth century
Ahzai	Jug inscription	Early fifth century
Nehemiah	Neh. 5.14; 12.26	445–432
Bahoi (Bagoas)	Cowley 30:1	407
Yehezqiya	Coins	330

Another indication that the book's author regarded the whole period as a cohesive unit is the summary list of Persian kings who furthered the temple rebuilding in Ezra 6.14, as referred to above. Whereas the limited field of vision of the immediate context leads modern readers to suspect an anachronism, the author's bird's eye retrospective view requires mention of Artaxerxes as well as Cyrus and Darius, while taking as read for himself and his contemporary readers the precise chronology of the period.[16]

3. The consciousness that the period constituted a unity has also determined the *portrayal of the adversaries* right at the start in Ezra 4. After relating the return and its troubled and modest beginnings in Ezra 3, the author turns to the difficulties experienced with the previous inhabitants. They continued to present a challenge in the author's own time, as the reference to the problem of intermarriage and loss of Israel's identity with which the book

---

15. Following E.M. Yamauchi, *Persia and the Bible* (Grand Rapids: Baker, 1996), 265; cf. H.G.M. Williamson, 'The Governors of Judah under the Persians', *TynB* 39 (1988), 59–82.

16. On the differing perceptions of reality in the ANE and modernity, cf. E. Brunner-Traut, *Frühformen des Erkennens: Am Beispiel Altägyptens* (Darmstadt: WBG, 1992).

closes (Nehemiah 13) is witness to. These continuing tensions obviously were already present under Zerubbabel.

The first source of problems was the returned exiles' refusal to let the previous inhabitants of the land participate in rebuilding the temple, which led to persistent animosity (Ezra 4.1). There may well have been many and various social and psychological grounds for the tensions between the new arrivals and the indigenous population, but they are only alluded to indirectly. For the reader the local inhabitants are immediately and unambiguously denoted *ṣārê yᵉhûdā*, 'enemies of Judah', an evaluation which also looks back on the whole period, since the desire to assist in the rebuilding referred to in Ezra 4.1 can hardly of itself be interpreted as hostile. The Yahwist reader will however have recognized implicitly how impossible it was to cooperate with those who describe themselves as descendants of the Assyrian king Esar-Haddon and who had settled in the land and claimed to have been worshipping Yнwн along with other deities (Ezra 4.2).

Subsequent experience proved this estimate from Zerubbabel's day to be correct, as is made clear to the reader in the form of the accusing letter against the Jews in Xerxes' time (Ezra 4.6) and, immediately following, the correspondence from the days of Artaxerxes as damning evidence of hostility (Ezra 4.7-23). These complaints led not only to a halt in the rebuilding but also to violence and the use of force in Jerusalem, and to the already laid foundations being destroyed (Ezra 4.23). The specific complaint in Artaxerxes' day was that the city was being rebuilt (Ezra 4.12), but the author sees this in continuity with attempts to hinder the temple reconstruction in Zerubbabel's day (Ezra 4.24). His rhetorical intention being to highlight the dangers of assimilation, the author sees this hostility as all of a piece, whereby it may be assumed he and his readers were fully aware of the chronological distances involved and the exact dates are always given. From the author's own perspective the events lay decades in the past but all fitted into the overall picture of the jeopardy to God's people which he wanted to communicate to his readers.

It is a justifiable assumption that Ezra-Nehemiah was written with the new generation in mind, on whom the responsibility falls for carrying on the work of renewal after the events narrated. The author is not interested in composing either a historical archive or a supposedly objective account of what is in fact a modest slice of history. He presents rather experiences gathered with the local inhabitants in the period 'from Cyrus to Artaxerxes' in which the 'enemies of Judah' have not really changed. His starkly drawn portrait early in the book underlines his concern to win his contemporary readers over to his own evauation of the local populations, for which the book furnishes sufficient evidence.

4. The value of the testimony of the *documents cited in Aramaic* is rhetorically underlined by the language used. The text is in Aramaic from the cited letter of accusation right through to the description of the completion of the temple (Ezra 4.8–6.22). The author not only proves his linguistic competence in Aramaic as well as Hebrew but by employing the lingua franca he hints that even with the finished temple Israel remains a dependent people. The correspondence reminds one that it is at once the language of the Persian hegemony and the language in which the hostility of those settled in the land from Assyria finds expression. The freedom from servitude celebrated at Passover (Ezra 6.10-22) has not yet been fully realized. There is still real dependence.

This sense of continuing dependence lies behind the denotation of Darius as 'King of Assyria'. While this was his official title for those of his subjects residing in Assyria, in this context it recalls the tradition of the occupying rural population and the inhabitants of Samaria. In their letter of accusation they described themselves as those whom 'the great and honourable Osnappar deported and settled in the city of Samaria and in the rest of the region beyond the River' (Ezra 4.2, 10). The reference to Darius as 'King of Assur' lets the reader know what the author thinks of the continuing support of the Persian monarchs. While there is no direct anti-Persian polemic nor call for independence from Persia in Ezra-Nehemiah, passages like this show that the lack of freedom colours the author's consciousness. At the close of their prayer of repentence (Neh. 9.36-37; cf. Ezra 9.8-9) the people remind Yhwh of their servitude, requesting him by implication to emancipate them from the still present burden of slavery and taxation. Freely admitting this situation has come about primarily through their own fault, their confession of guilt and prayer for forgiveness implies the hope of future emancipation.

5. Although a sense of longing for freedom from imposition is clearly recognizable in Ezra-Nehemiah, there is no expression of hope for a *restoration of the monarchy*. While valuable prescriptions for temple worship are more than once traced back to David (Ezra 3.10; Neh. 12.24) and to Solomon (Neh. 12.45-46), there is no evidence in the book for any political expectation in the Davidic line. Solomon is mentioned as the origin of the temple slaves (Ezra 2.55, 58) but also as a negative example of one who, through marriage alliances with foreign wives, brought calamity on the Davidic monarchy (Neh. 13.26). His role as temple builder is never referred to, although such a reference would have seemed appropriate given the topic of Ezra-Nehemiah. The location of the royal house, garden and tombs are explicitly mentioned in connection with the building and consecration of the city wall (Neh. 3.15-16; 12.37) and the Persians are familiar with the extent of the Davidic dominions in the Trans-Euphrates province (Ezra 4.16, 20), yet the

social ideal which inspires the author of Ezra-Nehemiah is not monarchy[17] but a communal life based on the Sinai Torah. Reference to the monarchy is restricted to David's role in connection with the temple, while the community ideal looks back before the monarchy to the Torah linked with the name of Moses.

6. In addition to the topical cohesion of the period as Israel's restoration as God's people it is clear from the outset that the ultimate initiative for the whole enterprise lay with God himself. The very first sentence of the book directs the reader's attention to the fact that the new start originated not with the Persian king Cyrus but with the God of Israel. The events of the period from Zerubbabel to Nehemiah are portrayed as the work of YHWH. It was YHWH who brought destructive retribution on Israel, as Jeremiah had predicted, and through the selfsame prophet he promised a return to the land after a period of 70 years. The same YHWH who had sent Jeremiah was now fulfilling his promise through the events described in Ezra.

It was Haggai and Zechariah prophesying 'in the name of the God of Israel' (Ezra 5.1) which led to a fresh start in rebuilding the temple under Darius. Their ministry bore such fruit that it could be said that not only the exiles' return to the land but also the completion of the temple took place 'according to the command of the God of Israel' and of the Persian kings (Ezra 6.14). Ezra's expedition from Babylon to Jerusalem proved a success because 'the hand of YHWH his God was upon him' (Ezra 7.6). Ezra blessed God that He had put it into the heart of the Persian king to send him to the land of his forefathers and to entrust him with this ministry (Ezra 7.27f.). He had affirmed to the king that God's hand is with those who seek after Him (Ezra 8.22). In his personal account Nehemiah also testified that God's hand of guidance and protection was on him too (Neh. 2.8, 18). His response to the now traditional adversaries is that their opposition will not be successful because YHWH Himself is behind the project to rebuild Jerusalem (Neh. 4.14), as they themselves are finally forced to admit once the work has been completed (Neh. 6.16). God Himself was the source of the people's joy at the consecration of the wall of Jerusalem. Ezra-Nehemiah portrays the whole period as an act of the God of Israel, a divine project in which the returning exiles, Ezra and Nehemiah assumed their respective roles.

7. This divine enterprise on behalf of the people of Israel as a whole, presented as one cohesive event, remains nevertheless in jeopardy because the

17. Cf. H.H. Klement, 'Monarchiekritik und Herrscherverheißung: Alttestamentlich-theologische Aspekte zur Rolle des Königs in Israel', in H.H. Klement and J. Steinberg (eds.), *Themenbuch zur Theologie des Alten Testaments* (Wuppertal: R. Brockhaus, 2007), 275–306.

adversaries who have been trying to undermine the project from the very beginning are still at work. The book closes with an account of disputes intended to prevent what has been achieved in the past from being put at risk (Nehemiah 13). It is rhetorically significant that the book ends on the note of the high-priestly family's implication in a mixed marriage (Neh. 13.28). The reference to Solomon, whose liaisons with foreign princesses led to the catastrophe of the divided kingdom (Neh. 13.26), shows that high rank is no ground for tolerating such practices. The rhetorical thrust of the book is thus *aimed at a readership which has not yet overcome the danger of assimilation*. There is a real risk of a relapse. The review of past history, especially in the penitential prayers (Ezra 9.6-15; Neh. 1.5-11; 9.5-37), make it clear that the success of the fresh start is in no way guaranteed.

The book was written to emphasize that the post-exilic community finds its identity in YHWH. The author identifies with YHWH's activity under Ezra and Nehemiah and invites his readers to adopt this perspective and commit themselves to the same concern. The future as YHWH's people lies with those who keep the Torah. The priority of the Torah over the cult shows this is equally valid for the priests who serve in the temple. The only figure in the book whose high-priestly genealogy is traced right back to Aaron is Ezra, the teacher of the Torah. The temple cult is not called into question but the priority of obedience to the Torah is demonstrated in the final chapter, where the officiating priests must bow to the Torah's demands (Neh. 13.4-13).

3. *Further Notes on the Chronology*

The insights thus far gained into particular rhetorical features permit a fresh approach to questions in other texts.

3.1 *The Twofold List of Inhabitants of the Jehud Province*
The list of the returning exiles in Ezra 2 is repeated in Nehemiah 7. This list bears the title 'These are the people of the province who came up from the captivity of the exiles . . .'. The designation 'people of the *medinah* (province)' is noteworthy, this being the Aramaic term for a Persian province, indicating this is not a list of members of an expedition but of inhabitants made up of the following elements (according to Stiegler):[18]

---

18. S. Stiegler, *Die nachexilische JHWH-Gemeinde in Jerusalem: Ein Beitrag zu einer alttestamentlichen Ekklesiologie* (BEATAJ, 34; Frankfurt a. M.: Peter Lang, 1994), 55.

a.	Frame	Ezra 2.1-2a	Neh. 7.6-7a
		Ezra 2.70	Neh. 7.72
b.	Lay people		
	By families	Ezra 2.3-20	Neh. 7.8-24
	By place of residence	Ezra 2.21-35	Neh. 7.25-38
c.	Cult personnel		
	Priests	Ezra 2.36-39	Neh. 7.39-42
	Levites	Ezra 2.40	Neh. 7.43
	Singers	Ezra 2.41	Neh. 7.44
	Gatekeepers	Ezra 2.42	Neh. 7.45
	Temple servants	Ezra 2.43-48	Neh. 7.46-60
d.	Returnees without proof of origin	Ezra 2.59-63	Neh. 7.61-65
e.	Total 42,360	Ezra 2.64-65	Neh. 7.66-67
f.	Mounts	Ezra 2.66-67	Neh. 7.68
g.	List of donations	Ezra 2.68-69	Neh 7.69-71

The 'list of the *medinah* (province)' is made up of lay people and cult personnel. The lay people are listed by family and clan and place of residence (Ezra 2.21-28). Stiegler[19] has suggested this list of the community of returned exiles may have originated in connection with the inspection under Tattenai,[20] who had demanded such a list be drawn up (Ezra 5.10). This would explain the presence of place names in the list and also the link to Zerubbabel rather than Sheshbazzar, referred to in Ezra 1.11. Lack of concrete information makes any hypotheses about Sheshbazzar's governorship speculative, but he may have returned to the Persian court after a brief period in office and so no longer belonged to the repatriated community, a scenario which in the light of the book's already observed chronological features is plausible if not demonstrable.

3.2 *The Dedication of the City Wall*
The book's already noted primacy of theological and topical concerns over a purely linear chronology means that the considerable segment of material lying between the actual completion of the city wall (Neh. 6.15) and its dedication with two processions (Neh. 12.27-43) may also mean it is not possible to assume the literary content is in chronological order. Not only does Nehemiah 12, with its list of priests and Levites from Zerubbabel's day, look

19. Stiegler, *Die nachexilische JHWH-Gemeinde in Jerusalem*, 57ff.
20. Tattenai was travelling as deputy of Ushtannu, Satrap 'over Babylon and Trans-Euphrates'; cf. Yamauchi, *Persia and the Bible*, 156.

back on the entire period, but a similar retrospective cannot be excluded for the material in between.

In the signing of the covenant in Nehemiah 10, for instance, Nehemiah appears in his role as governor. The wall was built in the first two months after he arrived in Jerusalem. Its dedication will hardly have taken place long afterwards. The ordering of the material according to literary concerns makes it impossible to identify at which point in Nehemiah's 12-year period of office the written commitment to keep the Torah was made.

3.3 *Nehemiah 8*

For literary-critical reasons Nehemiah 8 or even Nehemiah 8–9 is often removed from its present setting and placed after Ezra 8, a plausible historical reconstruction, since Nehemiah 8 narrates a gathering under Ezra's leadership, namely his first public reading of Moses' Torah. It is argued this publication (Ezra 7.25) can hardly have taken place 13 years after Artaxerxes' decree officially promulgating the God of Israel's Torah as law. Commencing with Neh. 7.72b, the reading would fit well into Ezra's time.

Date		Reference
1st day, 1st month 7th year of Artaxerxes	Expedition planned	Ezra 7.9
12th day, 1st month	Start from the River Ahava	Ezra 8.31
1st day, 5th month	Arrival in Jerusalem	Ezra 7.8
4th day	Delivery of donations	Ezra 8.33
1st day, 7th month	Public Torah reading	Neh. 7.72b–8.8
20th day, 9th month	Public meeting, decision on divorce	Ezra 10.9
1st day, 10th month	Measures taken	Ezra 10.16
1st day, 1st month	Measures completed	Ezra 10.17

The only problem with this arrangement is the reference in Neh. 8.9 to Nehemiah encouraging the people alongside Ezra. A similar explicit reference to both is found in the procession at the dedication of the wall (Neh. 12.36, 38).

The book's tendency to disconcert the modern reader by juxtaposing topical material which does not belong chronologically has already been observed.[21]

---

21. Readers of the New Testament Gospel material will be familiar with similar topical grouping such as Matthew's Sermon on the Mount, Luke's Sermon on the Plain, and John's three years compared with Luke's great journey to Jerusalem.

Were Nehemiah 8 to be seen as a narrative not only of Ezra's first proclamation of the law but in this context equally a review of its subsequent proclamation throughout the whole period, including Nehemiah's own contribution, then the major event could be situated in Ezra's seventh year. A textual displacement is however excluded on literary-critical grounds because the order of the material in Ezra-Nehemiah is to be interpreted topically according to theological criteria. The book's interpretation must derive from its rhetorical intention.

Part II

PROPHETS

Chapter 5

JUDAH AS ISRAEL IN EIGHTH-CENTURY PROPHECY

H.G.M. Williamson
University of Oxford

A familiar topic of scholarly discussion is the use of the name Israel in the Hebrew Bible with reference to the region/country/province that we should more normally and appropriately consider to be called Judah. While this is relatively uncontroversial, even though of continuing interest, so far as the post-exilic period is concerned, its occurrence in the pre-exilic period has always evoked more discussion. In recent years, two new factors have come into play that have raised this issue in fresh, and in some senses more radical, ways.

1. *A United Israel?*

On the one hand a growing number of historians question whether there was ever a united monarchy of Israel under kings David and Solomon.[1] On this view, whatever type of society inhabited the region in previous centuries, the state of Israel as such first came into existence in the ninth century BCE with the Omri dynasty in what we conventionally describe as the northern kingdom. The monumental buildings and fortifications at such sites as Megiddo and Hazor that were previously ascribed to the tenth-century reign of Solomon are dated later, on this view, in order to accommodate this new political understanding.[2] Judah was sparsely inhabited and Jerusalem was of no great significance, so that

---

1. For a full recent survey with abundant bibliography, see, for instance, W. Dietrich, *The Early Monarchy in Israel: The Tenth Century B.C.E.* (Biblical Encyclopedia, 3; Atlanta: SBL, 2007). The issue at stake is not whether there were 'kings' called David and Solomon, but whether the extent of their authority was sufficient to make meaningful the claim that the residents of the later kingdom of Judah had ever considered themselves to be part of a single 'Israel'.

2. See I. Finkelstein, 'Omride Architecture', *ZDPV* 116 (2000), 114–38.

the kingdom of Judah should be regarded as a later development, either along-side and in some measure in tandem with Israel or even, on the most extreme view, as a new entity as late as the period of Assyrian domination.

The importance of this new historical reconstruction for our present purpose is that Judah had never been, as in more traditional views, a part of a united entity called Israel which divided after the death of Solomon. There was no way, therefore, in which its pre-exilic inhabitants might somehow have retained a vestigial memory of their having once been a part of Israel and that in particu-lar circumstances this might have surfaced in an unexpected nomenclature. If the name Israel is applied to Judah in any text, that has simply to be regarded as anachronistic and therefore of obviously much later date than the time it purports to describe.

This relates loosely to the second consideration, therefore, which is of an exclusively literary-critical nature. While redaction criticism has long been use-fully applied to the prophetic and other texts, a trend has developed in recent years to take this very much further than previously. As we shall see, there are a few commentators now who would judge that this supposed anachronistic use of the name Israel is sufficient to date the relevant passage to the post-exilic period. Of course, this is not the sole, or even the main, reason for their overall position, but in association with the first, historical argument it plays its part in leading to a very different appreciation of early classical prophecy, whereby the once popular view that they spoke only words of judgment, with the salvation passages reflecting a later period, is now reversed and the prophets are regarded as far more supportive of the prevailing political establishment and the words of judgment are seen as later rationalizations for the disaster which overcame Judah at the hands of the Babylonians.[3]

If this represents the most extreme of the newer proposals, it should be noted that for similar reasons, though with somewhat less radical literary-critical conclusions, a number of others have recently taken the intermediate position that the name of Israel, which cannot originally have had any relation to Judah, probably travelled south, so to speak, after the fall of Samaria and the escape of a number of refugees to the south, bringing their name with them. On this view, a text referring to Judah as Israel might not necessarily be as late as the exilic (or later) period, but equally could not be earlier than the final decade or so of the eighth century. This intermediate position is obviously more difficult to assess because of the much tighter timeframe involved. Amos and Hosea ministered primarily to the northern kingdom of Israel in any case, so that the

---

3. For a prominent example in relation to the book of Isaiah, see U. Becker, *Jesaja – von der Botschaft zum Buch* (FRLANT, 178; Göttingen: Vandenhoeck & Ruprecht, 1997).

issue is not a live one in connection with them. Equally, Micah is generally agreed to be late eighth century (around the time of Sennacherib's invasion), by which time the transition could already have taken place. That leaves only Isaiah, and given that, on a standard view, he ministered after as well as before the fall of Samaria, it is a matter of fine judgment whether one can date particular passages in his work with the degree of precision necessary to reach a conclusion on our topic. Rost famously argued that the point of transition was the Syro-Ephraimite War, so that effectively all of Isaiah's ministry could stand in its wake.[4] This was modified by Høgenhaven to the fall of Samaria,[5] with the results that I have outlined, and this position's chronology, if not exactly its semantic significance, is also powerfully advocated by Kratz.[6]

2. *One Recent Reconstruction*

An interesting example of a thoughtful reconstruction that takes account of some of these points and yet recognizes that there is a significant question still to be answered is the recent monograph by Davies, who poses the first question he wishes to answer as 'Why did Judeans call themselves "Israel"?'[7] Noting that the name 'Israel' is variously applied in the Hebrew Bible, he dismisses most previous explanations as untenable for one reason or another; rather, he insists that the name as applied to Judah is not so much political as religious and ethnic. He then proceeds to an extensive survey of the historiographical literature both in order to buttress and refine this position and also to begin to explore the curious and yet important position of Benjamin in many narratives. On this basis he then postulates that there may have been a Benjaminite History of Israel which was later incorporated (with many changes, of course) into the Deuteronomistic History. Jeremiah is also invoked because of its evidence for the importance of Benjamin after the fall of Jerusalem. Davies then seeks to incorporate what is known from other sources, such as archaeology, to reinforce the conclusion that Mizpah, as regional capital for some 150 years, and Bethel, as its significant sanctuary, were the channels whereby the god of Israel came to be identified with the god of the Jerusalem sanctuary. In sum, the origins of Judah are revealed by archaeological surveys to have been separate from those of the heartland of Israel, and the literature relating to the reigns of Saul, David

---

4. L. Rost, *Israel bei den Propheten* (BWANT, 71; Stuttgart: Kohlhammer, 1937).

5. J. Høgenhaven, *Gott und Volk bei Jesaja: eine Untersuchung zur biblischen Theologie* (AThDan, 24; Leiden: Brill, 1988), 5–19.

6. R.G. Kratz, 'Israel in the Book of Isaiah', *JSOT* 31 (2006), 103–128.

7. P.R. Davies, *The Origins of Biblical Israel* (LHB/OTS, 485; New York and London: T & T Clark, 2007), 1.

and Solomon reflects that continuing separation (Saul never reigned over Judah, while David and Solomon reigned over each separately as a personal union). All this allows him to conclude that 'no text or passage in which Judah belongs to Israel should be dated before the Neo-Babylonian period at the earliest, and perhaps not before the Persian period'.[8]

At one level Davies's proposals have already encountered some criticism,[9] but his work both serves to underline the vibrancy of the question and also, I believe, to put a finger on an important aspect of the problem that deserves further consideration, namely the religious nature of this curious linguistic turn. However, as I shall attempt to show, the dates he works with may be unnecessarily late, and his insistence on the only very occasional use of this nomenclature in potentially earlier texts, which he thinks casts suspicion on their authenticity, has good reason.

3. *Judaean Identity and the Book of Micah*

The first point to be made is that, as with all the other discussions of this issue in recent times of which I am aware, there has been a curious tendency to ignore the potential contribution of the book of Micah. Focus has tended to concentrate on Isaiah, as already mentioned, while we have seen that Amos and Hosea, also much discussed, are inevitably somewhat less easy to evaluate because of their different primary audience. In the case of Micah, however, although there need be little doubt that significant parts of the book belong far later than the time of the eighth-century prophet, some of the material in chs. 1–3, at least, has a strong claim to authenticity. This is most obviously the case with the severe judgment saying at the end of ch. 3, because it was recalled specifically as having been spoken but not fulfilled at the time by the 'elders of the land' in Jer. 26.17-19. While the composition history of Jeremiah is itself an unusually complex subject, there seems to be no reason to doubt that at a time close to the Babylonian conquest (to be deliberately vague for the sake of the argument at this point) the written words of Micah were known and that they were already then ascribed to the reign of Hezekiah. This is unusual, if not unique, evidence for the secure dating of a prophetic text to a time well before the beginning of the exile.

In examining this text further, we find that it is integrally related to the city of Jerusalem; it is not a general judgment saying that might have been taken up from elsewhere (such as the northern kingdom) and reapplied to Judah. Its

---

8. Davies, *The Origins of Biblical Israel*, 176.
9. See, for instance, N. Na'aman, 'Saul, Benjamin and the Emergence of "Biblical Israel"', *ZAW* 121 (2009), 211–24 and 335–49.

wording is clear that it was formulated from the outset as a saying against Zion/ Jerusalem. The reference to the temple in the final line serves further only to reinforce this conclusion:

> Therefore because of you
> Zion shall be ploughed as a field;
> Jerusalem shall become a heap of ruins,
> and the mountain of the house a wooded height.

Turning to the addressees of this saying, it is striking then to observe that the same parallelism is in view, for they are called those 'who build Zion with blood and Jerusalem with wrong' (3.10). But this evident stylistic unity is introduced startlingly with an exhortation that inalienably identifies them further as members of the house of Jacob and Israel:

> Hear this, you rulers of the house of Jacob
> and chiefs of the house of Israel,
> who abhor justice
> and pervert all equity.

The one verse runs seamlessly into the next and, so far as I am aware, its literary unity has hardly ever been challenged.[10]

It should be noted, however, that this is not really just a simple case of Judah being called Israel, for the first element in the parallelism is Jacob, indicating that we are not dealing here with simple political terminology. The northern kingdom certainly had several names by which it was known internally and externally in ancient times, including (besides Israel) the land of Omri and Samaria, but 'the house of Jacob', while by no means unknown elsewhere, as we shall see, was not such a designation. In castigating the rulers for their failure in the administration of justice (vv. 9b-11a) the prophet then indicates that they are relying specifically on what has since come to be known as the Zion tradition (v. 11b, which clearly echoes Psalm 46), so tying the saying further with an exclusively Judaean motif and no doubt accounting for the climactic prediction of the destruction of the temple.

Given the closely integrated nature of this passage, we may move on with

---

10. For the discussion of one older exception, see W. McKane, *The Book of Micah: Introduction and Commentary* (Edinburgh: T & T Clark, 1998), 110-11. For a major discussion whose main conclusions are fully in line with the position defended here, see J.A. Wagenaar, *Judgement and Salvation: The Composition and Redaction of Micah 2–5* (VTSup, 85; Leiden: Brill, 2001), 241-61.

some confidence to find that a similar pattern is apparent elsewhere in Micah. At 3.1 the introductory 'And I said', strongly defended by Wolff as indicating Micah's own involvement in the later written recording/redaction of his own saying at this point,[11] introduces a saying which again condemns the leaders of the people for their failures with regard to justice and, closely similar to 3.9, calls them 'heads of Jacob and rulers of the house of Israel'.

In addition, at 3.8 the paragraph is concluded with a more general reference that the prophet will 'declare to Jacob his transgression and to Israel his sin'.

Further afield, the redactional history of Micah 1 is less clear, so that the status of v. 5, for instance, as a later, possibly exilic, reflection on the fall of Samaria and Jerusalem has been argued with some force.[12] If so, this may help account for the uncharacteristic application of Jacob and Israel explicitly to Samaria. The later part of the chapter, however, certainly has its origins in the eighth-century Assyrian invasion, and here the place names make the Judaean reference clear.[13] In this connection, the reference to Israel in the final line of v. 13 seems likely to be part of a small section of later commentary, in which the sins of the south are compared to those of the north: 'for in you were found the transgressions of Israel.' This usage, therefore, applies the name Israel to the north and is in line with common practice elsewhere.[14] In vv. 14 and 15, however, we find more tightly integrated references which it would be difficult to eliminate as later additions. Here, the 'kings of Israel' cannot be other than the kings of Judah, and when the next verse refers to 'the glory of Israel' it seems to have the same reference; the two occurrences thus support one another, making later scribal change an unlikely explanation and giving again, rather, a strong indication that for Micah, at least, the use of Israel for the southern kingdom was natural.

These five Mican references are split between religious and political usages (to the extent that such a distinction is appropriate for those times). At the

---

11. H.W. Wolff, *Dodekapropheton 4: Micha* (BKAT, 14/4; Neukirchen-Vluyn: Neukirchener Verlag, 1982), 64–65 (ET, *Micah: A Commentary* [Minneapolis: Augsburg, 1990], 95–96).

12. See J. Jeremias, 'Die Deutung der Gerichtsworte Michas in der Exilszeit', *ZAW* 83 (1971), 330–54.

13. In addition to the commentaries, see N. Na'aman, '"The House-of-no-shade Shall Take Away its Tax from You" (Micah i 11)', *VT* 45 (1995), 516–27 (repr. in *Ancient Israel's History and Historiography: The First Temple Period* [Collected Essays 3; Winona Lake: Eisenbrauns, 2006], 291–302).

14. So, for instance, W. Rudolph, *Micha – Nahum – Habakuk – Zephanja* (KAT, 13/3; Gütersloh: Gerd Mohn, 1975), 44. Indeed, this would seem to be the sense even if the integrity of the whole verse were to be upheld, *contra* B.K. Waltke, *A Commentary on Micah* (Grand Rapids: Eerdmans, 2007), 81.

simplest level we may conclude at once that to relegate all such uses to the exilic period at the earliest is therefore unjustifiably reductionist. We need to allow for a longer time span than some have recently allowed. At the same time, however, the natural, unselfconscious manner in which Micah speaks or writes on this leads us to question whether the explanation that the fall of Samaria was the single catalyst is adequate. The precise date of the passages in Micah is uncertain, of course, but presumably 20 years after the fall of Samaria is the longest period that can be accommodated. In addition, Micah was not a Jerusalemite (cf. Mic. 1.1), so that the usual view that this usage came south to Jerusalem with the refugees and was adopted from them is questionably adequate in this case. Some time would have to be allowed for this to develop, and all the more in the case of the resident of a country town with what is usually regarded as a moderately conservative social outlook.[15] If there were nothing in the culture to allow a sympathetic reception to such an innovation, it seems unlikely that it would have become as common as Micah's usage seems to suggest. Thus these few occurrences in a relatively understudied book may conceal more than at first meets the eye.

4. *Judaean Identity during the Divided Monarchy*

Can we then, we need to ask secondly, propose any means by which, in however muted a form, the name of Israel might have been preserved in the south as being in some way applicable to Judah and its inhabitants even during the long period of the divided monarchy? The obvious place to look, I suggest, is in connection with the liturgy (broadly understood) of the Jerusalem temple. The language of religious institutions is notoriously conservative, so that we might expect to find here traces of usage which had once been meaningful but which had passed from common parlance in the meantime. It might have sprung from the page with renewed force under radically changed circumstances such as those through which the region passed in the late eighth century.

In moving towards a positive response to this quest, a negative factor needs initially to be borne in mind, so reinforcing the plausibility of the exercise. To approach the point, I should wish to take strong issue with Davies's assertion that 'under the monarchies, Yhwh was the "god of Israel" and the "god of Judah," just as Chemosh was the "god of Moab"'.[16] Yhwh as 'the God of Israel'

---

15. See the appealing, though inevitably hypothetical, reconstruction of Micah's social background in H.W. Wolff, 'Wie verstand Micha von Moreschet sein prophetisches Amt?', in J.A. Emerton (ed.), *Congress Volume: Göttingen 1977* (VTSup, 29; Leiden: Brill, 1978), 403–17.

16. Davies, *The Origins of Biblical Israel*, 22.

is unexceptional, but what needs to be affirmed rather emphatically here is that, so far as I am aware, the name or title 'God of Judah' never appears, and that, given this god's centrality to the story of the Hebrew Bible, it is virtually certain that this argument from silence is indicative of the fact that there never was a deity who was so styled.[17] This point, on which scholars do not seem to have dwelt much in the past, raises the interesting question, to go no further, of how the Judaeans referred to their God during the period of the divided monarchy, for there is no reason to doubt that they could appeal to him in a nationalistic manner quite as much as any other people. Several answers – in addition to the Tetragrammaton, of course – emerge from the texts that most obviously offer themselves for study in this regard, of which three, to go no further, are prominent in that most Zionistic of Psalms, namely Psalm 46: the 'Most High' (v. 5) and the paralleled 'Lord of hosts' and 'God of Jacob' in vv. 8 and 12. A survey of the use of these names would take us far beyond the confines of the present study, but it would not be difficult to point to many another passage that supports the supposition that these names were common in the Jerusalem liturgy from early times. The use of Jacob in this connection is of particular interest because of its occurrence several times, as noted already, as a close and obvious parallel with Israel in Micah. If it seems clear and uncontroversial that the name of Jacob was familiar in the Jerusalem temple from early times, the prospect that we might find Israel in the same connection is strengthened.

More positively then, I should like to suggest that, alongside other possibilities, the name 'Holy One of Israel' was also preserved in the Jerusalem cult during the years prior to the fall of Samaria. I have dealt elsewhere with the use of this title in the book of Isaiah,[18] and can therefore be relatively brief here. So far as Isaiah of Jerusalem was concerned I defended the view that there were relatively few occurrences that could be attributed directly to him and that the increased usage by later writers (including especially in Isaiah 40–55) was strongly influenced in this as in other matters by reflection on the account of the vision in ch. 6. So far as this title is concerned, in other words, the prominence and, we may suspect, increasing familiarity with the hymnic trisagion, made the use of this particular divine title particularly attractive to later writers who followed to some extent in the footprints of the original prophet.

The title 'Holy One of Israel', it should be recalled, does not itself occur in

17. Passages in which God or the gods are spoken of in close association with Judah, such as Jer. 2.28, 13.9 and 51.5, can be easily seen by their rhetoric not to be presupposing a God named 'the God of Judah'.

18. H.G.M. Williamson, 'Isaiah and the Holy One of Israel', in A. Rapoport-Albert and G. Greenberg (eds.), *Biblical Hebrew, Biblical Texts: Essays in Memory of Michael P. Weitzman* (JSOTSup, 333; London: Sheffield Academic Press, 2001), 22–38.

ch. 6, so that the evidence available does not favour the view that Isaiah himself first coined it in connection with his early vision. Rather, I sought to suggest, he drew it from the cultic tradition with which he was most familiar – that of the Jerusalem temple itself. The evidence for this is modest, but in a way that is appropriate; use of such a title during the divided monarchy may well have been relatively sparse by comparison with others and it will have been precisely Isaiah's use of the title following the fall of the northern kingdom that led to its resurgence in popularity. Given that of its six occurrences outside the book of Isaiah four are certainly of a later date (2 Kgs 19.22; Jer. 50.29; 51.5; Ps. 71.22), that leaves only two occurrences, both in the Psalms, arguably of an earlier date. One of these is unlikely to convince those who are not already disposed to accept the position maintained here, namely Ps. 89.19. Some significant elements in the psalm may well reflect the exilic experience, but equally even those who accept this often find also earlier elements, including v. 19, which they believe were adopted and adapted by the later author.[19] Be that as it may, one could certainly not base a contentious case on such uncertainties.

The other example, Ps. 78.41, by contrast, is more promising from our perspective. While admittedly many possible dates have been proposed over the years,[20] the strong probability that this psalm was written before the fall of Samaria has been convincingly urged in two other separate studies.[21] Along with matters of detail, the single most telling argument, as advanced by Day, is that there is no reference to the fall of Samaria and the northern kingdom, a reference which would have clinched the psalmist's argument had he been able to make it and which is therefore an unusually powerful argument from silence. 'As it is, God's final judgement on Ephraim is represented as having occurred much earlier, ca. 1050 B.C., with the loss of the Ark and destruction of the Shiloh sanctuary. This makes sense only if the Psalm were written before 722 B.C.'[22]

On this basis I conclude that in all probability the divine name 'Holy One of Israel' was a long-established part of the Jerusalem liturgy. Psalm 78 seems to point clearly to that conclusion, while Psalm 89, even if written somewhat later (which is not certain), is best explained as drawing on the same tradition;

---

19. For surveys of opinion, see A.A. Anderson, *The Book of Psalms* (NCB; London: Oliphants, 1972), 630–31; M.E. Tate, *Psalms 51–100* (WBC, 20; Dallas: Word Books, 1990), 413–18.

20. For recent surveys, see, for instance, Tate, *Psalms 51–100*, 284–87, and J. Goldingay, *Psalms*, ii: *Psalms 42–89* (Grand Rapids: Baker Academic, 2007), 481–82.

21. J. Day, 'Pre-Deuteronomic Allusions to the Covenant in Hosea and Psalm lxxviii', *VT* 36 (1986), 1–12 (who lists many earlier scholars who agree with his conclusions), and P. Stern, 'The Eighth Century Dating of Psalm 78 Re-argued', *HUCA* 66 (1995), 41–65.

22. Day, 'Pre-Deuteronomic Allusions', 10.

the suggestion that the Psalm is here dependent on Isaiah seems to me to lack any supportive evidence in its favour.

As with Micah, so with Isaiah, unselfconscious references to his audience (evidently Judah) as Israel, even if a little later than the fall of Samaria, can also be more naturally understood if the way had already been prepared for him in this regard. Without total consistency, he tends to use names like Ephraim and Samaria for the northern kingdom that was still extant at the start of his ministry. 'Israel', therefore, was a name in some different sort of category for him, at least including Judah and serving for it alone sometimes later on. At Isa. 1.3, for instance, in a passage which I have argued elsewhere should be dated shortly before 701 BCE,[23] he has God refer to his audience as Israel in parallel with 'my people'. This contrast with his normal usage for the northern kingdom suggests that the name Israel resonated with him as some sort of ideal designation for the people of God, which at least will have included Judah, rather than being adopted merely from the regular designation for the northern kingdom. To postulate that it is no more than the latter would be a curious move on the part of so strongly nationalist a thinker.

In the nature of the case, it is unlikely that we should have access to much material that could provide further firm evidence on this topic. The amount of literature available to us that comes direct from Judaean writers referring to Judah working during the period of the divided monarchy (i.e. before the fall of Samaria) is, with the best will in the world, extremely limited. As already noted, only parts of Isaiah come in for consideration so far as the prophetic corpus is concerned. (Whatever their sources, the historical books were clearly worked up into their present shape long after.) No doubt some of the psalms originated at that time in Jerusalem, but we have already noted some uncertainties with regard to their use in this connection, and these derive mainly from the fact that their transmission was as part of a living community down to the post-exilic period, so that later modernization, if not more extensive reworking, is difficult to discount. There is no virtue, therefore, in trumpeting this sparsity of evidence as though it were surprising and hence an indication that a negative conclusion is more plausible. Rather, the facts of the situation should lead us to give due emphasis to such evidence as there is as valuable data of potential significance in seeking to recreate as many elements as possible of what must undoubtedly have been a far more complicated situation 'on the ground' than we are able at this great remove to reconstruct. To dismiss evidence too quickly as being late merely because it could be is historically impoverishing.

---

23. H.G.M. Williamson, *A Critical and Exegetical Commentary on Isaiah 1–27*, i: *Commentary on Isaiah 1–5* (ICC; London: T & T Clark, 2006), 28–30.

5. *Further Evidence from the Book of Isaiah*

Given, therefore, that I have argued that cultic usage may have been the channel through which politically curious usage might have been preserved and from which it could emerge with developed meaning in the light of later political upheaval, I turn finally to two last passages in Isaiah where there seems to me to be the strongest case (even if not all commentators would agree) for finding a related use of the name Israel from the period prior to the fall of Samaria.

I refer first to the well-known 'Song of the Vineyard' in Isa. 5.1-7. So far as the date is concerned, there are no direct references within the text that can lead to certainty, though most commentators, perhaps by presumption rather than argument, have placed it relatively early in Isaiah's ministry, something which its present position in the book might support, though it clearly cannot establish. I have suggested elsewhere, however, that within the web of literary dependencies which are such an important feature of the book of Isaiah, this passage seems to stand right at the start, indicative of an early date.[24] In particular, Isa. 3.13-15, which is itself relatively early, seems to be dependent on this passage. In addition, the pair שׁמיר ושׁית, 'briers and thorns', fits the present context both in terms of immediate sense and because stylistically its alliteration has other parallels in the passage, whereas later, even in 9.17, which is generally agreed to come from the eighth-century prophet, it is already being turned in a more metaphorical direction, so suggestive of dependency – and in this case the observation is of particular importance, since 9.17 presupposes that the northern kingdom is still in existence.[25]

Against this background, the concluding verse of the passage becomes of particular interest for our present discussion:

> For the vineyard of the Lord of hosts
> > is the house of Israel,
> and the people of Judah
> > are the planting in which he took delight.
> He expected justice,

---

24. Williamson, *Isaiah 1–5*, 330–31. Against the view of J. Vermeylen (followed by a few others), *Du prophète Isaïe à l'apocalyptique: Isaïe, I – XXXV, miroir d'un demi-millénaire d'expérience religieuse en Israël* (EB, 2 vols.; Paris: Gabalda, 1977–78), 159–68, that the passage shows Deuteronomic influence and so should be dated long after the time of Isaiah, see A.J. Bjørndalen, 'Zur Frage der Echtheit von Jesaja 1,2–3; 1,4–7 und 5,1–7', *NTT* 83 (1982), 51–62.

25. Other occurrences of this pair are probably all to be ascribed to later imitative authors or redactors: 7.23, 24, 25; 10.17; 27.4.

> but found only bloodshed,
> righteousness,
>   but heard only a cry of distress.

There are three possible ways in which 'the house of Israel' might be under-stood, and all have attracted significant support in the past. First, in view of the parallelism, it might be synonymous with 'the people of Judah'.[26] This seems unlikely, however, for if, as just argued, the passage dates from early in the prophet's ministry, when the northern kingdom still existed, such usage would at the least be confusing, and while there is no doubt that the name Israel was eventually adopted as an alternative designation for Judah alone, there is no strong evidence that Isaiah himself ever used it so.

Secondly, the two terms could be quite distinct (the term antithetical is hardly appropriate, but that is how this usage would conventionally be character-ized), so that Israel refers to the northern kingdom and Judah to the southern.[27] Although this interpretation has been quite popular, it seems to me to be the least likely of all. The 'vineyard' and 'the planting in which he took delight' are clearly not two wholly separate elements but at the least overlap in some measure, and it would be very strange if Judah were not also included within the referent of the vineyard. Furthermore, as we noted above, when Isaiah wants to refer explicitly to the northern kingdom in contrast with Judah as a separate political entity, he tends to use other terms, such as Ephraim.

Finally, therefore, this could be a case where the first line of the couplet is further specified by the second, so that Israel refers to the people of God as a whole, further defined more specifically as the people of Judah.[28] Formally, it fits best the form of parallelism here (nearer definition). In addition it reflects what we have seen to be probably Isaiah's most common use of Israel, namely the people of God as a whole, as, for instance, in the divine title 'the Holy One of Israel', as well as elsewhere (e.g. 1.3; 8.18, etc.). Here, Wildberger may be right to suggest that by choosing to use the name Israel 'the religious aspect is highlighted',[29] and of course the nearer definition of the second line makes

---

26. See, for instance, H. Wildberger, *Jesaja 1–12* (BKAT, 10/1; Neukirchen-Vluyn: Neukirchener Verlag, 2nd edn, 1980), 171–72 (ET, *Isaiah 1–12: A Commentary* [Continental Commentaries; Minneapolis: Fortress, 1991], 184).

27. e.g. R.E. Clements, *Isaiah 1–39* (NCB; Grand Rapids: Eerdmans, and London: Marshall, Morgan & Scott, 1980), 59–60.

28. This view too has attracted weighty support in the past. For a couple of significant examples, see A.J. Bjørndalen, *Untersuchungen zur allegorischen Rede der Propheten Amos und Jesaja* (BZAW, 165; Berlin: de Gruyter, 1986), 316–18; W.A.M. Beuken, *Jesaja 1–12* (HThKAT; Freiburg im Breisgau: Herder, 2003), 138–39.

29. Wildberger, *Jesaja 1–12*, 172 (ET, *Isaiah 1–12*, 184)

clear that Judah is the primary target of the polemic, but it is in their capacity as part of the people of God that they come in for judgment. Finally, we should note that the qualification of Judah as 'the planting in which he took delight' indicates that Judah was in an especially favoured or privileged section within the wider 'vineyard' that was Israel. If this is correct, then it fits well with what we have already seen, namely that a memory of the name Israel for the whole people of God, including both of the two political entities, survived, and that Judah could be regarded as an element of that.

Secondly, at 8.14 Isaiah speaks of 'the two houses of Israel', an unparalleled expression that deserves attention. As part of the extensive first-person material in Isaiah 6 and 8, the ostensible setting for the oral proclamation is during the Syro-Ephramite invasion and for the written form shortly after, if 8.16-17 are to be believed. This would certainly set it prior to the fall of Samaria. The overwhelming majority of commentators accepts this date.

In recent years, however, an alternative line of argument has been advanced by some to the effect that, on the basis of parallels with what we expect of an eighth-century prophet in the light of Neo-Assyrian prophets, Isaiah will have spoken only words of reassurance to the king (as, for instance, in 8.1-4), so that words of condemnation or judgment, such as 6.9-13, and most of ch. 8 other than vv. 1–4, must be later material, whether post-exilic,[30] from the early exilic period[31] or from the time of Hezekiah.[32] This startling new approach (mentioned briefly at the start of this article) deserves a thorough examination which cannot be undertaken here. I must therefore content myself with referring to the start of a riposte which is beginning to manifest itself in German-language scholarship[33] and to an article of my own which is devoted exclusively to that topic and which

---

30. Becker, *Jesaja*, 110–14.

31. M.J. de Jong, *Isaiah among the Ancient Near Eastern Prophets: A Comparative Study of the Earliest Stages of the Isaiah Tradition and the Neo-Assyrian Prophecies* (VTSup, 117; Leiden: Brill, 2007).

32. Høgenhaven, *Gott und Volk*, 95–98; see too his 'Prophecy and Propaganda: Aspects of Political and Religious Reasoning in Israel and the Ancient Near East', *SJOT* 3 (1989), 125–41 (138–40), and Kratz, 'Israel in the Book of Isaiah'.

33. See most directly E. Blum, 'Israels Prophetie im altorientalischen Kontext: Anmerkungen zu neueren religionsgeschichtlichen Thesen', in I. Cornelius and L. Jonker (eds.), *"From Ebla to Stellenbosch" – Syro-Palestinian Religions and the Hebrew Bible* (Abhandlungen des deutschen Palästina-Vereins, 37; Wiesbaden: Harrassowitz, 2008), 81–115; Blum refers to several other studies as well. See too J. Barthel's contribution to the discussion of 'Das Problem des historischen Jesaja', in I. Fischer, K. Schmid and H.G.M. Williamson (eds.), *Prophetie in Israel: Beiträge des Symposiums "Das Alte Testament und die Kultur der Moderne" anlässlich des 100. Geburtstags Gerhard von Rads* (ATM, 11; Münster: LIT, 2003), 125–35.

finds it wanting.[34] In my opinion, the essence of the case for retaining an early date for 8.11-15, presented there in full, is that the paragraph does not (*contra* some suggestions) allude to Isaiah 7 (which was added later to the first-person account), but that it does, on the other hand, show close literary affinity with the whole of 6.1-11[35] (and not just vv. 9–11, which some think were added later to the earlier core of 6.1-8) and with 8.1-8 (see immediately below). This tight network of allusions within a relatively restricted body of literature but without drawing at all on evidently later material in the context (6.12-13; 7; 8.9-10) is strongly suggestive of a single unit of composition, which is tied by its immediate continuation in 8.16-17 to a time quite soon after the events referred to and certainly prior to the more developed view of 30.8-11.

The particular significance of this conclusion for our present purposes is that the reference to 'the two houses of Israel' needs to be read explicitly in the light of the material which originally immediately preceded it, namely 8.1-8. Here we have judgment pronounced both on Samaria (note the avoidance of the name Israel for the northern kingdom here, as elsewhere in the earliest Isaianic material) in vv. 1–4 and on 'this people' of Judah in vv. 5–8. These two elements are then drawn together in our phrase as part of the summary paragraph in vv. 11–15 which deals with the response to the prophetic announcement.

If that is a correct understanding of the use of this unique expression in its context, then it shows once again that in the earliest phase of his ministry, prior to the fall of the northern kingdom, Isaiah took the name Israel to refer to both kingdoms together, with each one bearing its own separate name as political entities. I suggest this can best be explained once again as indicative of a memory of the name from much earlier times as transmitted to him, in all probability, through conservative liturgical uses in the Jerusalem temple.

---

34. 'Isaiah – Prophet of Weal or Woe?', in R.P. Gordon and H.M. Barstad (eds.), (Winona Lake: Eisenbrauns, forthcoming).

35. In both passages the prophet is distanced from 'this people' (twice in each passage – 6.9, 10; 8.11, 12); in both God is entitled 'Lord of hosts' in a climactic or emphatic position (6.5; 8.13), and the appropriate response to this exalted status is to be overwhelmed (with different vocabulary, however); part of this response in 8.13 is to 'sanctify' him, which ties in closely from a verbal point of view with the trisagion in 6.3; conceptually, the fate of the faithless people in 8.14 may be closely compared with that in 6.9-10 (note especially God's personal involvement in each case); finally, the unusual manner of expressing divine speech to the prophet in 8.11 may reflect the fact that this was once in much closer association with ch. 6 than is now the case.

Conclusion

In moving towards a conclusion of this analysis, it needs to be stressed once again that the likelihood of finding much evidence of relevance to our particular question is inevitably extremely slender. Most of the literature we have available for the self-understanding of Judah under the divided monarchy was certainly the product of later times. The relevant historical books, to whatever extent they incorporate earlier sources, were certainly not put together in anything approaching their present form until well after the fall of Samaria. The dating of the writings is too uncertain to command a consensus. And of the prophets, only Isaiah and Micah are of even possible relevance, being themselves of Judaean origin. In the light of this conclusion, the charge that the slender quantity of relevant material is evidence that we cannot say anything and should read all surprising elements as the inevitable result of later redaction is dangerously oversimplified. Historians will want to gather and evaluate the scarce evidence at their disposal with additional care so as not to forego insights into greater diversity and complexity than would otherwise be attained. The danger of flattening all data into a bland uniformity simply for the sake of tidiness is methodologically questionable.

As I have tried to show, by contrast, the two prophetic books just mentioned combine to suggest that there were memories in Judah of an 'Israel' inheritance. Writing after the fall of Samaria, Micah could simply adopt the name for Judah, but in circumstances which suggest, I have argued, that the ground had been prepared for him by earlier and inherited custom; in the light of his probable personal background, to claim that his adoption of the new nomenclature in so short a space of time was wholly novel flies in the face of historical probability. Pressing further backwards, we have found traces in Isaiah's writings that perhaps furnish us with the nature of that inherited custom. There are indications that the name Israel continued to be used in the Jerusalem cult during the previous centuries – and certainly the anticipated title 'God of Judah' never in fact appears to match the 'God of Israel'; the deity in Jerusalem had other names, if the evidence from the Psalms is to be believed, and among those, perhaps not very prominent at that time, was included 'the Holy One of Israel', as well as 'God of Jacob'. From this, in a couple of passages in Isaiah whose dating is most plausibly to be assigned to the period before the fall of Samaria, we find the name Israel used with reference to the combined peoples of north and south, matching the use in the divine title. From there, I suggest, it was explicable that when the name fell out of political use for the north because of the Assyrian conquest, it was understandable that what had been kept alive in the Judaean cult soon became even more widely used with reference to the heirs of the previous Israel in the southern component which we know of better as Judah.

Chapter 6

PAUL'S SELF-UNDERSTANDING IN THE LIGHT OF
JEREMIAH: A CASE STUDY INTO THE USE OF THE
OLD TESTAMENT IN THE NEW TESTAMENT

Hetty Lalleman
Spurgeon's College

Introduction

For more than a quarter of a century the book of Jeremiah has been the focus of much of my research[1] and today the book is no less intriguing to me than it was before. Gordon McConville has played an important part in this research journey, for he was the most helpful supervisor I could wish for during my doctoral research. He taught me not to be too quick in my conclusions and through him I learned how to take one step after the other in discovering more and more of the theology of the book of Jeremiah, for which I am ever thankful to him. The present contribution is a small token of this gratitude.[2]

In recent years one of the developments in biblical studies has been that much attention is being paid to the larger units to which individual texts and books of the Hebrew Bible belong. The work of B.S. Childs opened up the perspective of the place and function of texts within the canon of the church.[3] More recently

---

1. See in particular H. Lalleman-de Winkel, *Jeremiah in Prophetic Tradition. An Examination of the Book of Jeremiah in the Light of Israel's Prophetic Traditions* (CBET, 26; Leuven: Peeters, 2000), the publication of the PhD dissertation I wrote under the supervision of Dr McConville. Also my Dutch commentary *Jeremia* (De Brug, IX; Heerenveen: Groen, 2004).

2. I am also grateful to my husband, Dr Pieter J. Lalleman, for his help at various stages of this article.

3. B.S. Childs, 'The canonical shape of prophetic literature', *Interpretation* 32 (1978), 46–55; idem, *Introduction to the Old Testament as Scripture* (Minneapolis: Fortress, 1979); idem, *Old Testament Theology in a Canonical Context* (London: SCM, 1985).

intertextuality has become another way of opening up the meaning of texts in their wider context of the Old and New Testaments.[4] Texts were not written in isolation and they do not only have a meaning for the hearers or readers in the days they were written or edited; they rather take up previous texts and their echoes can be heard long after they were committed to paper.

I am deliberately using the word 'echo' here for I believe that texts from, *in casu*, the Old Testament, do not only play an important role in the New Testament when they are quoted literally; they may also have shaped the wording, choices, thinking and theology of a New Testament author without him being conscious of it. Texts which form part of the canon of Scripture may thus be viewed from two perspectives: looking forward we can trace Hebrew Bible texts and their *Wirkungsgeschichte* in the New Testament; looking backwards we can discover traces of Old Testament texts, concepts and ideas in New Testament texts, sometimes on the surface, sometimes hidden deep beneath it.

The present essay is not an attempt to add to the theory of *Wirkungsgeschichte* and intertextuality. It rather presupposes familiarity with the basic concepts and focuses on possible relationships between the book of Jeremiah and the Epistles of the apostle Paul, with particular attention to Paul's self-understanding as an apostle.[5]

In my *Jeremiah in Prophetic Tradition*, I have argued that the prophet Jeremiah was part of an ongoing prophetic tradition in Israel and that several strands of the book's theology are built on earlier traditions, in particular those found in the books of the prophets Amos and of Hosea. I argue that Jeremiah stands in a thoroughly prophetic tradition, which I define by means of themes such as the call to repentance, the covenant, and the role of the prophet in intercession and in suffering on behalf of his people.

In the second volume of his extensive commentary on Jeremiah, W.L. Holladay lists a whole range of subjects, words and verses which provide some form of evidence for the dependence of Jeremiah on previous biblical books, but he also shows how the book of Jeremiah had an impact on later literature, such as the Dead Sea Scrolls and the New Testament.[6] In his rather short section on the New Testament, Holladay mentions the obvious texts and concepts which are drawn from the book of Jeremiah, such as those which mention 'the new covenant' (possibly Mk 14.24-25, though the word 'new' is not used

4. See R.B. Hays, S. Alkier and L.A. Huizenga (eds.), *Reading the Bible Intertextually* (Waco: Baylor University Press, 2009).

5. See also K.O. Sandnes, *Paul – One of the Prophets? A Contribution to the Apostle's Self-understanding* (WUNT, 2.43; Tübingen: Mohr Siebeck, 1991).

6. W.L. Holladay, *Jeremiah 2* (Hermeneia; Minneapolis: Fortress, 1989), 92–95.

there; 1 Cor. 11.25; 2 Cor. 3.5-6; Heb. 8.8-12; 10.16-17). Another well-known theme used by Paul is that of 'boasting' (cf. Jer. 9.23-24 and 1 Cor. 1.31, also 2 Cor. 10.17). There are other clearly recognizable quotations such as the use of Jer. 31.15 in Matthew 2.17-18 ('Rachel weeping for her children') and Jesus' reference to the temple having become a 'den of robbers' (Mk 11.17 and Jer. 7.11).

Similar surveys of quotations, allusions and sometimes freely adapted words from Jeremiah in Paul's writings can also be found in the lists of 'places cited or alluded to'[7] in the edition of the Greek New Testament by Nestle-Aland.[8] The works of Hays and Moyise more or less follow the same method of tracing back words, expressions in the New Testament drawn from books in the Hebrew Bible including Jeremiah,[9] but they also deal with theological concepts adapted and shaped by the New Testament writers.

Interestingly enough, Holladay mentions one text which is not found in any of these discussions and lists. He states:

> ... in Gal 1:15 Paul uses the words of Jrm's call (Jer 1:5) to apply to himself: 'But when he who had set me apart before I was born, and had called me through his grace . . .'[10]

Holladay does not elaborate on this comment, but it leads us to the question: Did Paul understand himself as being a prophet in the tradition of Jeremiah? Was his self-understanding shaped by Jeremiah's mission and ministry?

The recent voluminous *Commentary on the New Testament Use of the Old Testament* contains some intriguing comments on this question. In dealing with the letter to the Galatians, Moisés Silva writes:

> In any case, Paul must have seen his own ministry as integrally related to the work of the OT prophets, and in some sense even as its culmination.[11]

---

7. *Loci citati vel allegati.*

8. K. Aland, *et al.* (eds.), *Novum Testamentum Graece* (Stuttgart: Deutsche Bibelstiftung, 27th edn, 1998).

9. R.B. Hays, *Echoes of Scripture in the Letters of Paul* (New Haven & London: Yale University Press, 1989); S. Moyise, *The Old Testament in the New: An Introduction* (London: Continuum, 2001); idem, *Evoking Scripture. Seeing the Old Testament in the New* (London: T & T Clark, 2008); also idem (ed.), *The Old Testament in the New Testament. Essays in Honour of J.L. North* (JSNTSup, 189; Sheffield: Sheffield Academic Press, 2000).

10. Holladay, *Jeremiah 2*, 95.

11. M. Silva, 'Galatians', in G.K. Beale, and D.A. Carson (eds.), *Commentary on the New Testament Use of the Old Testament* (Nottingham: Apollos, 2007), 786–87.

In what follows this statement is clarified: 'Now at last the message of salvation is breaking all national barriers.' Silva refers to the call of Paul in Gal. 1.15-16a, of which he says: 'It can hardly be doubted that in Gal. 1.15-16a the apostle is alluding to Jer. 1.5 . . . and Isa. 49.1-6 . . .'[12] So, along with Holladay, this is another example of a scholar who connects Paul's call to that of Jeremiah on the basis of what Paul himself writes. Yet, as we will see, others disagree and are convinced that Paul in Galatians 1 alludes only to Isaiah 49.[13]

The present essay will explore whether we can find echoes of Jeremiah in the way Paul's letters speak about the apostle's self-understanding. It will first look at the self-understanding of the prophet Jeremiah as it is presented in the book named after him and then will draw some lines of comparison to the self-understanding of the apostle Paul as presented in Galatians and 2 Corinthians.

1. *Prophetic Self-understanding in Jeremiah*

The time when scholars tried to understand the book of Jeremiah, and in particular the person of the prophet, in psychological terminology is over.[14] In the last decades two contrasting views on the book of Jeremiah have characterized research: R.P. Carroll denied any historical links between the book and the prophet whereas W.L. Holladay linked the events in the book to the historical reading of the Torah which he dated in every seventh year.[15] In between these two extreme positions other studies have appeared which concentrate more on the redactional layers[16] or on later communities and theological traditions which created the book as we now have it.[17] J.R. Lundbom's recent commen-

12. Silva, 'Galatians', 786.

13. See the discussion below.

14. An example of that approach is P. Volz, *Prophetengestalten des Alten Testaments* (Stuttgart: Calwer Vereinsbuchhandlung, 1938).

15. R.P. Carroll, *The Book of Jeremiah* (OTL; London: SCM, 1986); W.L. Holladay, *Jeremiah 1* (Hermeneia; Minneapolis: Fortress, 1986); Holladay, *Jeremiah 2*.

16. An example of redaction criticism which defends an overall Deuteronomistic influence on the book of Jeremiah is W. Thiel, *Die deuteronomistische Redaktion von Jeremia 1–25* (WMANT, 41; Neukirchen-Vluyn: Neukirchener Verlag, 1973); see the critical evaluation of this method in H. Weippert, *Die Prosareden des Jeremiabuches* (BZAW, 132; Berlin and New York: De Gruyter, 1973).

17. E.W. Nicholson, *Preaching to the Exiles: A Study of the Prose Tradition in the Book of Jeremiah* (Oxford: Blackwell, 1970); L. Stulman, *The Prose Sermons of the Book of Jeremiah: A Redescription of the Correspondences with Deuteronomistic Literature in the Light of Recent Text-critical Research* (SBLDS, 83; Atlanta: Scholars Press, 1986) and idem, *Jeremiah* (Abingdon Old Testament Commentaries; Nashville: Abingdon, 2005). In the latter work Stulman writes: 'The Jeremiah corpus would address the needs

tary on Jeremiah puts the words of the prophet in a historical context, but also pays much attention to literary structures in the book, which reflects the trend to read texts in a more synchronic way than in a diachronic manner.[18]

After the demise of the psychological interpretation, is there anything that we can still say about how the prophet understood himself in terms of his message and ministry? The only way to answer this question is to follow the perspective that the texts themselves present, whoever may have been responsible for the final edition of the book of Jeremiah as we have it. This is the text we should study in order to discover what picture is given of the prophet.[19] Our task as readers is to listen to this text.[20]

1.1 *Jeremiah 1*

Jeremiah 1 can be seen as the programme for the whole book. The first three verses put the prophet and his ministry in a historical context, but they also emphasize that it is the 'word of the LORD' (v. 2) which is heard through this particular human being's 'words' (v. 1), thus linking the message and person of the prophet with his 'sending authority'. This link is also emphasized in the verses that follow, which tell about Jeremiah's call to the role of prophet. In the remainder of ch. 1 there is an interaction between God's words and the person of the prophet. Verses 4–19 bring out that the prophet does not just speak words of his own but that he is commissioned by the God of Israel, who even 'knew' him before he was formed in the womb of his mother and who 'consecrated' him before he was born.

This election even from before Jeremiah's birth has the effect of emphasizing his ministry as being founded solely in God's choice and being based on his authority. This notion gets even more attention due to Jeremiah's objection that he is no skilled speaker. The divine reply makes it clear that it is not Jeremiah's own competence which makes him fit to be a prophet; rather it is the LORD who gives words which are 'put in the mouth of the prophet'. The chapter as a whole makes it crystal clear that Jeremiah is to be seen as a prophet in

---

and concerns of later communities of faith as it was read and reinterpreted. This is why one should consider the book of Jeremiah to be a trajectory rather than a fixed point: it must have been continually changing and developing over a period of several centuries, albeit slowly' (9).

18. J. Lundbom, *Jeremiah* (3 vols.; Anchor Bible; New York & London: Doubleday, 1999, 2004, 2004). Of course there is much more to be said about modern research on Jeremiah but that is not the scope of this article.

19. I am aware of the differences between the MT and the LXX but for the purposes of the present essay these do not need to be discussed.

20. The NRSV is used unless otherwise indicated.

the line of Moses (Deut. 18.18).[21] He is a 'true' prophet, sent by Yahweh and he is therefore to be taken seriously. Yet, whereas Moses was mainly sent to the people of Israel, Jeremiah's mission is worldwide: 'I appointed you a prophet to the nations' (Jer. 1.5).

His call is confirmed by the receipt of two messages which are both linked to 'what he sees'. In these messages the content of his role as 'a prophet to the nations' is clarified. He is to proclaim judgment to Judah which involves foreign kingdoms and which is addressed to all of the different layers of the population of Judah.

1.2 *Jeremiah 52*
At the other end of the book of Jeremiah stands ch. 52 which contains the narrative account of the fall of Jerusalem and the restoration of King Jehoiachin. This chapter seems to be a mere appendix to the book. However, in the context of the entire book as it stands, it has an important although often overlooked role. It provides the evidence that Jeremiah was indeed a 'true prophet' by showing that his words were fulfilled. The narrative thus demonstrates that he did not speak his own words but God's words, and that God affirmed his message by establishing what he had spoken. This affirmation is one of the criteria mentioned in Deuteronomy 18 as proof of a true prophet (Deut. 18.21-22).

1.3 *The central section*
When we consider the rest of the book, we see that the theme of false and true prophecy is of major importance, in particular in the central section. This part of the book as we have it – in the Masoretic Text – contains several chapters on the theme of false and true prophecy: 23.9-40; 26, 27, 28 and 29. In these chapters the message of Jeremiah is heavily criticized by his opponents, who say that everything will be 'peace'. Jeremiah's message on the other hand is one of judgment, as is also clear from ch. 25. In Jeremiah 24 the prophet makes clear that hope comes from an unexpected side. It is as if he turns all the popular expectations upside down. The building and planting (1.10) will come by means of the horrible experience of the exile (24.6; 29.5) and the promised salvation of the LORD will only come after severe judgment. Only through judgment will there be a new beginning which is initiated by God's grace alone (24; cf. 29.10-14).

---

21. See W.L. Holladay, 'The Background of Jeremiah's Self-Understanding: Moses, Samuel and Psalm 22', *JBL* 83 (1964), 153–64, repr. in L.G. Perdue and B.W. Kovacs (eds.), *A Prophet to the Nations: Essays in Jeremiah Studies* (Winona Lake: Eisenbrauns, 1984), 313–23; also W.L. Holladay, 'Jeremiah and Moses: Further Observations', *JBL* 85 (1966), 17–27.

Jeremiah is heavily criticized for this message of doom and judgment. People want to kill him (ch. 26), others oppose him publicly (ch. 28). A more 'theoretical' reflection on false prophecy is given in 23.9-32. This passage underlines that the lifestyle of the false prophets shows that they are wrong. This lifestyle is characterized by elements such as abuse of power (v. 10), adultery (v. 14) and speaking 'visions of their own minds, not from the mouth of the LORD' (v. 16), which includes words of peace when there is no peace. The false prophets do not call Israel to repentance nor do they challenge their moral behaviour. They say what people want to hear: 'It shall be well with you . . .' (v. 17). Their own immoral behaviour is in fact a stimulus for the people to continue in their immorality. For Jeremiah all this is evidence that they were not sent by God (v. 21) nor did they 'stand in his council' (v. 22), which we may interpret as not having an intimate relationship with God by which they might know his will and proclaim it. They claim that they dream God-given dreams, but in actual fact their message is in contradiction to that. The people are not challenged to repent and return to God (v. 22b).

Exactly this criterion of dreams and repentance is also used in Deut. 13.1-5 to expose false prophets. The fact that God did not send these false prophets (Jer. 23.32) makes them the opposite numbers of the prophet Jeremiah about whom chs. 1 and 52 testified; the role of these chapters in the book is to affirm that Jeremiah *was* sent by God. The coverage of the fall of Jerusalem, not only in ch. 52 but also in ch. 39, underlines the fact that Jeremiah was indeed a true prophet, chosen and sent by God to speak his word, whereas his authenticity and authority as God's true prophet are emphasized by the wording of his call.

Even in his struggles Jeremiah is aware of these things. In fact, they are the reason why he suffers. He knows he cannot escape his divine call, even if he wanted to (20.9). Reversing his birth and with it his call from before birth is an impossible option (20.14-18). Thus even his suffering proves that Jeremiah is a true prophet: he did not choose this role out of a desire to be popular – as the false prophets did. His family (12.6) and other opponents, even from royal descent (Jeremiah 36), must have thought he was a failure. However, God was on his side in all tribulations (1.18-19, repeated in 15.20). Jeremiah's message survived.

2. *Apostolic Self-understanding in the Pauline Corpus*

Having reconstructed the basic elements of Jeremiah's self-understanding, we now turn to Paul. It will become evident that when we look for traces of the book of Jeremiah in the way Paul expresses his self-understanding, it is in the context of the need to defend his ministry as that of a true apostle, sent by God, that he does so. In two of his letters he specifically has to defend his apostolic authority, 2 Corinthians and Galatians, and it appears that Jeremiah plays an important part in each. The first passage we look at is Galatians 1.

2.1 *Galatians 1*

The context of Gal. 1.15-16 is one of defence. Jewish people have entered the churches in Galatia and are trying to convince the new Christians from a gentile background that circumcision is an essential part of being saved. In doing so, they deny the validity of the Gospel as preached by Paul and the apostle uses heavy weapons in combating their thoughts. He knows that the heart of the Gospel is at stake. If anything can be added to 'being saved by grace alone' it means that Christ's death on the cross has effectively been made redundant. Hence in Galatians 1 Paul strongly emphasizes that the good news of salvation through Christ is the only true Gospel and nothing should be added to it (1.1-9). In v. 10 he argues that his proclamation is not his own but that it is based on what God wants him to say. Paul is in no way 'inventing' his own message in order to please people.

He then launches an elaborate attempt to prove that his ministry and his message are authorized by God and not by human beings (1.11-24). Without any human intervention he 'received it [viz. the Gospel] through a revelation of Jesus Christ' (1.12). Hence his authority as an apostle to the nations, in proclaiming Christ 'among the Gentiles' (v. 16), is based on God's direct call. Paul even brings to bear that he knows that he was 'elected' before birth:

> But when God, who had set me apart before I was born and called me through
> his grace, was pleased to reveal his Son to me, so that I might proclaim him
> among the Gentiles . . . (1.15-16a)

The NRSV translation 'before I was born' is not the only one suggested. NIV has 'from birth'. The Greek text reads ἐκ κοιλίας μητρός μου. Here the preposition ἐκ could indeed mean 'from'. F.F. Bruce mentions both possibilities:

> . . . lit. 'from my mother's womb [. . .]; it may mean either 'since my birth'
> or 'since before my birth' (here the latter would be apposite). Before ever he
> was born, Paul means, God had his eye on him and set him apart for his apos-
> tolic ministry.[22]

Whichever rendering we prefer, the expression 'the womb of my mother' (which makes for the translation 'from the womb of my mother onwards') seems to be a

---

22. F.F. Bruce, *The Epistle of Paul to the Galatians* (NIGTC; Exeter: Paternoster, 1982), 92.

clear echo of Jer. 1.5, as is suggested by a variety of scholars.[23] Although there
are more Old Testament characters of whom we read that they were called 'from
birth on' (Moses in Exodus 2, Samuel in 1 Samuel 1, the 'servant' in Isa. 49.1;
cf. also Isa. 44.2, 24; 49.5), Lundbom comments on Jer. 1.5: 'The clearest echo
of the present call comes in Paul's statement in Gal 1.15, where he says, "(God)
set me apart before I was born".'[24] As was mentioned above, Holladay and Silva
interpret Gal. 1.15-16 as a clear allusion to Jer. 1.5.

However, several scholars argue it is primarily Isaiah 49 to which Paul
is referring, in particular in view of the verses following Gal. 1.15-16. K.O.
Sandnes, after comparing Gal. 1.15b, Jer. 1.5 and Isa. 49.1, 5, concludes that
the similarities between the verses from Galatians and Isaiah are more significant than the similarities with Jeremiah.[25] He argues that the verb καλέω
is used in both Galatians and Isaiah, and that Paul's mission to the Gentiles
in 1.16b corresponds to that of the Servant in Isa. 49.6, whereas 'Jeremiah's
commission to the nations is different in its purpose'.[26] Furthermore, Sandnes
sets out correspondences between Gal. 1.24 and Isa. 49.3, and Gal. 2.2b and
Isa. 49.4. These similarities suggest that Paul had Isaiah 49 in mind when writing Gal. 1.15-16.[27] F. Wilk even denies an allusion to Jer. 1.5 and only focuses
on Isaiah 49. He states:

> By contrast, only a loose linguistic connection exists with Jeremiah 1.5;
> in addition, that passage is shaped as an oration of God (cf. 1.4) that turns
> Jeremiah (1.10) from his birth into a prophet of salvation and disaster.[28]

The second part of Wilk's phrase seems to me only to confirm that there *is* a
relationship between Jeremiah 1 and Paul's statement: it is God who made the
decision to call both men to his service. The emphasis in both cases falls on the
non-human origin of their call. It was not an office they desired for themselves.

---

23. See for example P. Bonnard, *L'épitre de St. Paul aux Galates* (CNT; Paris:
Delachaux et Niestle, 1953); J.L. Martyn, *Galatians: A New Translation with Introduction
and Commentary* (New York: Doubleday, 1997); F. Mussner, *Der Galaterbrief* (Herder's;
Freiburg: Herder, 1997); S.J. Hafemann, *2 Corinthians* (NIV Application Commentary;
London: Hodder & Stoughton, 2000), 127–28; A.C. Thiselton, *The First Epistle to the
Corinthians* (NIGTC; Carlisle: Paternoster, 2000), 548, 695–96.

24. Lundbom, *Jeremiah 1–20*, 231.

25. Sandnes, *Paul – One of the Prophets?*, 61.

26. Sandnes, *Paul – One of the Prophets?*, 61.

27. Sandnes, *Paul – One of the Prophets?*, 61–62.

28. F. Wilk, 'Paul as User, Interpreter, and Reader of the Book of Isaiah' in Hays,
Alkier and Huizenga (eds.), *Reading the Bible Intertextually*, 83–99; quotation from
285, n. 85.

Both of them have a divine Sender whose message they proclaim. Besides, the words used in Galatians ('set me apart before I was born') seem to be more than merely a 'loose linguistic connection' to Jer. 1.5. Both the Servant and Jeremiah are said to be called at a very early stage, even before birth, and the same is claimed by Paul who, however, quotes neither Isaiah 49 nor Jeremiah 1 literally. Yet all three passages emphasize the purpose that God had in mind for his servants even before they were born and this is done in quite specific language (all three mentioning the mother's womb).

Is Isa. 49.1-6 then closer to Gal. 1.15-16 than Jer. 1.5? Sandnes mentions the presence of the verb καλέω in the former two but not in Jeremiah. However, the verb 'set apart' in Gal. 1.15a corresponds with the idea of 'made holy', which can be interpreted as 'set apart for God's purpose' in Jer. 1.5. Furthermore, the 'Gentiles' mentioned in Gal. 1.16b may correspond to the 'nations' in Isa. 49.6 *as well as* to Jer. 1.5, where God appoints the prophet as 'a prophet to the nations' (Jer. 1.5). I agree with Sandnes that Jeremiah's commission to the nations differs from Paul's. Yet I do not think this is the most important issue in Gal. 1.15-16. That seems to me the statement of Paul's call as a call directly and only from God, not received 'from a human source' (Gal. 1.12).

In his discussion of Rom. 3.21–4.25, D. Chae connects Paul's call to preach the Gospel to the Gentiles to that of Jeremiah who is also called as a prophet to the nations.[29] In referring to Romans 3.29-30, Chae says:

> Jeremiah was called a prophet *to* the nations . . . and appointed *over* the nations
> . . . His call was primarily to deliver the message of wrath to the nations
> (Jer 1.10); his message to the nations is full of woes and disasters, and it
> extends to many chapters . . .
>
> Paul is, however, very different from Jeremiah, though he is also called 'to
> the nations' . . . Above all, he is apostle *of* the Gentiles . . . He *belongs to the*
> *nations*. He was called to be an apostle *to* the Gentiles, *of* the Gentiles and *for*
> the Gentiles. He is a Jewish apostle *for the nations* to bring them the message
> of *good news* from the God of the Jews who *is also* the God of *Gentiles* . . . His
> self-understanding is much deeper and more radical than that of the prophets
> of the OT, even more profound than that of Jeremiah, as far as their relation
> with Gentiles is concerned.[30]

Though the context of Chae's argument differs from ours (he tries to prove that

---

29. D.J.S. Chae, *Paul as Apostle to the Gentiles. His Apostolic Self-Awareness and its Influence on the Soteriological Argument in Romans* (Carlisle: Paternoster, 1997), 153–205.

30. Chae, *Paul as Apostle*, 178–79; italics his.

Paul's apostolic self-awareness plays a significant role in Romans when arguing for the inclusion of Gentiles), his comparison between Jeremiah and Paul
is worth considering.

However, to see Jeremiah as mainly proclaiming a message of doom to the
nations is a rather one-sided view of his ministry: Jer. 1.10 speaks of 'building and planting' just as much as about judgment, and some prophecies to the
nations do contain words of restoration and hope, e.g. Jer. 46.26; 48.47; 49.6
and 49.39. Paul's mission may have been more 'positive' in that he proclaimed
salvation even to the Gentiles, but that this is due to a deeper self-understanding
of his relationship with the Gentiles seems unlikely. After all, from the very
beginning Jeremiah received a call as 'a prophet to the nations'. The difference
between the two lies in the different stage in salvation-history to which they
belong, not in a difference in their self-understanding.

To conclude, both Jeremiah 1 and Galatians 1 underline the authority of the
person who is commissioned not by human beings, but by God. As a consequence of this commissioning, Jeremiah is a 'true prophet' and Paul is a 'true
apostle'. As we saw, this emphasis on Jeremiah being God's true prophet to
the people and the nations is a major theme in the book that bears his name.
In Galatians Paul declares that his message is not of human origin but that he
is truly sent by God. In this way he shows himself superior to the 'people who
came from James' (2.12) and exposes them as false teachers.

2.2 *Second Corinthians 10–12*
A similar issue is at stake in another passage in which Paul is confronted
with opponents who consciously undermine his apostolic authority, namely
2 Corinthians 10–13.[31] Paul has to argue that he is a true apostle, commissioned by God, and this long section contains several allusions to and echoes
of Jeremiah. In arguing like this the apostle apparently places himself in the
tradition of the prophets as a *true* messenger of God. The first allusion is in
2 Cor. 10.8:

> Now, even if I boast a little too much of our authority, which the Lord gave for
> building you up and not for tearing you down, I will not be ashamed of it.

Paul is defending himself against the accusation that he is 'tearing down' the
church in Corinth by writing 'weighty and strong' letters to them whereas he is
weak in person and speech when he meets with his readers (v. 10). In reply he

---

31. Whether 2 Corinthians 10–13 was originally part of the same letter as chs. 1–9
is immaterial to the present discussion since those who doubt this still attribute the text
to Paul.

argues for the unity of his message and person, which is based on the mission given to him by God – a mission he sticks to, not overstepping its boundaries. That mission is described as proclaiming 'the good news in lands beyond you . . .' (v. 16). The terminology of 'building up and not tearing down' is obviously an allusion to verses from Jeremiah, as several commentators have noted.[32]

At the end of the long section the theme of building up and tearing down recurs so that it forms an *inclusio* around Paul's self-defence:

> So I write these things while I am far away from you, so that when I come, I
> may not have to be severe in using the authority that the Lord has given me
> for building up and not for tearing down (2 Cor. 13.10).

The 'building' and 'planting' metaphors had already been used in the earlier 1 Corinthians to indicate the work which 'servants of God' such as Apollos and Paul are commissioned to do (1 Corinthians 3), but in 2 Corinthians 10–13 the metaphors are much more obviously derived from Jeremiah than in 1 Corinthians. It is the intended positive effect of his admonitions that Paul tries to highlight by using this terminology.

Commentators have puzzled about the apparent contrast with 2 Cor. 10.4-5, where Paul speaks of the destruction of 'strongholds', 'arguments' and 'every proud obstacle', whereas in v. 8 his intention seems to only 'build up'.[33] Does he more or less automatically echo Jeremiah's words? M.E. Thrall states that the motif of building and destroying should be interpreted within Paul's own thinking and that the second verb should not be regarded as a thoughtless quotation.[34] She concludes that Paul sees the negative and destructive effects of his opponents' actions and wants to destroy their thoughts and attitudes without destroying them themselves.[35]

It appears that the Jeremianic context may shed even more light on this point. The phrases in Jeremiah which contain the terms 'building up' and 'tearing down' are summaries of the calling and the commissioning of the prophet, the content of his message and the effect of his ministry. The book as a whole shows that his ministry goes through the different stages of prophetic warnings, divine

---

32. C.K. Barrett, *A Commentary on the Second Epistle to the* Corinthians (London: Black, 1973), 258; M.E. Thrall, *A Critical and Exegetical Commentary on the Second Epistle to the Corinthians Vol. 2: Commentary on II Corinthians VIII–XIII* (Edinburgh: T & T Clark, 2000), 625; Hafemann, *2 Corinthians*, 398.

33. For an overview of the alternative explanations see Thrall, *II Corinthians VIII–XIII*, 625.

34. Thrall, *II Corinthians VIII–XIII*, 625.

35. Thrall, *II Corinthians VIII–XIII*, 626.

judgment, and prophetic promises after judgment. The metaphors of 'building up' and 'tearing down' are used throughout (see Jer. 1.10, 18.7-10 [with reference to any nation or kingdom], 24.6, 31.28 and 42.10). In Jer. 29.5 the terms 'building' and 'planting' are used in the most literal sense, with reference to that which must take place in exile; in this way they contribute to an unexpected message for those remaining in Judah! In the structure of the book of Jeremiah the 'building' and 'planting' come after the 'tearing down' and 'destroying'. The latter are necessary to make way for God's forgiveness and restoration. Jeremiah, as God's agent and messenger, has to perform the difficult task of analysing Israel's sin and announcing its consequent judgment before he can begin to proclaim a time of restoration. Yet the 'grace of God' is never totally absent.

Paul understood his work of naming and shaming the sin and injustice among the Corinthians in the same way. It is obvious from both 1 Corinthians and 2 Corinthians 10–13 that there was 'rubbish' which needed to be cleared. The 'weeds' of sins such as argumentativeness, boastfulness, strife and sexual misbehaviour needed to be plucked up in order to be able to 'build up' the church again. Yet like the Israelites of old, the Corinthians were apparently unaware that their behaviour was wrong in the eyes of God. Paul does not address these issues with the purpose of hurting people deliberately but in order to free up the way to a deeper relationship with God (2 Cor. 12.19-21; cf. 1 Corinthians 5–7). Apparently the false apostles with whom he wrestles in 2 Corinthians 10–13 had not dealt with these issues, just as the false prophets in Jeremiah's time would not address the people's sins, however blatant they were from the perspective of God's true servant (see e.g. Jer. 6.13-14; 23.9-32). Chapters 10–13 in 2 Corinthians do not reveal much about the false apostles but the fact that Paul repeatedly defends himself against the charge that his approach is negative suggests that these rival leaders did not tackle sins in the way he did.

The ultimate goal of Paul's stern letters is to save the churches from further trouble and to keep them in the way of Christ. 'Destroying' things is not Paul's primary goal, but the destruction of 'arguments and every proud obstacle raised up against the knowledge of God' (2 Cor. 10.4-5) is done with God's authority. As Paul puts it, 'Everything we do, beloved, is for the sake of building you up' (2 Cor. 12.19). Thus Paul's work resembles Jeremiah's ministry which also seemed to be merely negative, yet was meant to have a purifying effect. Only by tearing down false beliefs and behaviour was a new beginning possible.

From this perspective the contrast between Jeremiah and Paul is by no means as great as some think it is. Hafemann, in his otherwise fine commentary on 2 Corinthians, emphasizes the contrasts between Paul and Jeremiah more than seems warranted by the text. He states:

> In fulfilment of Jeremiah's promise, the Lord (i.e., Christ) gave Paul authority

to be a minister of the new covenant 'for building you up rather than pulling you down,' whereas under the old covenant the emphasis of Jeremiah's ministry was just the opposite . . . This is why Paul's role as a minister of the new covenant is to mediate the Spirit, since as an apostle his primary purpose is the salvation of God's people, not their judgement . . . Though Jeremiah and Paul were each called both to save and to judge, their *primary* purposes within redemptive history have been reversed. As the introduction to the promise of the new covenant puts it (Jer. 31.27-28) . . .[36]

Paul is indeed a minister of the *new* covenant rather than a prophet of the *old* covenant (cf. 2 Cor. 3.3-6 and Jer. 31.31-34).[37] Furthermore, there may seem to be more emphasis on 'tearing down' than on 'building up' in Jeremiah – which contrasts with Paul's words in 2 Cor. 10.8 and 13.10. Yet the similarities between Jeremiah and Paul are worth considering. Despite Jeremiah's numerous oracles of judgment the primary purpose of his mission, in particular that to his own nation, was redemptive. Hafemann acknowledges this but connects 'judgement' more with the 'old covenant' and 'salvation' with the new covenant. Yet the mere fact that the new covenant promise in Jer. 31.27-28 sits in the context of prophecies to the nation of God then and there means that the concept of ultimate salvation through judgment was already part of Jeremiah's theology. On the other hand, Paul's letters to the Corinthians contain not a few cautions and warnings; their overall effect on the hearer is not dissimilar to that of the book of Jeremiah! The entire passage 2 Corinthians 10–13, which forms the context of 10.8 and 13.10, resounds with stern warnings and corrections, so much so that many scholars wonder whether these chapters were originally part of the same letter as 2 Corinthians 1–9.[38]

2.3 *Boasting and sufferings*

The theme of 'boasting' which we met in 2 Cor. 10.8 plays a significant role in Paul's first letter to the Corinthians. It is not difficult to see that 1 Cor. 1.31 is a clear reference to Jer. 9.23-24: '. . . as it is written, "Let the one who boasts, boast in the Lord".' In the context Paul argues at length that God's way is in contrast to that of human beings; what is of value in the world, be it wisdom or power or richness, should not play a role in the Christian church, not even in giving certain leaders more honour than others (1 Cor. 3.21).

In 2 Corinthians boasting occurs in even more places, in fact throughout

---

36. Hafemann, *2 Corinthians*, 398; italics his.

37. Hafemann, *2 Corinthians*, 127–28.

38. See e.g. the contrasting views of Hafemann, *2 Corinthians*, 31–33 and Thrall, *II Corinthians VIII–XIII*, 595–96.

chs. 10–12: We find it in 10.8, 13, 15, 16, 17 (a clear reference to Jer. 9.24); 11.10, 12, 13, 16–18, 21, 30; 12.1, 5, 6, 9. It is obvious that Paul is being challenged by people who 'boast' about being apostles and being of far more weight than he (11.12-13). To Paul's dismay, these false apostles (2 Cor. 11.13) are leading the Corinthian church astray. We saw above that they probably did not challenge the people's sinful behaviour as Paul did, which made them more popular than he. And this despite the fact that there were many issues to be addressed (2 Cor. 12.21), some of which may have been left over from the time Paul wrote 1 Corinthians 5–7. The struggle against opponents who claim to act with God's authority is one which must have been familiar to Paul from Jeremiah's life. The false prophets in his days claimed to receive revelations with which they impressed the people. From 2 Cor. 12.11-12 and Paul's long digression about his visionary experience in vv. 1–7 we may conclude that the false apostles also claimed to have extraordinary gifts and experiences.

For Paul the only proper boasting is in God and he refuses to boast in any human efforts, revelations or works performed. If he does so, it is with irony (2 Cor. 11.16-17). It is interesting that Paul's 'boasting' is eventually in his 'suffering' (2 Cor. 11.21–12.10). His sufferings and his weakness as result of 'a thorn in the flesh' are God's power and work in his life. They are all 'for the sake of Christ' (12.10) and to ensure 'that the power of Christ may dwell in me' (12.9). So in his body and through his life's experiences Paul is a living illustration of the message he proclaims. Paul's message is that it is only by grace and not by any effort of his own that God saves in Christ. His message that human power and impressions are no ground for boasting and that it is through the 'weakness' of the cross that God's power is manifested, is illustrated through his own sufferings and weaknesses (cf. 1 Cor. 1.23-25).

We tend to underestimate Paul's suffering, partly because the book of Acts does not pay much attention to it, partly due to his seemingly joyful attitude towards it. The latter is illustrated most poignantly in the letter to the Philippians, written from prison yet containing many exhortations to 'rejoice in the Lord'. Nonetheless, the list of 2 Cor. 11.21-33 is impressive and the hurt of rejection by those who were physically closest to him, his fellow Jews, must have been enormous (cf. Rom. 9.2-3).

In his life Paul embodies the suffering of Christ, experiencing rejection from his own people whom he loves. In this respect Jeremiah can be seen as a forerunner not only of Jesus Christ, but also of the apostle Paul, the apostle to the nations. Both Paul and Jeremiah were involved in the battle of false versus true messengers of God and both saw their mission questioned and rejected, even by their fellow countrymen (Jer. 11.21; 12.6).

In this respect Paul also stands in the tradition of other servants of God for whom suffering was part of God's call and mission, such as Moses, the 'suffering servant' in Isaiah, Ezekiel, Hosea and John the Baptist. In view of his allusions to the book of Jeremiah it is most likely that Paul recognized his own life and sufferings in those of Jeremiah. Yet Paul realizes what Jeremiah did not yet realize – that the 'cross' is the embodiment of God's grace.

Conclusion

Although Paul was, of course, thoroughly familiar with the Hebrew Scriptures, there are good reasons to think that in his self-understanding as a true messenger of God he was particularly influenced by his predecessor Jeremiah, another unmarried God-sent messenger from the tribe of Benjamin, who defines himself as untrained in speaking (compare Jer. 1.6 with 2 Cor. 11.6). In his defence against false apostles (2 Corinthians 10–13) and false doctrine (Galatians 1) Paul uses words from Jeremiah to claim God's authority as a true apostle. In their sufferings both men experience rejection by fellow Israelites and both do not receive human glory. The parallels between the two thus include their divine calling, their message of 'tearing down and building up', their life experiences and the need to defend themselves against a multitude of adversaries who claimed to be true messengers of God. It was only God's grace and power which sustained them both.

Chapter 7

'PROPHET TO THE NATIONS': MISSIONAL REFLECTIONS ON THE BOOK OF JEREMIAH

Christopher J.H. Wright
International Director, Langham Partnership International

Introduction

It is a joy to contribute to this volume in honour of Gordon McConville, with whom I have shared scholarly interest in the Old Testament throughout our careers, along with the natural friendship of our common roots in Northern Ireland. Gordon's theological interests in the Old Testament texts have over-lapped with and informed my own over many years. Some indication of my own journey will help to explain the choice of topic for this contribution – apart from the fact of Gordon's well-known interest in the book of Jeremiah.

My doctoral work and early publications were in the field of Old Testament economic ethics. After some years of pastoral ministry, I taught at All Nations Christian College (a training institution for people involved in cross-cultural Christian mission) for a year prior to going to teach in India. During that year I heard Martin Goldsmith talking about the missiological context out of which New Testament texts had arisen. That is to say, he urged us to see that it was not enough merely to exegete the text and then ask 'What are the missiological implications?' Rather, we needed to take into account that the circumstances that had led to the writing of the text in the first place were missional. Mission was intrinsic to the texts, not merely an extrinsic implication or application. I was struck by that insight and began to apply it to Old Testament texts, finding the results interesting and hermeneutically fruitful.

I then went to teach the Old Testament in India for five years, and found enormous stimulation in reading these texts with students who were going to be engaged in ministry and mission in that cultural and religious context. The ethical and spiritual challenges for God's people living in the midst of a poly-theistic context seemed to step off the pages of the Old Testament straight onto the streets of India in remarkably relevant ways. Missional reading of the Bible seemed very appropriate in that environment and my combination of ethical and missiological appropriation of the texts continued to develop.

Back in the UK and teaching again at All Nations, I inherited Martin Goldsmith's course, *The Biblical Basis of Mission*. I applied the hermeneutical approach I had first learned from him, and used to tell the students that I would like to change the title of the course to 'The Missional Basis of the Bible', i.e. to help them read the whole Bible for mission, not just to collect a few 'missionary texts' like beads on a string. At the same time, I encouraged a number of our MA students to explore a missiological reading of Old Testament books, and some interesting dissertations emerged on Deuteronomy, the Deuteronomic History, Wisdom Literature, the Book of the Twelve, and Ezekiel. In my own writing of commentaries on Deuteronomy[1] and Ezekiel,[2] I sought to apply some missiological reflection, with sections in the introductions devoted to the hermeneutical challenge that involved.

Eventually, all of this came together in my book, *The Mission of God: Unlocking the Bible's Grand Narrative*.[3] This was the culmination of those years of reflection and teaching, and an attempt to argue for the validity of a missional hermeneutic of scripture in principle, and to offer some outline of what it might look like in practice.

Then, just as that was coming to completion, I was introduced to a group of biblical and missiological scholars, mostly from Canada and the USA, who had been meeting annually since 2002 in the context of SBL to wrestle with a missional hermeneutic of scripture. I found even more encouragement and stimulation in that group of cheerfully encouraging fellow-travellers who welcomed my own contribution to the task.

In the 2008 meeting of that group, George Hunsberger offered a most helpful summarizing paper, analysing some key ways that the contributors to the group's reflection over seven years had developed. His paper, 'Proposals for a Missional Hermeneutic: Mapping the Conversation',[4] proposed that the phrase 'missional hermeneutic' was being used in four complementary ways in the discussion. In the hands of different scholars it could mean: the missional direction or framework of the biblical narrative; the missional purpose of the

---

1. *Deuteronomy* (NIBCOT; Carlisle: Paternoster, 1996).
2. *The Message of Ezekiel* (BST; Nottingham: IVP, 2001).
3. *The Mission of God: Unlocking the Bible's Grand Narrative* (Nottingham: IVP, 2006).
4. The full paper, and its bibliographical references, is available online at: http://www.gocn.org/resources/articles/proposals-missional-hermeneutic-mapping-conversation (accessed 26.02.10).

biblical texts; the missional locatedness of readers of the Bible; and the missional engagement of the gospel with cultures. For the purpose of this essay, I am taking the first three of Hunsberger's definitions as ways of thinking about a missional hermeneutic of the book of Jeremiah, and then adding a fourth of my own.

1. *The Missional Framework of the Biblical Narrative*

This is the approach that is developed most fully in my own book. It is to view the whole Bible as rendering to us the mission of God. The Bible is the witness to, and the product of, God's mission, through God's people, in God's world, for God's purpose – which is the restoration of all creation populated by a redeemed humanity drawn from every nation. This is the overarching narrative that spans the Bible from creation to new creation. The mission of God is what fills the gap between, on the one hand, the spoiled creation and the nations scattered in rebellion of Genesis 3–11, and on the other hand, the nations gathered in worship and the new creation of Revelation 21–22.

Such a view of the whole canon of scripture sets the Old Testament in continuity with the New, moving from beginning to climax in a single great universal narrative. Thus, God's election of Abraham and gift of a land is instrumental in God's plan for the blessing of all nations and the whole earth. The sequence of election, redemption, covenant and land-gift is thus paradigmatic for the wider story of God's multinational people, redeemed to inhabit the earth. This, according to Paul, is the narrative heart of the Gospel promise (cf. Gal. 3.6-8; Romans 4).

But the failure of Old Testament Israel, and the broken covenant, led to both *judgment* (in the immediate history of Old Testament Israel this meant exile), and also to *future hope* (the eschatology of restoration for Israel and ingathering of the nations). This is a theme that is found in poetic anticipation in Deuteronomy 32, but gathers clarity and emphasis in the prophets, especially during and after the exile itself. All this prepares the way for the New Testament proclamation of the embodiment and fulfilment of God's mission through Israel in the person and accomplishment of Jesus of Nazareth, and the New Testament mission of the church in the power of the Spirit to accomplish the ingathering of the nations by going to them with the message of the Gospel.

Where does the book of Jeremiah fit into this great matrix?[5] Although no

---

5. For the sake of the argument of this essay, I am not concerned to engage in critical questions of authorship of specific texts, or to distinguish the poetic and prose materials. The 'he' of the discussions above refers to the prophetic voice of Jeremiah as presented in the overall book in our hands.

single passage expresses the whole sweep of the scenario sketched above, it is clear that Jeremiah endorses its broad contours in at least four ways. He sees the wider purpose of Israel's election; he exposes the reality of failure and judgment; he holds out hope for restoration; and he envisages blessing for the nations alongside the hope of Israel.

1.1 *He sees the purpose of Israel's election and covenant (Jer. 13.1-11)*

> 'For as a belt is bound round a man's waist, so I bound the whole house of Israel and the whole house of Judah to me,' declares the LORD, 'to be my people for my renown and praise and honour. But they have not listened'. (Jer. 13.11)

This text uses the same triplet of words, '*renown* (or fame; Heb. *šēm*, 'name'), *praise and honour*', as in Deut. 26.19, where they are applied to Israel among the nations. But it is clear in both cases that the beneficiary is God himself. Whatever levels of renown, praise and honour may come Israel's way among the nations is actually for YHWH, the God who chose them as his covenant people.

The imagery of Jeremiah's acted parable expresses this well. He was to select a bright, new piece of clothing (probably a sash, not just a belt), and then very likely was to wear it with pride as something that was beautiful in itself. But the point of wearing it was to bring praise to the wearer, not to the sash. That was how God regarded Israel. He wanted to 'wear them'. Election here is expressed under the figure of choosing a piece of clothing to put on. The intention is to enhance the wearer before a watching world. It was doubtless an incredible privilege and honour for Israel to be chosen as YHWH's covenant partner, but that in itself was not the reason for YHWH making the choice. God had a wider agenda, namely the exaltation of his own name among the nations through what he would ultimately accomplish 'dressed with' Israel. The purpose of election was to bring glory to the electing God among the nations, for whose benefit the election had taken place.

Another hint of Jeremiah's awareness of the wider international scope of God's dealings with Israel is found in Jer. 4.1-2. The challenge is to get Israel to repent and show evidence of it in ethical transformation. The result of such repentance would be, not merely that Israel would be blessed or spared God's judgment (which are passed over in silence as perhaps too obvious to need stating), but also that '*the nations* will be blessed by him and in him they will glory', which seems like a very clear echo of the promise to Abraham. If Israel would repent, the nations would benefit. God's dealings with Israel have wider goals in view. We will return to this text below.

1.2 *He exposes the reality of failure and judgment*

This hardly needs stating for it is the unmistakeable burden of the message of Jeremiah in chapter after chapter, especially in the early part of the book. Chapter 2 accuses Judah of being worse than the polytheistic nations that surround it by imitating all their idolatries. The covenant is shattered (Jeremiah 11), and the curses will fall.

The tragedy was that Israel, by its failure to respond in trust and obedience to their covenant Lord, was thwarting the purpose of God in and through them. As the acted parable of the sash vividly portrayed, God simply couldn't wear such a people.

> And it is that wider purpose of God that Israel were frustrating by their disobedience. They had become as corrupt as a new sash that has lain in wet soil for many months – to return to Jeremiah's graphic acted parable. God simply couldn't wear them anymore. Far from bringing him praise and honour, they brought him disgrace and contempt.[6] For that reason, if God's purpose for the nations is to proceed, God will have to deal with Israel first. Hence the promises in Jeremiah 33 and the surrounding context. The restoration of the elect is not for their sole benefit, but so that the mission of God, for which they had been elect in the first place, can be accomplished among the nations. This is why, in broader canonical terms, the restoration of Israel had to happen before the ingathering of the nations – a sequence that Paul profoundly understood in his own mission theology.[7]

1.3 *He holds out the hope of new covenant restoration*

The 'Book of Consolation' (Jeremiah 30–33) is well known for its rich and moving theology of restoration and renewal. Primarily, of course, this is addressed to Israel. But there are glimpses of the wider significance of Israel's restoration – analogous to the wider significance of their failure.

> I will cleanse them from all the sin
> > they have committed against me
> and will forgive all their sins of rebellion against me.
> > Then this city will bring me
> renown, joy, praise and honour before all nations on earth
> > that hear of all the good things I do for it;

---

6. This is what Ezekiel means in ch. 36 when he speaks of Israel 'profaning the name of Yʜᴡʜ' (i.e. 'bringing Yʜᴡʜ into disrepute').

7. *Mission of God*, 259.

and they will be in awe
> and will tremble at the abundant prosperity
and peace I provide for it. (Jer. 33.8-9)

We see here the same three words (with the addition of 'joy') as we found in 13.11 and Deut. 26.19, and the same international resonance as in Deuteronomy. God's actions in relation to Israel – in judgment or in restoration – have their impact on the nations. In this text, the impact is simply one of awe and trembling, but Jeremiah is aware that more is on offer than gawping admiration.

1.4 *He envisages the resultant blessing of the nations*
There is nothing in Jeremiah that remotely compares with the symphony of universality and hope for the nations that we find in Isaiah. But still, there are some significant notes from the same score, as the following four illustrative texts indicate.

Jeremiah 6.18-19; 31.10
The parallels between these two texts are striking. Nothing that God does in Israel is done in vacuum-sealed isolation. The nations are summoned as witnesses, whether of the making and breaking of the covenant, or of its restoration. When God acts to redeem Israel, it will be a matter of proclamation among the nations. This theme is of course much stronger in Isaiah, but Jeremiah, 'prophet to the nations', is fully aware of this wider horizon of his message and ministry.

Jeremiah 18.1-10
Here we have another acted prophecy, or at least one illustrated by the actions of a third party – the potter. It presents the remarkable message that *any nation* can be the recipient of God's mercy, as well as the target of his judgment. Not many Israelites wanted to hear that about themselves or about other nations.

> The same universality by which all nations stand under the judgment of God for their wickedness and idolatry is also deployed in Old Testament thinking about the mercy of God. 'I will have mercy on whom I will have mercy, and I will have compassion on whom I will have compassion,' said Yhwh, in the course of his remarkable self-revelation to Moses, and in definition of his goodness and his name (Exod. 33.19, cf. 34.6-7). This is a principle that operated not only in, or on behalf of, Israel. Any nation could benefit from it.
>
> The lesson that Jeremiah draws from his observation of a potter who declared an initial intention, but then changed his plans and therefore the end result because of some 'response' in the clay, is that God likewise responds to

human response to his declared intentions. The focal point of the potter metaphor in Jeremiah 18 is not so much on the unquestionable sovereignty of the
divine potter, but on the potential that resides in the clay to cause the potter
to change his intention. And that provides an opportunity that God extends,
by way of general principle, to any nation at any time. If a nation repents in
the face of God's declaration of impending judgment, they will be spared that
doom. On the other hand, if a nation does evil in spite of God's declaration
of blessing, then they will suffer his judgment (Jer. 18.7-10). This point is
established as general principle of God's dealings with all nations, before it is
applied in urgent specificity to Judah.[8]

The message that any nation could in principle benefit from the mercy of God,
embodied in the potter story, is made even more explicit and specific in the
next remarkable passage.

Jeremiah 12.14-17
Here, God offers to the nations the same promise of divine forgiveness and
restoration as to Israel, if only they would turn to him and learn the ways of
YHWH.

It was the same offer, in virtually the same language, as Jeremiah held out to
Judah – and probably with as little hope of it being accepted. The point is, how-
ever, that there is no favouritism in God's dealings with Israel and the nations.
All stand under YHWH's judgment. All can turn to YHWH and find his mercy.

This, surely, has to be one of the most foundational elements of the Old
Testament contribution to our theology of mission.
- *If it were not the case that all nations stand under the impending judgment
  of God, there would be no need to proclaim the gospel.*
- *But if were not for the fact that God deals in mercy and forgiveness with
  all who repent, there would be no gospel to proclaim.*[9]

Jeremiah 3.17
This little text about the nations is virtually buried in God's appeal to Israel to
repent. But once again, in the indefinite eschatological future that lies beyond
such hope (forlorn as it was for Jeremiah's own generation), there is a place for
the nations. They will come to worship and honour YHWH. *The nations* 'will no
longer follow the stubbornness of their evil hearts', which is exactly what God
wanted to see in Israel.

---

8. *Mission of God*, 460.
9. *Mission of God*, 462.

This theme of the gathering of the nations to worship the living God is barely hinted at here, but it does show Jeremiah's awareness of a tradition that is embedded in other places, notably Psalms (such as Pss. 22.27-28; 86.9), Isaiah strongly, and, see also, Mic. 4.1-5; Zeph. 2.11; 3.9; Zech. 8.20-22; 14.16; Mal. 1.11.

So then, Jeremiah can be seen to fit coherently within the great overarching structure of biblical narrative and worldview. The God of Israel, from his covenant with Abraham, has called Israel to be a blessing to the nations. That mission is gravely threatened by their rebellion and the inevitable judgment that is falling upon them. But beyond that judgment lies a restoration of Israel that will inevitably involve a comparable hope for the nations – for whose ultimate blessing Israel had been created and chosen.

2. *The Missional Purpose of the Texts*

The second dimension of a missional hermeneutic surveyed by Hunsberger focuses on the purpose inherent in the text itself. Building on the work of Darrell Guder, he notes that the purpose of the written texts of the New Testament was the same as that of the spoken teaching and preaching of Jesus and the apostles. That is, for the formation of missional communities of disciples. The texts arose with the purpose of shaping and equipping the church for its witness, and for carrying forward the mission of God in the world. So a missional hermeneutic asks of any given text: How *did* this text function to equip and shape God's people for their missional witness, and how *does* it continue to shape us today? Such a hermeneutic takes the Bible as *formative* in its own context, and for the life of God's people ever since.

Where and how, then, might we see such a dimension in the book of Jeremiah? What was the purpose of Jeremiah's preaching, and therefore of the texts that arose from it? In what sense can we discern a missionally shaping intent here?

The first thing we have to say, depressingly, is that the task of shaping and equipping God's people needed to start a long way back, since by the time of the late monarchy, Israel had got very 'out of shape' indeed, and were barely distinguishable from the nations around them, and in some ways even worse. The preaching of Jeremiah can be summarized in two major thrusts (the rejection of idolatry; and the challenge of ethical change), both of which can then be seen, thirdly, to have a strongly missional dimension in relation to Israel's role in the midst of the nations.

2.1 *Rejection of idolatry and return to radical monotheism*
Jeremiah's earliest sustained preaching majors on this – the exposure of the continuing idolatry at the heart of Israel's life – even in the wake of Josiah's

reforms. Jeremiah 2 is probably something of a summary of the themes that filled Jeremiah's message, and the portrayal of Israel's addiction to idolatry and abandonment of their one covenant Lord is scorching in its intensity and metaphorical power. In rapid succession Jeremiah presents idolatry as a matter of:

Disappointment (1–3) and divine nostalgia. Their present apostasy made even the wilderness feel like a honeymoon period – but it is now heading for divorce (3.1-2).

a. Ingratitude (3–8), evidenced in the pursuit of worthlessness, the waste of what was precious, and the failure of leadership.
b. Disloyalty (10–12), on a scale that was shocking even in comparison with the surrounding nations.
c. Futility (13), the stupidity of abandoning God and going after unreliable substitutes (religious or political).
d. Delusion (22–23), they denied that they were involved in idolatry at all while claiming they had no option but to go after other gods!
e. Disaster (19, 37), for there would be tears in the end. Idolatry is ultimately self-destructive.

The themes of this powerful chapter ring through so much of the first half of the book.

> Given, then, that the gods of the nations were a disappointing failure even to the nations who worshipped them, and given that YHWH alone was the living God who could be trusted not to fail, it was doubly tragic that Israel should even think of exchanging the one for the other. There was something grossly unnatural about it, as Jeremiah observed in shocked disbelief.
>
> > Has a nation ever changed its gods?
> > (Yet they are not gods at all.)
> > But my people have exchanged their Glory
> > for worthless idols.
> > Be appalled at this, O heavens,
> > and shudder with great horror.
>
> How could anyone abandon a guaranteed source of life for a guaranteed source of disappointment? Yet that is what Israel had done, in forsaking the living spring for a leaking cistern. 'Broken cisterns that can hold no water' are a powerful image of disappointment, futility and wasted effort.[10]

---

10. *Mission of God*, 175–76.

In place of such futile idolatry, Jeremiah, like Isaiah especially, calls Israel back to radical monotheism: to the worship of the one and only true and living God. Jeremiah 10.1-16 is probably the most sustained piece of rhetoric against the falsehood of other gods and the reality and power of the living, creator God. It is a chapter that in many ways matches the rhetorical power of Isaiah 40–55 in its monotheistic thrust. And, like Isaiah, Jeremiah sees the universal significance of the affirmation that YHWH the God of Israel is the sole transcendent God. It is a fact that ultimately all nations must acknowledge.

> No one is like you, O LORD;
>> you are great,
>> and your name is mighty in power.
> Who should not revere you,
>> O King of the nations?
>> This is your due.
> Among all the wise men of the nations
>> and in all their kingdoms,
>> there is no one like you.
> the LORD is the true God;
>> he is the living God, the eternal King.
> When he is angry, the earth trembles;
>> the nations cannot endure his wrath (Jer. 10.6-7, 10).

Elsewhere I have explored in greater depth the missional significance of Old Testament monotheism,[11] for it is fundamental to all biblical theology of mission. The mission of God could be summed up as the will of the one God to be known throughout the whole earth as sole creator, ruler, judge, and saviour for all nations. Furthermore, this Old Testament teaching on the uniqueness and universality of YHWH is applied directly in the New Testament to the uniqueness and universality of Jesus Christ, which is the primary fount of all Christian mission. Remarkably, according to varied New Testament witness, the same four great functions that are the sole prerogative of YHWH are now exercised by Jesus Christ, who is presented to us as creator, ruler, judge and saviour of the world.

So while Jeremiah tackles Israel's idolatry head on, with only sidelong glances at the nations around, those glances are significant. The need for Israel to return to the radical monotheism of their covenant faith was not just a matter of getting them to believe in the right God. It was an essential part of their

---

11. *Mission of God*, ch. 3, and 126–35.

very reason for existence – to serve the mission of God to make himself known to the nations.

Recalling Israel to their covenant monotheism was thus profoundly missional in its *shaping* function. Those who refuse to worship the one living God are simply misshapen. They cannot fittingly participate in God's mission to be known to the nations if they themselves participate in the futile idolatry of the nations.

2.2 Challenge to ethical change (Jeremiah 7)

A return to the true God would necessarily mean a return to the *ways* of the true God; i.e. to the ethical demands of the covenant. This ethical thrust is felt widely in Jeremiah's preaching, but perhaps the 'Temple Sermon' of Jeremiah 7 is the clearest example of his point.

> This is what the LORD Almighty, the God of Israel, says: Reform your ways and your actions, and I will let you live in this place. Do not trust in deceptive words and say, "This is the temple of the LORD, the temple of the LORD, the temple of the LORD!" If you really change your ways and your actions and deal with each other justly, if you do not oppress the alien, the fatherless or the widow and do not shed innocent blood in this place, and if you do not follow other gods to your own harm, then I will let you live in this place, in the land I gave your forefathers for ever and ever. But look, you are trusting in deceptive words that are worthless. (Jer. 7.3-8)

'Reform your ways and your actions': that is the challenge to change summarized in v. 3. But the explanation in vv. 5–6 makes clear that such change had to be radical, practical, social, and transformative. It involved, in short, a return to the covenant ethics of Sinai. This is the 'shaping' work of the text. The people seemed to think they could have the right religious terminology, but Jeremiah tells them they are the wrong ethical shape. God would no longer tolerate such a mismatch of claims and realities.

So the call for repentance was urgent and repeated – and went on for decades. At first it seemed Jeremiah genuinely hoped that they would respond to his call, and he may even have written liturgies of repentance for them (3.22-25), but all to no avail (25.4-7; 36.3).

2.3 The impact on the nations

But what if they had repented? What was at stake? How did Jeremiah envisage the difference it would make, if the people could be shaped by his words back into a repentant and reformed people?

Jeremiah 4.1-2 addresses this very question. Note its combination of *both* rejection of idolatry, *and* a call to return to ways of truth, justice and righteousness.

> 'If you will return, O Israel, return to me,'
> > declares the LORD.
> 'If you put your detestable idols out of my sight and no longer go astray;
> > and if in a truthful, just and righteous way
> > you swear, "As surely as the LORD lives,"
> then the nations will be blessed by him
> > and in him they will glory.'

Jeremiah was appointed a 'prophet to the nations' (Jer. 1.5), and he has many things to say concerning them . . . Here, however, he links the destiny of *nations* directly to the response of *Israel* to God. The appeal for Israel genuinely to repent is familiar enough from the surrounding chapters of Jeremiah's early ministry, when he seems to have passionately believed that they could be induced to do so. The emphasis on the truly spiritual and ethical nature of such repentance is also familiar: it must involve the radical rejection of all other gods and idols, and it must combine genuine worship of YHWH with social integrity and justice. So far, we might say, we have heard this before in all the law and the prophets.

Previously, however, we might have expected the conditional phrases of vv.1–2a to be followed by an assurance that God would withdraw his threat of judgement against Israel. If only *Israel* will truly repent, then God will not have to punish *them*. In what Jeremiah actually does say, however, it feels as if he almost impatiently brushes that aside as self-evident: ('Yes of course, if *Israel* repents, *Israel* will be blessed'), and jumps ahead to a much wider perspective altogether. If Israel will return to their proper place of covenant loyalty and obedience, then God can get on with the job of blessing the *nations*, which is what Israel was called into existence for in the first place. 'It becomes clear that true repentance on Israel's part would have far-reaching consequences not merely for Israel but also for mankind in general.'[12]

The Abrahamic echo in the final two lines is very clear,[13] but the logic of the whole sentence is remarkable. God's mission to the nations is being hindered

---

12. J.A. Thompson, *The Book of Jeremiah* (NICOT; Grand Rapids: Eerdmans, 1980), 213.

13. 'The consequence of repentance and reorientation of life is the implementation of God's promise to Abraham . . . The restoration of covenant thus will benefit not only Judah but the other nations that derive new life from that covenant' (W. Brueggemann,

because of Israel's continuing spiritual and ethical failure. Let Israel return to *their* mission (to be the people of YHWH, worshipping him exclusively and living according to his moral demands), and God can return to *his* mission – blessing the nations.

> This interesting perspective sheds fresh light on the full scale and depth of God's problem with Israel. Rebellious Israel were not just an affront to God; they were also a hindrance to the nations. Ezekiel will make the same point even more sharply to Israel in exile. Not surprisingly, then (and for both prophets), the restoration of Israel to covenant obedience, and thereby to covenant blessing (peace, fruitfulness, abundance), will make a corresponding impact on the nations also (cf. Jer. 33.6-9; Ezek. 36.16-36).[14]

The missional purpose of the text of Jeremiah, then, was to bring Israel back to their covenant shape. But the longer-distant purpose of *that* was to enable them to fulfil their mission of bringing blessing to the nations. In other words, here as in so many places in the Old Testament, there is a fundamental, inextricable connection between the ethical quality of life of the people of God and their mission to the nations. There is no biblical mission without biblical ethics, and Jeremiah would agree.

3. *The Missional Locatedness of the Readers*

Hunsberger's observation of a third way that the phrase 'missional hermeneutic' has been used draws on Michael Barram's work. Missional hermeneutics emerge from within the community doing the reading – in their context and location. All communities of believers who read and listen to the scriptures together are rooted in a particular time and place, and they need to engage their own context in line with God's missional agenda, as they perceive it in their own generation and situation. Thus they should seek to read scripture in a way that is not only faithful to the original context (the world of and behind the text), but also faithful to its significance for their own present context (the world in front of the text). Thus, a missional reading takes account not only of the 'what' of the text's content along with the 'where' of the text's location in the wider biblical canon, and the 'why' of the text's formative purpose, but also of the 'who' and 'where' of the readers of the text in any situation.

All post-biblical readers of the book of Jeremiah can find responsible points

---

To Pluck Up, to Tear Down: A Commentary on the Book of Jeremiah 1–25 [ITC; Grand Rapids: Eerdmans, 1988], 46–47).

   14. *Mission of God*, 240–41.

of contact and application for their own context and mission as God's people in their contemporary world, and this is still true for us today. We can briefly think of that first of all, below. But the book had its readers even within the biblical period and it will be worthwhile, secondly, to think about the 'missional locatedness' of those original readers to whom the edited book itself was addressed.

3.1 Reading Jeremiah today

There are many ways in which the world into which Jeremiah spoke is reflected in today's international world, and the message that Jeremiah brought has continuing sharpness. So our missional reading of Jeremiah engages the text from the perspective of the many concerns of our own context, which find matching concerns in the text. All of the list below could be teased out in fruitful discussion, relating text to modern context in richly suggestive and challenging ways. We can do no more than mention them here, rather than explore them in depth. That should be the task of biblical preaching and teaching in the community of the church.

Here then are some features of the book of Jeremiah that deserve missiological reflection in our world:

a. The international scene: collapse of an old world order, fear over new threats to world stability.
b. Religious confusion among God's own people: Josiah's reformation had produced enormous social and religious change and stress, but there was continuing idolatry, and misplaced nationalism posturing as patriotism.
c. Social evils abounded: inequality, cheating, injustice, immorality.
d. Political abuse of power to stifle dissent: prophets who spoke the truth were silenced; Jeremiah, for opposing the official position of the political and religious establishment, was treated with hostility, ostracism, false accusation, physical abuse and even death threats.
e. Abuse of religious power: false prophets and corrupt priests cushioned the government from the voice of God or conscience, and colluded in social evils and immorality.
f. The message of God's sovereignty in history: in the midst of all the confusion, Jeremiah affirmed that God was ultimately in control, including contemporary events, and saw his hand even in the attack upon the homeland; the moral inevitability of judgment is an uncomfortable theme.
g. The mission of God's people even in exile: even after the collapse of their whole world and culture under God's judgment, God had a mission for his scattered people – to carry on with the Abrahamic mandate of being a blessing among the nations, seeking their welfare and praying for them.

h. Grace in the end: as with other prophetic books, Jeremiah is finally a hopeful book, for it sees restoration after judgment, and, in the promise of a new covenant, sets the scene for the unquenchable hope that undergirds Christian mission to the ends of the earth and the end of the world.

So, yes, in our own missional locatedness in the twenty-first century, we can read the words and themes of Jeremiah against the background of his day and discern multiple messages of power and relevance to our own. Such reading gives biblical missiology a sharp prophetic cutting edge that is vital to all our engagement with our world for God's sake and in Christ's name.

3.2 *Reading Jeremiah with the exiles*

However, the missional locatedness of contemporary modern readers of the book is not the only horizon of hermeneutical interest. We can also consider the missional locatedness of the original readers of the whole book. Who were they?

The opening and closing editorial sections of the book tell us by referring to the event that was the defining experience of those who edited the book into its present form, and those who read it in that form (1.1-3; 52.27-34). The book has been put together for those who had experienced the ending of it: i.e. the Babylonian exile.

Thus, when we read the text of Jeremiah's preaching, we need some 'double listening'. Of course we try to listen with the ears of those who first heard Jeremiah in person (and failed to respond to his message). But then also, we need to read these texts through the eyes of those who would read them in the circumstances that Jeremiah had predicted for 40 years. This is the thrust of Ernest Nicholson's book, *Preaching to the Exiles*,[15] except that the point applies not just (as he argues) to the prose sermons in the book. In fact the whole book is exactly that: preaching again the sermon of Jeremiah's whole life and ministry to the exiles.

Did they have a 'missional location'? They probably did not think so. We can read Psalm 137 and Lamentations to feel the mood on the street in the first traumatic years of exile. But in Jeremiah's letter to the exiles (Jer. 29.1-4) we have nothing less than a powerful piece of 'located missiology'. It is profoundly surprising – to them, no doubt, as much as to us – in at least three ways.

3.2.1 A surprising new perspective (Jer. 29.1, 4)

Notice the difference between the narrator's description of events and the repeated emphasis of the letter itself. The narrator speaks of the people whom

---

15. E. Nicholson, *Preaching to the Exiles: A Study of the Prose Tradition in the Book of Jeremiah* (Oxford: Blackwell, 1970).

Nebuchadnezzar had carried off into exile. That was a matter of historical observation and fact. The letter speaks of those whom *God* had carried (indeed, 'sent') into exile. That was a matter of prophetic interpretation. Behind the hammer of Nebuchadnezzar was the hand of God. This was doubtless surprising to the exiles, some of whom at least thought that YHWH had been defeated by the gods of Babylon. But it should not actually be surprising to us (or them), since it only repeats a truth as old as the story of Joseph in Egypt (delivered there by callous brothers, but 'sent' there by God for a purpose). Even the direst circumstances that (in the exiles' case) mediate the judgment of God can be viewed from the perspective of God's sovereign control of events, and therefore turned to missional advantage. God's purposes go on. This is a perspective that turned refugees into residents – as Jeremiah told them to settle down for the long haul. Babylon would be their 'locatedness' for several generations, so they had better 'be there' with God for the duration.

3.2.2 A surprising new mission (Jer. 29.7)

This is an amazing verse, which probably gave serious and fearful pause to whoever had the task of reading this letter aloud to the exiles. The ending of Psalm 137 gives us some hint of what the exiles thought about Babylon. Psalm 122 shows us what city they knew they ought to be praying for. And yet here Jeremiah boldly reverses that sentiment and instructs the exiles to pray for, and seek the welfare of *Babylon*! The exiles possibly had doubts whether it was possible to 'pray to YHWH' *in* Babylon, let alone pray to him *for* Babylon. But that was now their task. And the reason was surely not merely the most self-interested reading of the verse. In any case, Jeremiah knew that within a generation or two Babylon also would stand in the blast-path of God's judgment (Jeremiah 50–51). Nevertheless, he reminds the Israelites of their Abrahamic calling to be a blessing to the nations, not excluding their enemies. This is a perspective that turned mourners into 'missionaries', that is, a people with a sense of purpose. The stories in Daniel 1–6 seem to illustrate what was meant by such a perspective. There we see young Jewish men able to discern the hand and purpose of God, able and willing to serve Nebuchadnezzar's state in constructive and beneficial ways, almost certainly praying for Babylon as Jeremiah's letter instructed, and able, when the opportunities arose, to speak up and stand up for their covenantal faith in the living God without compromise.

3.2.3 A surprising new hope (Jer. 29.10-14)

The exile was not the end, contrary to the assumptions of many who suffered it and thought they might as well be dead (Ezek. 37.11) as far as their national future in the purposes of God was concerned. God still had his plan for them, as he had ever since they existed only in the loins of Abraham, and that plan was for good, for a future filled with hope. What is so surprising about Jer. 29.11 (probably one of the favourite promises that Bible readers like to claim) is that it is offered to people smarting under the direct judgment of God. It was meant to induce not comfortable feelings of security but earnest repentance and radical seeking of God. Those who read this text in exile knew their own exilic 'locatedness', but were being offered a 'way back to God from the dark paths of sin'. This was a perspective that could turn victims into visionaries. It was a long-term vision, for none of those who heard the letter first read in exile would see its fulfilment in the return to Jerusalem. But they could rest assured that God's purpose for Israel would go on and future generations would participate in it. Such vision and hope constitute the only foundation for missional investment such as v. 7 commanded.

And when they read the 'Book of Consolation', they would see that the promise of restoration for Israel would ultimately extend the knowledge of God among the nations, so that the hope of Jeremiah 13 would eventually be fulfilled.

> I will cleanse them from all the sin they have committed against me
>> and will forgive all their sins of rebellion against me.
> Then this city will bring me renown, joy, praise and honour
>> before all nations on earth that hear of all the good things I do for it;
> and they will be in awe and will tremble
>> at the abundant prosperity and peace I provide for it. (Jer. 33.8-9)

4. *The Missional Cost to the Messenger*

We have been thinking of 'mission' primarily in terms of the mission of God, through his people, for the nations of the world. But 'mission' includes the concept of sending, and the prophets had this in common that they were 'sent' by God, with their mission and message for God's people (and the nations, sometimes).[16]

Jeremiah 1 has featured in many a missionary sermon, since it articulates so clearly the prophetic calling and sending. It expresses, with its succinct narrative and dialogue, all the essential ingredients of what it means to be a 'sent one' of God. We observe God's sovereign choice (5), his sovereign command (7, wherever I send you; whatever I tell you to say); his sovereign care (8), and

---

16. I have explored further the biblical concept of sending and being sent, which includes a very broad range of purposes, in Christopher J.H. Wright, *The Mission of God's People: A Biblical Theology of the Church's Mission* (Biblical Theology for Life; Grand Rapids: Zondervan, 2010), ch. 12.

his sovereign authority (9–10, my words in your mouth). The parallels with the calling and commissioning of Moses are interesting, and these are probably intentional. So the prophet as a 'missionary', a sent one, is emphatic. Jeremiah's age, inexperience, reluctance, etc. were all irrelevant. A prophet's gotta do what a prophet's gotta do.

However, the cost of being such a sent one was extremely high. Jeremiah gives us more insight into his life and struggles, his suffering and emotional response, than any other prophet. Again, space precludes commenting on all the following in depth, but the personal cost of fulfilling God's mission included: Rejection and attack from his own family (11.18-23); Unpopularity with the whole nation (15.10; 20.7-8); Disillusionment and frustration with the failure of his ministry (15.10, 15–17); Suicidal rejection of his calling (20.14-18); Disappointment with God (15.18b); Aching grief (15.18a; 8.21–9.2); Profound and lifelong loneliness (16.1-9; 15.17); Being branded as a traitor (37–38); Suffering beatings, imprisonment and near-lynching (20.1-2; 26; 37–38); Seeing his words ignored, burnt, disobeyed (28, 36).

At least some of these were experienced by Jesus too (who was likened to Jeremiah in the word on the street), and others of them certainly also by Paul – in both cases because of their Jeremiah-like faithfulness to God's calling and sending.[17] So a missional reflection on Jeremiah cannot be confined only to the theological and ethical challenges of the book, but must also include the recognition of the man behind the book – the prophet himself, in the missionary nature of his being called and sent, and in the remarkable resilient faithfulness with which he carried out his mission in God's name. And such considerations should include his faithful servant, Baruch, who clearly shared Jeremiah's grief and pain (Jeremiah 45), and to whom, possibly, we owe the collected words of the book that bears his name.

---

17. See Hetty Lalleman's essay in this volume for a more detailed comparison of the missionary calls of Jeremiah and Paul.

Chapter 8

REMNANT MOTIF IN AMOS, MICAH AND ZEPHANIAH

Alison Lo

London School of Theology

'Remnant' is one of the significant motifs in the Minor Prophets. This essay will examine the remnant motif in Amos, Micah and Zephaniah, seeking to find out the commonality of this concept between these three pre-exilic books.

In order to facilitate this study, finding the remnant terminology[1] helps us locate the remnant passages. In Amos the term שארית is used with reference to Israel, i.e. the 'remnant of Joseph' (Amos 5.15). It also refers to other peoples, like the remnant of the Philistines (Amos 1.8) and Edomites (Amos 9.12). The term שארית is used five times in Micah (Mic. 2.12; 4.7; 5.6, 7 [7, 8]; 7.18) and another term יתר 'the rest/remainder/remnant' appears once in Mic. 5.2 [5.3]. In Zephaniah, the term שאר (1.4), which is translated as 'remnant' in many English versions, does not refer to the same concept of remnant as the rest of the book, but rather 'the last vestige of Baal' (NAB translation).[2] The term שארית occurs three times (Zeph. 2.7, 9; 3.13), יתר once in Zeph. 2.9; and the verb השארתי only in Zeph. 3.12. Some passages which are closely related to the remnant motif will also be studied despite the fact that there is a lack of specific remnant terminology there.

According to Meyer, a remnant is the left-over of a community, who survive the calamity of judgment.[3] This term contains both negative and positive connotations. Negatively a remnant has to first undergo a catastrophe, but positively a remnant can survive that dreadful time. House rightly states, 'Judgment creates

---

1. יתר, פליטה, שריד, שאר, and שארית are the common terms related to the remnant idea. These Hebrew words are often used interchangeably. E.W. Conrad, 'Remnant', in K. Doob Sakenfeld (ed.), *NIDB* (vol. 4; Nashville: Abingdon, 2009), 761–62.

2. The ESV version is used in this essay unless it is noted otherwise.

3. L.V. Meyer, 'Remnant', in David Noel Freedman (ed.), *ABD*; vol. 5; New York: Doubleday, 1992), 669–70.

the remnant as distinctly as it removes the rebellious'.[4] This essay, therefore, first addresses the issue of judgment in Amos, Micah and Zephaniah before examining the concept of remnant in these books.

1. *Judgment in Amos, Micah and Zephaniah*

Amos, Micah and Zephaniah all point out that sin is the reason for God's judgment upon His people. As shown in the table below, this can be seen through the repetition of the words פשע 'transgression', חטא 'sin', עון 'iniquity' and עולה 'wrongdoing', all of which are more general terms designating punishable offences.

פשע 'transgression'	Amos	1.3, 6, 9, 11, 13; 2.1, 4, 6; 3.14; 4.4 x2; 5.12
	Micah	1.5 x2; 1.13; 3.8; 6.7; 7.18
	Zephaniah	3.11
חטא 'sin'	Amos	5.12; 9.10
	Micah	1.5, 13; 3.8; 6.7, 13; 7.9, 19
	Zephaniah	1.17
עון 'iniquity'	Amos	3.2
	Micah	7.18, 19
עולה 'wrongdoing'	Micah	3.10
	Zephaniah	3.5, 13

The terms listed above indicate the problems of God's people, which justify God's intervention.

1.1 *Specific Reasons for Judgment*

Sin takes many specific forms, which are quite similar between Amos, Micah and Zephaniah. They include religious malpractice, pride and complacency, social injustice and oppression, corrupt leadership (religious, official, royal and judicial), and corruption in the marketplace and high society in the table that follows:

4. P.R. House, 'Dramatic Coherence in Nahum, Habakkuk, and Zephaniah', in J.W. Watts and P.R. House (eds.), *Forming Prophetic Literature: Essays on Isaiah and the Twelve in Honor of John D. W. Watts* (Sheffield: Sheffield Academic Press, 1996), 204.

	Amos	*Micah*	*Zephaniah*
Religious practices	4.4-5; 5.21-24, 26; 8.14	1.7; 5.12-13 [13–14]	1.4-6
Pride and complacency	5.18; 6.1, 8; 9.10	2.6; 3.11	1.12; 3.11
Social injustice and oppression	2.6-8; 4.1; 5.10-12; 8.3, 6	2.2; 3.1-3	1.9; 3.1-3
Religious leaders	7.10-17	3.5-7, 11	3.4
Official, royal, judicial leaders	7.11; 5.12	3.1-3, 9–11a; 7.3	1.8; 3.3
Marketplaces	8.5-6	6.11	1.10-11
Rich people	3.10, 12, 15; 4.1-3; 6.4-7	6.12	1.11, 18

In face of the great sins of God's people, Amos proclaims, 'The end has come upon my people Israel' (Amos 8.2). Micah announces, 'All this is for the transgression of Jacob and for the sins of the house of Israel' (Mic. 1.5). Zephaniah utters repeatedly, 'In the fire of His jealousy, all the earth shall be consumed' (Zeph. 1.18; 3.8). These prophets all proclaim that on the Day(s) of the LORD[5] (Amos 5.18-20; 8.1-3, 9; Mic. 5.9-14 [10–15]; Zeph. 1.4-6) God will pour out His punishment, with a combination of military defeat (Amos 2.13-16; 3.11; 4.1-3; 5.3; Mic. 5.9-10 [10–11]; Zeph. 1.10, 13–14, 16), exile (Amos 4.2-3; 5.5, 27; 6.7; 7.11, 17; Mic. 1.16; Zeph. 3.10), disasters (Amos 2.13; 4.6-10; 9.1; Mic. 6.13–7.1; Zeph. 1.2-3, 18), death (Amos 5.3, 16–17; 6.9-10; 7.17; 8.3; 9.1, 4, 10; Mic. 2.5; Zeph. 1.2-3, 17, 18, 3.8) and desolation (Amos 7.9; 9.11; Mic. 3.12; 6.13, 16; Zeph. 1.13[6]).

1.2 *Totality and Inescapability of Judgment*

The judgment announced by Amos, Micah and Zephaniah is sheer and inescapable. Regarding the fate of Israel, Amos says, 'As the shepherd rescues from the mouth of the lion two legs, or a piece of an ear, so shall the people of Israel who dwell in Samaria be rescued, with the corner of a couch and part of a bed' (3.12). The remains of the prey in the simile prove that 'rescue came too late

---

5. Here the concept of the Day of the LORD is not confined to the precise phrase יום יהוה, but it includes other terms like 'on that day', 'at that time' and so on. See J.D. Nogalski, 'The Day(s) of YHWH in the Book of the Twelve', in P.L. Redditt and A. Schart (eds.), *Thematic Threads in the Book of the Twelve* (Berlin: Walter de Gruyter, 2003), 192–93.

6. Most of the 'desolation' punishments declared by Zephaniah are directed against the nations. These passages include Zeph. 2.4, 13, 15; 3.6.

– surely an ironic thrust!'[7] Mockingly the total loss of the nation is the reality. The Samaritan women in high society are also singled out for accusation. Even 'the last' (אחרית) of them will be deported to exile (Amos 4.2). Their dead bodies will be taken out of the city through the breaches and cast into Harmon (Amos 4.3). The judgment is again absolute. Amos 6.9-10 points out that 'if ten men remain in one house, they shall die'. The single survivor will be fearful of God's anger falling on him. Hasel rightly states, 'Amos leaves open the possibility of a remnant being left in a house, but he emphasizes the utter ineffectiveness and hopelessness of this remnant'.[8]

Amos vividly describes how the people of Israel cannot escape the Day of Yahweh. Their situation is 'as if a man fled from a lion, and a bear met him, or went into the house and leaned his hand against the wall, and a serpent bit him' (Amos 5.19). The inescapability of judgment is once again pinpointed by the fact that 'those who escape the initial onslaught will be hunted down one by one' (Amos 9.1-4).[9] The stunning reality is 'not one of them shall flee away; not one of them shall escape' (9.1); and 'All the sinners of my people shall die by the sword' (9.10). The above passages contain allusions to the remnant concept, ironically bringing out the message that '[o]nly a remnant of Israel will remain but not Israel as a remnant'.[10]

Micah points to Israel as a model for the fate of Judah and Jerusalem (1.5),[11] and it looks towards the Babylonian exile (3.12; cf. 1.16; 4.9-10a) from the perspective of the Assyrian period (1.6). The fourfold repetition of 'I will cut off' (כרת) in Mic. 5.9-12 [10–13], says Mays, 'sketches a programme of the eradication and removal of things offensive to Yahweh's sovereignty'[12] – horses, chariots and strongholds (vv. 9–10 [10–11]), sorceries and fortune tellers (v. 11 [12]), carved images and pillars (v. 12 [13]). His people will be utterly devastated (2.4) and the guilty land-grabbers will have no descendants to claim their heritage in the congregation of Yahweh (2.5). There is no resting place because of uncleanness that destroys with a grievous destruction (2.10). Total desolation will become a reality because 'Zion shall be plowed as a field; Jerusalem shall become a heap of ruins, and the mountain of the house a wooded height' (3.12).

The sheer scale of God's punishment is revealed in Zephaniah's warning that

7. J.L. Mays, *Amos* (OTL; London: SCM Press, 1969), 67.

8. G.F. Hasel, *The Remnant: The History and Theology of the Remnant Idea from Genesis to Isaiah* (Berrien Springs, MI: Andrews University Press, 1972), 184.

9. Meyer, 'Remnant', 669.

10. Hasel, *The Remnant*, 189.

11. Regarding the function of Mic. 1.5, see J.D. Nogalski, *Literary Precursors to the Book of the Twelve* (Berlin; New York: Walter de Gruyter, 1993), 131–37.

12. J.L. Mays, *Micah* (OTL; Philadelphia: Westminster, 1976), 125.

God will utterly sweep away everything 'from the face of the earth', including man and other living creatures (1.2-3); all the earth will be consumed in
the fire of His jealousy (1.18; 3.8); and Yahweh will suddenly and completely
destroy all the inhabitants of the earth (1.18). This is a 'reversal of creation'.[13]
Ball establishes that the exact Hebrew phrase מעל פני האדמה 'from the face of
the earth' is used 13 times in the MT, all of them except Gen. 8.8 involving
punishment.[14] People can hardly hide and escape as God will search Jerusalem
with lamps (1.12).

1.3 *Yahweh's Personal Intervention*
Amos, Micah and Zephaniah portray Yahweh as a god who is personally
involved in human affairs. They cite Yahweh in the first person when He proclaims the planned judgment upon His people. Regarding the book of Amos,
Wolff rightly observes, 'At least two thirds of the announcements of punishment attribute the impending end to Yahweh's own intervention, always using
the first person of the messenger speech'.[15] Take Amos 8.9-11 for instance.
Yahweh declares, 'I will make the sun go down at noon'; 'I will turn your feasts
into mourning'; 'I will bring sackcloth on every waist'; 'I will make it like the
mourning for an only son'; and 'I will send a famine'. Similarly in Mic. 5.9-14
[10–15], Yahweh's first person announcement of judgment is quoted: 'I will cut
off'; 'I will destroy'; 'I will throw down'; 'I will root out'; and 'I will execute
vengeance'. In Zephaniah, God's relentless personal involvement in judgment
is also clearly seen: 'I will sweep away' (1.2-3); 'I will cut off' (1.3, 4); 'I will
stretch out My hand' (1.4); 'I will punish' (1.8-9, 12); 'I will search' (1.12); and
'I will bring distress' (1.17). Unequivocally, these three prophets all underscore
that 'Yahweh is the agent of judgment, the driving force behind it'.[16]

   God's personal involvement in His judgment in Amos, Micah and Zephaniah
ironically contradicts the belief of some people. The sinners in Amos' time
say, 'Disaster shall not overtake or meet us' (Amos 9.10). The land-grabbers,
who stop Micah from preaching the doom message, say that 'disgrace will not
overtake us' (Mic. 2.6). The peace prophets preach, 'Is not the LORD in the

---

   13. M. DeRoche, 'Zephaniah 1 2–3: The "Sweeping" of Creation', *VT* 30 (1980),
104–109 (106).
   14. The 13 occurrences are: Gen. 4.14; 6.7; 7.4; 8.8; Exod. 32.12; Deut. 6.15; 1 Sam.
20.15; 1 Kgs 9.7; 13.34; Jer. 28.16; Amos 9.8; Zeph. 1.2, 3 (I.J. Ball, *A Rhetorical Study
of Zephaniah* [Berkeley: Bibal, 1988], 46).
   15. Wolff lists God's first-person declarations, highlighting His personal intervention
in judgment. See H.W. Wolff, *Joel and Amos* (trans. W. Janzen, S.D. McBride, Jr., and
C.A. Muenchow; Hermeneia; Philadelphia: Fortress, 1977), 102–103.
   16. G.A. King, 'The Message of Zephaniah: An Urgent Echo', *Andrews University
Seminary Studies* 32 (1996), 211–22 (215).

midst of us? No disaster shall come upon us' (Mic. 3.11). In Zephaniah the Jerusalemites' pride is well reflected by what they say in their hearts – 'The Lord will not do good, nor will he do ill' (Zeph. 1.12), which Achtemeier regards as the central indictment in the book.[17] Instead of being passive and detached, God takes an active role in cleansing the evil. However, God did not stop thereafter removing the wicked ones. More importantly, this purging of impurities gives birth to a remnant. The next section proceeds to investigate the common characteristics of remnant in Amos, Micah and Zephaniah.

2. *Remnant in Amos, Micah and Zephaniah*

Inevitably, the investigation of the remnant idea will have to tackle some important interpretative issues in the course of discussion, such as: the tension between total destruction and salvation; the tension between a remnant's vulnerability and strength; and the tension between human deeds and divine grace. First, we will examine the issue of total annihilation and salvation.

2.1 *Tension between Total Annihilation and Salvation*
Earlier in the essay, the totality of judgment in Amos, Micah and Zephaniah has been examined. It begs the question how a remnant can arise amidst total destruction. Take Amos as an example. In the face of the destruction of the sanctuary, Amos claims that no one can escape the calamity (Amos 9.1-6). Unexpectedly the juxtaposition of Amos 9.8b-10 with 9.1-6, 7–8a oddly displays a tension between the totality of punishment and the salvation of survivors. Some key verses are singled out to demonstrate the dilemma:

> not one of them shall flee away;
> > not one of them shall escape.   (9.1b)
> 'Behold, the eyes of the Lord God are upon the sinful kingdom,
> > and I will destroy it from the surface of the ground,   (9.8a)
> *except that I will not utterly destroy the house of Jacob,*' declares
> > the Lord.
> > 'For behold, I will command, and shake the house of Israel
> among all the nations as one shakes with *a sieve*,
> > but no pebble shall fall to the earth.
> All the sinners of my people shall die by the sword,
> > who say, "Disaster shall not overtake or meet us."'   (9.8b-10)

---

17. E. Achtemeier, *Nahum – Malachi* (Interpretation; Atlanta: John Knox, 1986), 69.

Nogalski rightly comments that Amos 9.8b-10 serves as an 'interpretative correction' to 9.7-8a. He further points out:

> It [Amos 9.8b-10] seeks to explain the existence of survivors in light of an authoritative text which 'on the surface' appears to say there would be no survivors. By subtly altering the perspective through the use of a sieve metaphor, the author is able to keep the totality of judgment (all experience great upheaval), while at the same time limiting and accentuating the idea of the total destruction of those who paid no heed.[18]

That is to say, Amos 9.7-8a 'applies the message of judgment in its radical form' while Amos 9.8b-10 'qualifies the idea of total destruction' in 9.1-6, 7–8a 'by allowing the existence of a remnant and attempting an explanation for those who did not escape the fate of judgment'.[19] Therefore, the sieve metaphor is skillfully used to unlock the dilemma between total destruction and the survival of the remnant.

In Micah the childbirth metaphor vividly exhibits the tension between the wailing pain of distress and great joy of salvation, which are juxtaposed in Micah 4.9-10. The writhing and groaning pain of deportation and exile is compared to the pains of a woman in labour (4.9-10a). However, the dilemma is resolved as Smith points out, 'The pains in childbirth can be excruciating but they normally conclude with a new life'.[20] Then there comes God's deliverance from the hands of the enemies (4.10b). It gives birth to a remnant. The totality of punishment is again implied as no one can escape such great pain.

Zephaniah desperately exhorts Judah, 'Gather (קשׁשׁ) together, yes, gather (קשׁשׁ), O shameless nation' (2.1). The Hebrew verb קשׁשׁ 'gather' is generally used in the sense of gathering straw or sticks, instead of gathering people.[21] Here the straw metaphor is used to echo the preceding verse (1.18), which tells us that God's wrath will consume the world like fire. Now Judah is like straw, quickly burned. In Zeph. 2.3, however, the shelter/refuge metaphor is used and points out the possibility that a humble and righteous remnant might be 'hidden' (Niphal of סתר) and thus spared on the day of Yahweh's wrath. As Berlin comments, '[t]he totality and finality of the prophecy of destruction is moderated by

---

18. Nogalski, *Literary Precursors*, 103–104.

19. Nogalski, *Literary Precursors*, 121.

20. R.L. Smith, *Micah – Malachi* (WBC, 32; Nashville: Thomas Nelson, 1984), 40.

21. F. Brown, S. Driver and C. Briggs, *BDB* (Peabody: Hendrickson, 1996), 905; A. Berlin, *Zephaniah* (AB, 25A; New Heaven; London: Yale University Press, 1994), 95–96; M.A. Sweeney, *Zephaniah* (Hermeneia; Minneapolis: Augsburg Fortress, 2003), 114–15.

a ray of last-minute hope'.[22] The certainty of the remnant's salvation is affirmed later in 3.12, where the shelter metaphor is once again used, stating that God will leave (שאר) a humble and lowly people, who shall 'seek refuge' (חסה) in the name of the LORD. On the one hand, the shelter metaphor qualifies the total destruction announced by Zephaniah (1.2-3, 18; 2.1; 3.8), but on the other it explains the existence of a remnant.

Throughout Amos, Micah and Zephaniah, the totality of God's judgment seems to contradict His salvation at first glance. However, the use of different metaphors in these books serves to explain such a paradox.

2.2 *Tension between the Remnant's Vulnerability and Strength*

The remnant is described as both weak and strong. Picking up some points from both Amos and Micah, Zephaniah brings such a stark contrast to a fuller expression. In His future plan, Yahweh has a special purpose for them – a people with special characteristics.

2.2.1 Powerlessness

Regarding the characteristics of a remnant, both Zephaniah and Micah identify this group of survivors as 'the lame' (הצלעה; Mic. 4.7; Zeph. 3.19) and 'the outcast' (הנהלאה Mic. 4.7; הנדחה Zeph. 3.19) who have gone into exile and are dispersed over different places. The Lord will assemble and bring them back to their homeland (Mic. 2.12-13; 4.6; 7.12; Zeph. 3.18-20; cf. Isa. 11.11-16). They are afflicted and taunted by their oppressors (Mic. 7.10; Zeph. 2.8, 10; 3.15, 19). Zephaniah gives a fuller description of this remnant: they suffer without appointed feasts because they cannot worship in Jerusalem during the diaspora (Zeph. 3.18); they are depicted as 'all the humble of the earth' (כל־ענוי הארץ), who 'seek humility' in Zeph. 2.3, and 'a people humble and lowly/poor' (עם עני ודל) in Zeph. 3.12 (cf. Isa. 2.11-12; 3.16–4.4). A summary of this section shows that Yahweh is the defender of the humble, poor and needy.

2.2.2 Spiritual Strength

As Anderson points out, the concept of remnant must be understood in a positive instead of a negative sense. They are not survivors, who represent the doom of the disaster.[23] Instead, they are survivors of past punishment, who exemplify the quality of the people of God, which will constitute a purified community. Both Amos and Zephaniah imply that the remnant is a people, who respond

---

22. Berlin, *Zephaniah*, 100.

23. G.W. Anderson, 'The Idea of the Remnant in the Book of Zephaniah', *ASTI* 11 (1977–78), 11–14; idem, 'Some Observations on the Old Testament Doctrine of the Remnant', *TGUOS* 23 (1969–70), 1–10.

positively to the prophets' exhortation to seek Yahweh (בקשׁ Zeph. 2.3; דרשׁ Amos 5.4-6). They do justice (משׁפט Amos 5.15; Zeph. 2.3), seek righteousness (צדקה Amos 5.24; צדק Zeph. 2.3) and humility (Zeph. 2.3; 3.12). They hate evil and love good (Amos 5.14-15). Specifically they exhibit justice and righteousness in their treatment of others: doing no injustice (עולה), speaking no lies and refraining from deceitful tongue (Zeph. 3.13).

Even though Micah does not explicitly tell us the spiritual qualities of a remnant as Amos and Zephaniah do, he does spell out what God requires of His people: 'He has told you, O man, what is good; and what does the LORD require of you but to do justice (משׁפט), and to love kindness (חסד), and to walk humbly (הצנע לכת) with your God?' (Mic. 6.8). Micah implies that a remnant who truly repents is presumably willing to live up to this expectation. 'The characteristics of the remnant mark them as the true people of God. They are in a right relationship with their Lord, being deeply committed to Him.'[24]

2.3 *God's Transformation to the Remnant*

Apart from the distinct characteristics discussed above, the remnant will be further transformed by God to be a strong and glorious nation. Before addressing how Yahweh transforms them, it is important to recognize who this Transformer is.

2.3.1 Yahweh as King of kings

The theme of the restoration of the Davidic kingdom is stressed in both Amos and Micah. On that day Yahweh will raise up, repair, and rebuild the 'booth of David', which is fallen (Amos 9.11). Here the 'booth of David' refers to the 'united Israel' instead of the house 'in the sense of dynastic lineage'.[25] The fallen 'booth of David' refers to the division of the united monarchy after the death of Solomon. Not only does the remnant enjoy the restoration of the Davidic kingdom (9.11), but also they enjoy peace and security (9.15), which is bestowed by Yahweh God of Hosts (יהוה אלהי צבאות). The variant forms of יהוה אלהי צבאות occur 9 times in Amos (3.13; 4.13; 5.14, 15, 16, 27; 6.8; 6.14; 9.5).[26] This divine epithet 'designates the enthroned, powerful god in his majesty'.[27]

---

24. G.A. King, 'The Remnant in Zephaniah', *BS* 151 (1994), 414–27 (420).

25. Hasel, *The Remnant*, 210.

26. The variant expressions are: אדני יהוה אלהי הצבאות (3.13); אלהי הצבאות (6.14); and אדני יהוה הצבאות (9.5).

27. S. Kreuzer, 'Zebaoth – Der Thronende', *VT* 56 (2006), 347–62 (362). See also J.P. Ross, '*Jahweh Seba'ot* in Samuel and Psalms', *VT* 17 (1967), 76–92; E. Jenni and C. Westermann, *Theological Lexicon of the Old Testament* (vol. 2; trans. M.E. Biddle; Peabody: Hendrickson, 1997), 1045.

Yahweh is the majestic God-King, who is able to judge all nations and restore the Davidic rule and the remnant.

Micah parallels Amos in highlighting God's restoration of the Davidic kingdom (Mic. 5.1-4a [2–5a]). A king will emerge from Bethlehem Ephrathah. Both Bethlehem and Ephrathah are related to David in terms of 'geographical location and family identification'[28] – low status, small size, no power and influence (cf. Ruth 1.2; 1 Sam. 17.12; Ps. 132.6). God chooses someone, who is considered as the most impossible candidate to carry out His mission. God says that this new ruler will come forth 'for me' (5.1 [2]) and he will find strength and authority in the Lord to stand and feed his flock (5.3 [4]). The new ruler's submission to God – the True King of Israel – is vividly indicated here. With his total subordination to God, he brings peace to his people ('the remnant', 5.4a [5a]), who can dwell securely (5.3 [4]). He will become great among the nations (5.3 [4]).

Both Micah and Zephaniah portray Yahweh as the King who will rule over the restored community and personally dwell in their midst. Micah proclaims, 'The LORD will reign over them (the remnant) in Mount Zion from this time forth and forevermore' (Mic. 4.7). Not only does Yahweh appoint a new king (Mic. 5.1-4a [2–5a]), but also He will be the King among the restored in Mount Zion (Mic. 4.7). No wonder they become a strong and secure nation (4.7; 5.3 [4]). Without mentioning the restoration of the Davidic Kingdom, Zephaniah in turn echoes Micah, announcing 'The King of Israel, the LORD, is in your midst' (Zeph. 3.15c; cf. 3.17). Because of the presence of their God-King the restored remnant shall never again fear evil (Zeph. 3.15d).

This analysis reveals that Yahweh, who appoints the new ruler of the Davidic kingdom, is the True King of Israel. He is actually the King of kings, who brings true security and peace to His people. How this Transformer will transform His people is discussed below.

2.3.2 Victory over the Enemies

The identification of a remnant as 'the lame', 'the outcast', 'the sufferer' and 'the oppressed' seems to highlight the lowliness, vulnerability and weakness of this people. However, this is not the whole picture of the remnant. Actually the Lord will transform them into a strong nation.

The remnant's victory over their enemies is reiterated throughout the book of Micah. God clearly states that He will turn the remnant into 'a strong nation' (4.7; גוי עצום), which contrasts sharply with the present image of 'powerlessness'

---

28. D.J. Simundson, 'The Book of Micah', in L.E. Keck (ed.), *NIB* (vol. 7; Nashville: Abingdon, 1996), 570.

in 4.6,[29] where the 'lame female' (הצלעה) metaphor is used to depict the remnant as an afflicted woman being driven away. Then Zion will repossess her former dominion and have their king again (4.8). When God gathers the nations to punish Zion, she suffers like a woman in labour pain (4.9-10a). However, God will redeem His people from the hand of the enemies (4.10b). Instead of being like a woman in labour, Zion now becomes like a mighty threshing cow with iron horns and bronze hoofs, beating many peoples (like sheaves) into pieces (4.12-13). Again, the remnant's defeat of their enemies is vividly portrayed when God promises them: 'Your hand shall be lifted up over your adversaries, and all your enemies shall be cut off' (5.8 [9]; cf. 5.5b-6) and 'in anger and wrath I will execute vengeance on the nations that did not obey' (5.14 [15]).

Micah 7.7-10 highlights that God will vindicate Zion by shaming her enemy,[30] who is rejoicing over Jerusalem's defeat (7.8) and taunting her by asking: 'Where is the LORD your God?' (7.10a). But when God brings justice to Zion, calamity and humiliation will in turn befall her enemy (7.10b). The situation will be reversed, even though the enemy is now enjoying the upper hand. Further vindication is promised in Mic. 7.11-13.[31] People from all nations will come to Jerusalem, from Assyria and Egypt, and from Egypt to the River, from sea to sea and from mountain to mountain (7.12; cf. 4.1-2). And the rest of the earth will become desolate (7.13).

In the oracles against the nations (Zeph. 2.4-15), God declares His punishment upon: a) Judah's smaller neighbouring rivals, i.e. Philistia in the *west* (2.4-7), Moab and Ammon in the *east* (2.8-11), the Ethiopians/Cushites in the *south* (2.12); and b) larger distant superpowers, i.e. Assyria in the *north* (2.13-15). Floyd rightly states that the two geopolitical categories of nations and their four cardinal directions 'represent the totality of the world situation viewed from Judah's perspective'.[32] God's intervention in punishing the nations paves the way to Judah's possession of their enemies' land, which will be discussed in the next section.

---

29. For the discussion of the contrast, see E. Ben Zvi, *Micah* (FOTL, 21B; Grand Rapids: Eerdmans, 2000), 112.

30. In this section the speaker and enemy are not identified, but both are female. They may refer to two countries or cities. Zion is most probably the speaker. D.N. Freedman, *Micah* (AB, 24E; New York: Doubleday, 2000), 576.

31. Here it is a different voice (a priest or a prophet) asserting the congregation about God's future acts for them. Zion (feminine pronominal suffix) now shifts from speaker to addressee (Ben Zvi, *Micah*, 175–76).

32. M.H. Floyd, *Minor Prophets II* (FOTL, 22; Grand Rapids: Eerdmans, 2000), 204.

2.3.3 Territorial Extension

Amos, Micah and Zephaniah all speak of the remnant's territorial expansion. Apart from enjoying their own land, the remnant even extends their borders by defeating their former enemies and possessing their territories.

Amos 9.12 points out that in the restoration they will 'possess the remnant of Edom and all the nations who are called by my name'. Israel and Edom have a long history of rivalry, which dates back to the time of the Exodus and Israel's journey to Canaan (Exod. 15.15; Num. 20.14-21; Judg. 11.17-18; 1 Sam. 14.47; 2 Sam. 8.13-14; 1 Kgs 11.15-16; 2 Kgs 8.20-22; 14.7-10; 2 Chron. 25.11-12; 28.16-18, etc.). Edom may well represent Israel's enemies throughout the Israelite history. Now God promises that Edom and all other nations will be in the remnant's control.

The theme of territorial extension appears in Micah too. On that day, Jerusalem's broken city walls will be rebuilt. Such a rebuilding points to the restoration of the nation's fortune. Not only will she restore the domination of her territory, but her border will also be far extended (ירחק־חק, Mic. 7.11).

In Zephaniah God not only cuts off the nations (Zeph. 2.4-15; 3.6) and clears away the remnant's enemies (Zeph. 3.15), He even allows the remnant of Judah to possess the former territories of Philistia, Moab and Ammon (Zeph. 2.7a, 9b). The seacoast (Philistia) belongs to the remnant of Judah, who will lie down in the houses of Ashkelon in the evening (Zeph. 2.7a) because God will be mindful of them and restore (פקד) their fortunes (Zeph. 2.7b). The verb פקד is usually used in contexts where God will 'visit' or 'punish' (e.g. Zeph. 1.8, 9, 12; 3.7). However, in Zeph. 2.7b, פ connotes a positive meaning of 'restore' instead of a negative sense of punishment.[33] Because of their arrogance and taunt against God's people, Moab and Ammon will be laid waste like Sodom and Gomorrah (Zeph. 2.8-9a). The remnant of Yahweh's people shall plunder them and possess their land (Zeph. 2.9b).

2.3.4 Complete Security

After describing how God deals with the people's enemies, Amos, Micah and Zephaniah all describe the restored remnant enjoying the complete security with nothing to fear (Amos 9.15; Mic. 5.3-4 [4–5]; Zeph. 3.13). The metaphor of planting is employed in Amos 9.15 to assure Yahweh's promises of security to Israel. Yahweh will plant Israelites upon their own land and never again pluck them up (Amos 9.15; cf. Jer. 1.10; 18.7; 31.28) when the Davidic Rule is restored (Amos 9.11).

Micah 5.3-4 [4–5] uses the metaphor of a shepherd to highlight the Davidic Ruler's protection over the remnant, as a shepherd watching over his flock.

33. For the diametrically different meanings of פקד, see Sweeney, *Zephaniah*, 131.

Israel will dwell securely (5.3b [4b]) when the new monarch is established and it shall be recognized until the ends of the earth. And this will be peace to them (5.4 [5]).

In Zeph. 3.13 the remnant of Yahweh's people, as sheep, shall 'pasture/ graze' (רעה) and 'lie down' (רבץ) in their land (cf. Zeph. 2.7; Hos. 2.20 [18]; Ps. 23.1-2) with none to disturb them (cf. Ps. 23.4). The image of Israel as sheep indicates that 'the enemies of the remnant of Israel, both external and internal, are no longer present to endanger God's flock'.[34] Echoing Amos and Micah, Zephaniah also underscores the complete peace and security that the remnant will enjoy.

2.3.5 Remnant's Elevation among the Nations

Micah and Zephaniah travel beyond Amos regarding God's raising the remnant over the nations. In Micah the remnant's relationship to the nations is first described as 'dew' or 'rain', giving life to the natural world (5.6 [7]). They are then portrayed as a 'lion', threatening its prey (5.7 [8]). The remnant of Jacob, as Waltke says, 'will be at the same time a source of benediction and a fomenter of misfortune; a channel of salvation and a cause of punishment; an instrument of hope and tragedy'.[35] Their relationship to the nations can be both beneficial and threatening.

In addition to God's gathering the exiles and delivering them from the oppressors, God also promises the remnant in Zeph. 3.19, 'I will change their shame into praise and renown in all the earth'. Then He reiterates the same point in the next verse, 'Indeed I will make you renowned and praised among all the peoples of the earth, when I restore your fortunes before your eyes' (Zeph. 3.20). The 'praise' and 'renown' of the remnant among the nations will 'provide a basis by which Yahweh will be praised and recognized throughout the entire world', as Sweeney comments.[36]

2.4 *Tension between Human Repentance and Divine Sovereignty*

House rightly points out that 'the Twelve argues for the need of repentance'.[37] Regarding the survival of the remnant, repentance is required in each of the three books under consideration. In Amos the significance of repentance is

---

34. Berlin, *Zephaniah*, 137.

35. B.K. Waltke, *A Commentary on Micah* (Grand Rapids: Eerdmans, 2007), 317.

36. M.A. Sweeney, *The Twelve Prophets* (vol. 2; Berit Olam; Collegeville: The Liturgical Press, 2000), 524.

37. P.R. House, *The Unity of the Twelve* (JSOTSup, 97; Sheffield: Almond Press, 1990), 88.

showed by God's fivefold repetition of 'yet you did not return to me' (4.6, 8, 9, 10, 11), which is uttered after each of the past punishments – famine (4.6), drought (4.7-8), agricultural disaster (4.9), pestilence and war (4.10) and the fates of the cities of the plain (4.11). Obviously the Israelites did not return to God despite the divine judgment. Therefore, the worst is yet to come (4.12). In this context Amos exhorts the Israelites in 5.4, 'Seek (דרש) Yahweh, then you shall live (חיה)'.

The second imperative 'live' (חיה) states the result of the first imperative 'seek' (דרש).[38] Amos warns against the seeking of the sanctuaries (Bethel, Gilgal and Beersheba) in 5.5. The Israelites are challenged to choose between God Himself and mere cultic activities (e.g. feasts, solemn assemblies, burnt offerings, grain offerings, peace offerings and songs in 5.21-23). 'Their sanctuaries will be destroyed; their Saviour will not.'[39] Amos 5.6 and 5.14-15 serve as an 'interpretation' of 5.4-5.[40] 'Seek God' is the way to avoid the fate of death (5.6). 'Seek God' (5.4) is to 'seek good, and not evil' (5.14) and to 'hate evil, and love good, and establish justice in the gate' (5.15a). 'Perhaps' (אולי) Yahweh will be gracious to the remnant of Joseph (5.15b).

Amos reiterates the need for turning to God. However, the adverb 'perhaps' (אולי) indicates that good deeds cannot guarantee God's deliverance on the day of Yahweh. It is all from His grace. The flickering possibility of salvation is finally assured in Amos 9.8: 'Behold, the eyes of the Lord GOD are upon the sinful kingdom, and I will destroy it from the surface of the ground, *except that I will not utterly destroy the house of Jacob.*' It is only until God promises the restoration of the Davidic kingdom (9.11-15) that the salvation of the remnant is further affirmed. After all, the remnant cannot owe their salvation to their good deeds.

Micah also stresses the need of repentance for both Israelites and the nations. The sins of Judah have reached the climax in the final chapter when the speaker of the lament points out that 'the godly has perished from the earth, and there is no one upright among mankind' (Mic. 7.2). Sin infects everyone, from the leaders (7.3) to the individuals among the neighbours, friends and family members (7.5-6). The personified Zion confesses her sin on behalf of her people (7.9). Smith makes a good observation, 'For the first time in Micah we read of the people's confession of sin'.[41] More importantly, such a confession serves as

---

38. The first imperative carries the sense of a condition, whereas the second functions as a telic clause. H.F.W. Gesenius, E. Kautzsch and A.E. Cowley, *Gesenius' Hebrew Grammar* (New York: Oxford University Press, 2nd edn, 1910), § 110–11.

39. D. Stuart, *Hosea – Jonah* (WBC, 31; Nashville: Nelson, 1987), 346.

40. Wolff, *Joel and Amos*, 240, 250.

41. Smith, *Micah – Malachi*, 58.

a bridge between all the sins in the preceding contexts (6.9–7.6) and the final conclusion (7.18-20). They must confess their sins if they are to be forgiven (7.18-20). House states, 'Even the hopeful conclusion to Micah (7.18-20) is based on a confession of sin and plea for pardon'.[42] When the hymn of doxology spells out, 'Who is a God like you, pardoning iniquity and passing over transgression for the remnant of his inheritance?' (7.18a), it shows clearly that the remnant must confess their sins. It is God's own nature – slowness to anger, steadfast love, compassion and faithfulness – that He treads our iniquities under foot and cast all our sins into the depths of the sea (7.18b-20). Confession of sin is no doubt necessary, but forgiveness of sin is mainly because of God's grace and mercy. So no human deeds can earn salvation.

In face of the impending threat posed by the Day of Yahweh, Zephaniah addresses the humble, who do God's commands and who seek (בקׁש) Yahweh, righteousness and humility (Zeph. 2.3). This verse contrasts with 1.6: 'Those who do not seek the LORD'. The verb בקׁש usually refers to oracular divination or cultic inquiry. Sweeney rightly points out that 'the present context requires only that it functions in its general sense of seeking or turning to Yahweh'.[43] Actually, Zephaniah's exhortation is a call to repentance. Similarly to Amos 5.15b, 'perhaps' (אולי) is used to highlight the possibility of being sheltered from the day of Yahweh's wrath. Smith makes the following comment:

> The word 'perhaps' speaks volumes. The prophet would not presume on the prerogative of Yahweh to determine who would or would not be hidden. Zephaniah, like Amos (cf. 5.15), knew that not even righteousness nor humility could guarantee a person's safety. That was all in the hand of Yahweh.[44]

Human repentance is significant, but it cannot manipulate God. People may hope for His forgiveness and compassion, but they cannot command it. The note of 'perhaps' (אולי) 'preserves the absolute sovereignty and freedom of Yahweh'.[45] The LXX in turn removes the ambiguity of אולי in both Amos 5.15 and Zeph. 2.3 by employing ὅπως ('in order that' in English translation) to give a sense of certainty as to the remnant's deliverance on the Day of Yahweh if they follow the prophets' instructions.[46]

The existence of a remnant is affirmed in Zephaniah when God promises that the remnant will possess the deserted Philistine territory (2.7) and disinherit the

---

42. House, *The Unity of the Twelve*, 87.
43. Sweeney, *Zephaniah*, 119.
44. Smith, *Micah – Malachi*, 132.
45. King, 'The Remnant in Zephaniah', 421.
46. Sweeney, *Zephaniah*, 119–20.

land of Moab and Ammon (2.9). The assurance of the remnant's deliverance has become crystal clear when God unequivocally utters: 'But I will leave in your midst a people humble and lowly. They shall seek refuge in the name of the LORD' (3.12). Zephaniah demonstrates a gradual movement from a doubtful uncertainty (2.3) to a full assurance (3.12) regarding God's saving the remnant.

To sum up, Amos, Micah and Zephaniah all stress the need of repentance. By using the adverb 'perhaps' (Amos 5.5; Zeph. 2.3) both Amos and Zephaniah 'do not compel Yahweh's decision to save a remnant'.[47] However, they both affirm the existence of a remnant later in the books (Amos 9.11-15; Zeph. 2.7, 9; 3.12). Micah highlights God's nature of compassion, faithfulness, slowness to anger and forgiveness (7.18-20), which cannot substitute human repentance (7.9). The balance between human deeds and divine sovereignty is appropriately concluded by Hasel's statement:

> Human action cannot be a substitute for God's action nor can God's action be a substitute for human action. Each has its proper sphere. There will be no remnant without God's grace just as little as there will be a remnant without man's return to God.[48]

2.5 *Equalization between Israel and the Nations*
Amos, Micah and Zephaniah all point out that Yahweh is the universal God, who treats Israel and the nations equally. Amos uses the oracles against the foreign nations (Amos 1.1–2.3) to engage the Israelites in their own violation of God's commands. The accusations directed against the nations, with which Israel agrees, in turn point against the Israelites themselves. Amos tries to make his audience admit thoroughly that they are transgressors, like other nations. The equal status between Israel and the foreign nations is well expressed by the following rhetorical questions:

> Pass over to Calneh, and see,
>   and from there go to Hamath the great;
> then go down to Gath of the Philistines.
>   Are you better than these kingdoms?
> Or is their territory greater than your territory?   (Amos 6.2)
>   Are you not like the Cushites to me, O people
>   of Israel?

---

47. King, 'The Message of Zephaniah', 217.
48. Hasel, *The Remnant*, 206.

> Did I not bring up Israel from the land of Egypt,
>   and the Philistines from Captor and the Syrians from Kir? (Amos 9.7)

Israel is no better and no worse than other nations (Amos 6.2). God saved Israel from Egypt, in the same manner that He saved the Philistines from Captor and the Syrians from Kir (Amos 9.7). Overall, Amos emphasizes more God's equal treatment to both Israel and the nations regarding His judgment. Wolff aptly remarks, 'The most surprising consequence is therefore the equalization of the nations with Israel and of Israel with the nations; the nations stand, just as does Israel, under Yahweh's guidance'.[49] Despite a brief declaration about God's salvation of a remnant of His people (Amos 5.4-6, 14–15; 9.8-15), Amos does not mention anything about the nations' future restoration, to which more weight is given by both Micah and Zephaniah.

Like Amos, both Micah and Zephaniah target foreign nations for punishment (Zeph. 2.4-15; 3.6-8; Mic. 5.14 [15]; 7.13). Unlike Amos, Micah and Zephaniah take God's salvation of the nations into account. Alongside the future restoration of the remnant of all Israel in Zion (Mic. 4.6-7), Micah sketches a picture of worldwide peace in which the nations will stream to Zion to learn the law of Yahweh and to walk in His way (Mic. 4.2). Peace is made possible because Yahweh shall judge between many peoples and shall arbitrate between strong nations far off. Their military weapons will become agricultural tools. There will be no more war and threat between the nations (Mic. 4.3-4). 'This universal empire will be ruled by Yahweh'[50] and Zion will be the centre of the universal worship, to which the remnant's restoration is closely tied.

Like Amos (1.3–2.3), Zephaniah deals with specific foreign nations (2.4-15). Zephaniah proclaims that Moab and Ammon will be like Sodom and Gomorrah because of their pride (Zeph. 2.10) and Nineveh will be destroyed because of her sense of invincibility (Zeph. 2.15a). Yahweh will pour out upon the nations His indignation and consume all the earth in the fire of His jealousy (Zeph. 3.6-8). However, '[God's] punishment of all nations is intended to bring about a transformation of human nature'.[51] Like Micah (4.1-4), Zephaniah speaks of the nations' future conversion and their universal worship. Yahweh will change the speech (שׂפה) of the peoples to a pure speech, so that all of them may call upon Yahweh's name and serve Him with one accord (Zeph. 3.9-10). The story of the Tower of Babel (Gen. 11) is reversed. God restores 'precisely the capacity that was lost when Yahweh disrupted humanity's unified attempt to build a towering city, confused their "speech" (שׂפה, Gen. 11.9a), and scattered

---

49. Wolff, *Joel and Amos*, 106.
50. Ben Zvi, *Micah*, 105.
51. Floyd, *Minor Prophets II*, 209.

them over the face of the earth', as Floyd maintains.[52] The transformation of the nations (Zeph. 3.10) is brought out side by side with the restoration of the remnant of Israel (Zeph. 3.11-20).

Overall, Amos, Micah and Zephaniah all point out the equalization between Israel and the nations with their different foci. God treats both Israel and the nations equally in terms of their punishment and salvation.

2.6 *Yahweh's Joy over His People's Salvation*

It is worth noting that the description 'He [Yahweh] will rejoice over you with gladness; he will be silent in his love; he will exult over you with loud singing' in Zeph. 3.17 adds a unique nuance to the concept of remnant.[53] The Hebrew clause יחריש באהבתו in Zeph. 3.17 is rendered differently among scholars. The translation varies from 'he will renew you in his love' (NRSV) to 'he will quiet you with his love' (NIV). However, the literal sense 'He will be silent in his love' is preferred here. Explaining Yahweh's silence, Keil remarks: 'Silence in His love is an expression used to denote love deeply felt, which is absorbed in its object with thoughtfulness and admiration'.[54] King's comment resonates with Keil's:

> Perhaps the greatest difficulty with this understanding of the word is how to conceive of Yahweh having such great love for His people. The thought of Yahweh being so enraptured in His affection for the remnant that He lapses into silence is almost unfathomable for some people. But regardless of the reason for Yahweh's silence, though He may be initially mute in His immense love for the remnant, He cannot remain that way. His joy over the remnant is so great that He cannot contain it. He bursts into joyful cheers, cheers that echo those the remnant shouted when they were delivered (Zeph. 3.14).[55]

Zephaniah's most thrilling description of Yahweh's joy over the remnant's salvation has contributed to our understanding of His unfathomable love and passion for His people.

---

52. Floyd, *Minor Prophets II*, 209.
53. King, 'The Message of Zephaniah', 221, n.22.
54. C.F. Keil, *The Twelve Minor Prophets* (vol. 2; Commentaries on the Old Testament; Grand Rapids: Eerdmans, 1954), 161.
55. King, 'The Remnant in Zephaniah', 424.

3. *Summary*

In Amos, Micah and Zephaniah the remnant witnesses to both judgment and salvation. 'As this concept was deepened by the prophets it expressed no facile optimism, but a faith purged in the fire.'[56] The remnant is made up of those who are lowly, lame and outcast. However, they witness how God transforms them into a strong people and how He takes care of the needy and vulnerable. In addition, the remnant well demonstrates the quality of the true people of God – faith, humility, righteousness, goodness and so on. However, they cannot owe their salvation to this good quality because it is only by God's grace that they are able to survive. That is to say, 'the remnant witnesses to the grace of God'.[57] Furthermore, the remnant witnesses to the conversion of the nations, to world peace and to universal worship at Zion. The remnant people witness to the universal God, who reigns over all nations and equalizes Israel with the nations. Most thrillingly, they witness to a god who rejoices over their salvation with loud singing. From Him, a remnant receives 'true security', 'real peace', 'genuine love' and 'lasting hope'.[58]

56. D.M. Warne, 'The Origin, Development and Significance of the Concept of the Remnant in the Old Testament' (unpublished doctoral dissertation; University of Edinburgh, 1958), 144.

57. Warne, 'The Origin, Development and Significance', 145.

58. Hasel, 'The Remnant', 403.

Chapter 9

THE THREE SHEPHERDS: READING ZECHARIAH 11 IN THE LIGHT OF JEREMIAH

Michael R. Stead

Moore Theological College, Sydney

Zechariah 11.8 declares 'I destroyed the three shepherds in one month'. This verse has been described as 'probably the most enigmatic in the whole Old Testament'.[1] The problem is not that there is any lack of possible interpretations – writing a century ago, H.G. Mitchell was aware of more than 40 proposals regarding the identity of the three shepherds,[2] and the last hundred years of scholarship have only added to this number. What is needed is not yet another speculation about the three shepherds, but some means by which we might evaluate and decide between the myriad interpretations.

In this essay, I argue that an intertextual approach to Zechariah 11 provides a way both to unlock the enigma of 'the three shepherds' and to make sense of Zech. 11.4-17 more broadly. In particular, I will argue that the book of Jeremiah provides primary intertexts for Zechariah 11, and will demonstrate that reading Zechariah 11 in the light of the book of Jeremiah helps to unravel some of its enigmas.

My rationale for pursuing an intertextual approach is that the text of Zechariah 11 points us back to the book of Jeremiah.[3] The 'shepherd allegory' in Zech. 11.4-17 is immediately preceded by an unmistakeable intertextual echo of Jer. 25.36 in Zech. 11.3.

---

1. J.G. Baldwin, *Haggai, Zechariah, Malachi* (Tyndale Old Testament Commentaries; London: Tyndale, 1972), 181.

2. H.G. Mitchell, J.M. Smith and J.A. Bewer, *Haggai, Zechariah, Malachi and Jonah: Critical and Exegetical Commentary* (Edinburgh: T & T Clark, 1912), 306.

3. For an explanation of, and justification for, my intertextual approach more generally, see M.R. Stead, *The Intertextuality of Zechariah 1–8* (London; New York: T & T Clark, 2009).

Jer. 25.36	Hark (קוֹל), the cry of the shepherds (רעה)
	and the wail (יְלָלָה) of the majesties (אדיר) of the flock
	for the LORD is destroying (שדד) their pasture.[4]
Zech. 11.3	Hark (קל), the wail (יללה) of the shepherds (רעה)
	for their glory (אדרת) is destroyed (שדד).

The effect of this intertext is to orient the reader towards Jeremiah's understanding of the 'shepherds' of the people of God – the shepherds in Zechariah 11 are like the shepherds in Jeremiah's day. This is reinforced by a further series of intertextual parallels in the shepherd allegory itself, most notably:

Jer. 12.3	Sheep (צאן) set apart for the day of slaughter (הרגה)
Zech. 11.4	Sheep (צאן) doomed to slaughter (הרגה)
Jer. 19.9	A man (איש) will eat (אכל) the flesh (בשר) of his neighbour (רע)
Zech. 11.9	Let a woman (אשה) . . . eat (אכל) the flesh (בשר) of her neighbour (רעות)
Jer. 23.2	shepherds (רעה) who have not tended (פקד) the flock (צאן)
Zech. 11.16-17	a shepherd (רעה) who will not tend (פקד) but abandons the flock (צאן)

These intertextual clues in Zechariah 11 direct the reader to Jeremiah to find keys to unlock the enigmas of the imagery of the shepherd allegory.[5]

---

4. Cf. also Jer. 25.34 'Weep and wail (ילל), you shepherds (רעה), . . . you majesties (אדרת) of the flock'. See further R. Nurmela, *Prophets in Dialogue: Inner-Biblical Allusions in Zechariah 1–8 and 9–14* (Åbo: Åbo Akademi University Press, 1996), 135–36, who registers this as a 'sure allusion'.

5. Of course, the book of Jeremiah is not the only intertext of Zechariah 11. The book of Ezekiel provides other secondary intertexts for this passage, and we shall examine some of its parallels in the analysis that follows. Most scholars recognize that Zechariah 11 draws heavily on parts of Jeremiah 22–25 and/or Ezekiel 34 and 37 – see, e.g. M. Sæbø, *Sacharja 9–14: Untersuchungen Von Text Und Form* (Neukirchen-Vluyn: Neukirchener Verlag, 1969), 236; R.A. Mason, 'The Use of Earlier Biblical Material in Zechariah 9–14: A Study in Inner Biblical Exegesis. Phd Diss. 1973 University of London', in M.J. Boda and M.H. Floyd (eds.), *Bringing out the Treasure: Inner Biblical Allusion in Zechariah 9–14* (London; New York: Sheffield Academic Press, 2003), 1–208 (150–53); W. Rudolph, *Haggai, Sacharja 1–8, Sacharja 9–14, Maleachi* (Gütersloh: Gütersloher Verlagshaus Mohn, 1976), 205; L.V. Meyer, 'Allegory Concerning the Monarchy: Zech 11:4–17; 13:7–9', in A.L. Merrill and T.W. Overholt (eds.), *Scripture in History and Theology* (Pittsburgh: Pickwick Pr, 1977), 225–40 (229–30); P.D. Hanson, *The Dawn of Apocalyptic: The Historical and Sociological Roots of Jewish Apocalyptic Eschatology* (Philadelphia: Fortress Press, rev. edn, 1979), 343–49; M.A. Sweeney, *The*

1. *The Identity of the Three Shepherds*

As noted above, there is a bewildering number of interpretations of 'the three shepherds' in Zech. 11.8. For example, it has been suggested that they represent three specific kings of Israel/Judah,[6] three leaders of God's people,[7] three officials,[8] three pagan rulers,[9] three empires,[10] governors of Yehud during the Persian period,[11] false prophets,[12] the priesthood,[13] or the three offices of prophet, priest and king.[14]

Twelve Prophets: Micah, Nahum, Habakkuk, Zephaniah, Haggai, Zechariah, Malachi (Collegeville, MN: Liturgical Press, 2000), 677.

6. Suggestions range from the nation's first three kings – Saul, David and Solomon – as argued by B. Otzen, *Studien Über Deuterosacharja* (Copenhagen: Prostant Apud Munksgaard, 1964), 156, to the near-to-last three kings of Israel – Zechariah, Shallum and Menahem – as argued by H. Ewald, *Commentary on the Prophets of the Old Testament* (vol. 1; London: Williams and Norgate, 1875), 329–30 – to the last three kings of Judah – Jehoahaz, Jehoiakim and Zedekiah, as argued by D. Kimchi, *Commentary Upon the Prophecies of Zechariah* (London: James Duncan, 1837), 122.

7. The candidates suggested for this set of three leaders spans from Moses, Aaron and Miriam (as suggested by Jerome, 'Commentariorum in Zachariam Prophetam Libri', in J.P. Migne (ed.), *Patrologia Latina*, vol. 25, 1503, to the governor, High Priest and officials at the time of Ezra's reforms (as argued by H. Gese, 'Nachtrag: Die Deutung Der Hirtenallegorie Sach 11,4ff', in H. Gese (ed.), *Vom Sinai Zum Zion, Alttestamentliche Beiträge Zur Biblischen Theologie* (München: Kaiser, 1974), 231–38 (233).

8. See e.g. M.H. Floyd, *Minor Prophets* (Grand Rapids: Eerdmans, 2000), 487, who argues that 'shepherds' includes 'the entire class of those who govern'.

9. See e.g. Sweeney, *The Twelve*, 677–78, who suggests Cyrus, Cambyses and Darius. Cf. C.H.H. Wright, *Zechariah and His Prophecies* (London: Hodder and Stoughton, 1879), 316, who argues for Antiochus Epiphanes, Antiochus Eupator and Demetrius I.

10. C.F. Keil, *The Twelve Minor Prophets* (Grand Rapids: Eerdmans, 1961), 363–64, identifies the three shepherds with three empires – the Babylonian, the Medo-Persian and the Greek.

11. See e.g. R.L. Foster, 'Shepherds, Sticks, and Social Destabilization: A Fresh Look at Zechariah 11:4–17', *Journal of Biblical Literature* 126 (2007), 735–53 (740–43).

12. See e.g. C.L. Meyers and E.M. Meyers, *Zechariah 9–14: A New Translation with Introduction and Commentary* (New York: Doubleday, 1993), 265.

13. Hanson, *Dawn of Apocalyptic*, 345–46, argues that 'the shepherds' refers to the hierocracy led by the Zadokites.

14. This interpretation goes back at least to Theodoret (c.430 AD), who in his commentary on Zech. 11.8 writes Τοὺς Ἰουδαίων λέγει βασιλέας, καί προφήτας, καί ἱερέας· διὰ γὰρ τούτων τῶν τριῶν ἐποιμαίνοντο ταγμάτων ('He speaks of the kings of the Jews and prophets and priests; for by the three orders they were shepherded'). This interpretation (with variations) is followed, for example, by E.W. Hengstenberg, *Christology of the Old Testament: And a Commentary on the Messianic Predictions* (tr. from Christologie des Alten Testaments; vol. 4; Grand Rapids: Kregel, 1956; repr. of Edinburgh: Clark,

However, if we let the echoes of Jeremiah be our guide to the interpretation of Zechariah 11, then one interpretation comes to the fore. To arrive at this interpretation, the first question we must ask is 'Who are the shepherds in the book of Jeremiah?'

'Shepherds' is characteristically a plural designation in the book of Jeremiah. While it is clear that the Davidic king is *a* shepherd (see e.g. Jer. 23.4-5), the term must encompass more than the king alone. That much is clear from Jer. 17.16, where we see that the *prophet* Jeremiah functions as Yahweh's under-shepherd – he declares 'I have not run away from being shepherd after you (מרעה אחריך)'.

Jeremiah repeatedly condemns 'the shepherds' (plural) who have scattered the flock through their failure to lead/guide/protect the people (Jer. 10.21; 23.1-2; 25.34; 50.6). Similarly, Yahweh promises King Jehoiakim that 'the wind will drive all your *shepherds* away' (Jer. 22.22). Jeremiah's characteristic way of referring to the leadership of Israel is 'their kings and officials, and their priests, and their prophets' (e.g. Jer. 2.26; cf. 4.9; 8.1), or more succinctly as 'the kings who sit on David's throne, the priests, and the prophets' (Jer. 13.13). This suggests that the role of 'the shepherds' encompasses royal rule, the priesthood and prophetic leadership.

This observation is supported by the flow of Jeremiah 22–23. Jerermiah 23.1 pronounces a word of woe against the bad shepherds who destroy the flock. The royal administration ('O King of Judah . . . and your servants' – Jer. 22.2), who are condemned in Jeremiah 22, are clearly part of this set of 'bad shepherds', but Jeremiah 23 goes on to condemn two other groups – prophets and priests. The best way to explain their inclusion in this chapter is that they too are part of the set of 'bad shepherds' condemned in Jer. 23.1. Jeremiah 23.9-40 condemns the 'ungodly prophets and priests' (23.11), who claim to speak an oracle of Yahweh when they are only speaking their own words (23.34-36). From this grouping of condemnations, it seems reasonable to conclude that the 'bad shepherds' in Jeremiah 22–23 encompasses the royal administration, the prophets and the priests.

Further evidence that 'the shepherds' in Jeremiah emcompasses the three leadership roles of kingly rule, prophet and priest can be found in Jeremiah's critique of the bad shepherds:

Jer. 50.6   Their *shepherds* have led them astray (תעה).

1854–58), 26; see also D. Baron, *The Visions and Prophecies of Zechariah: An Exposition* (London: Morgan & Scott, 1918), 397; and C.L. Feinberg, *God Remembers: A Study of Zechariah* (Portland, OR: Multnomah Press, 3rd edn, 1977), 206.

Jer. 10.21   The *shepherds* are senseless and do not inquire (דרשׁ) of
             Yahweh.

According to Jer. 23.32, it is the [*false*] *prophets* who have 'led the people astray
(תעה)', and Jer. 21.2 demonstrates that it is a *prophetic role* to 'inquire (דרשׁ)
of Yahweh'. But it is not the prophets alone who are to blame – according to
Jer. 8.10, 'prophets and priests alike all practice deceit', and Jer. 2.8 tells us
that 'The priests did not say, "Where is Yahweh?" Those who handle the law
did not know me; the shepherds transgressed against me; the prophets proph-
esied by Baal'.

Based on this evidence, we may justifiably conclude that 'the shepherds'
in the book of Jeremiah refers to the combined leadership of the royal administration, [false] prophets and priests.[15] We see this same tripartite division of
leadership elsewhere in the Old Testament.[16]

Whether or not the above is sufficient to demonstrate that Jeremiah used
'shepherds' to refer to all of Israel's leadership, there is clear evidence elsewhere in Zechariah that this is how the author of Zechariah 9–11 has understood
the term. Zechariah 10.3 describes Yahweh's anger which burns against 'the
shepherds' who have been leading his flock astray. These 'shepherds' are false
prophets: 'the idols speak deceit, diviners see visions that lie; they tell dreams
that are false' (Zech. 10.2a), and it is because of them that 'the people wander
like sheep oppressed for lack of a shepherd' (Zech. 10.2b).

For all of the reasons above, we may justifiably conclude that the book of
Jeremiah has shaped Zechariah's understanding of 'the shepherds' – the shepherds of God's people are king, priest and prophet. This conclusion is crucial for
our understanding of Zech. 11.8, which states 'I destroyed the three shepherds in
one month'. The phrase 'the three shepherds' (את־שׁלשׁת הרעים) is definite, which
suggests that it is not merely any combination of three kings or three priests or
three prophets, but rather the summation of *the* three roles. That is, Zech. 11.8
announces the termination of royal rule, the priesthood and the prophetic office.
Moreover, it tells us that this is to happen 'in one month' (בירח אחד). According
to Jer. 52.6-27, this is exactly what happened in 587 BCE. The famine reached
crisis point on the 'ninth day of the fourth month' (52.6), and King Zedekiah and
his soldiers fled that night, but were pursued and captured by the Babylonians

---

15. I echo the conclusion of C. Brouwer, *Wachter En Herder: Een Exegetische Studie
over De Herder-Figuur in Het Oude Testament, Inzonderheid in De Pericopen Zacharia
11 En 13: 7–9* (Wageningen: H. Veenman En Zonen, 1949), 25, who argues that 'De
priesters, vorsten en profeten zijn de herders en bezitters der kudde' (The priests, princes
and prophets are the shepherds and owners of the flock).

16. See e.g. Mic. 3.11; Neh. 9.32; Zeph. 3.3-4.

on or after the *tenth day of the fourth month*. The next time marker we get is in Jer. 52.12 – '*on the tenth day of the fifth month*'. In the space of that single month, the king's sons and officials were put to death (52.10), the temple and palace were burnt to the ground (52.13), and the chief priest and other key figures were exiled or killed (52.15, 24–27). In exactly one month, Yahweh cut down the city of Jerusalem and all its leadership – prophet, priest and king.

Before we explore the significance of this for our interpretation of Zechariah 11, there is a second question that the intertextual connections with Jeremiah can help to answer. The question is this – who is the shepherd being portrayed in Zech. 11.4-15? For each of the four key clauses in Zech. 11.8-9, there is an intertextual parallel in the book of Jeremiah – the first two parallels are thematic, and the second two are partial verbal parallels.

Zech 11.8b	I grew weary of them and they detested me.
Jer.15.6	You rejected me . . . so I stretched out my hand against you; I am weary of relenting.
Zech. 11.9a	I will not be your shepherd.
Jer. 13.14	I will show no pity (לא חמל) + Zech. 11.5 – shepherds have no pity (לא חמל).
Zech. 11.9b	Let the dying die (המתה תמות), and the perishing perish.
Jer. 15.2	Those for death, to death (למות למות), and those for the sword, to the sword.
Zech. 11.9c	Let a woman (אשה) who remains eat (אכל) the flesh (בשר) of a neighbour (רעות).
Jer. 19.9	A man (איש) will eat (אכל) the flesh (בשר) of his neighbour (רע).

In each of the four intertextual parallels in Jeremiah, it is Yahweh who speaks these words (through the mouth of his prophet). To make the same point in a different way, the figure being portrayed in Zech. 11.8-9 says the same kinds of things that Yahweh said to Jeremiah's generation about the impending judgment and exile. These intertextual parallels suggest that the shepherd being portrayed in Zech. 11.4-14 is Yahweh himself.[17]

---

17. See similarly Rudolph, *Sacharja*, 205; cf. Keil, *The Twelve*, 358, Otzen, *Studien Über Deuterosacharja*, 156; D.R. Jones, 'A Fresh Interpretation of Zechariah 9–11', *Vetus Testamentum* 12 (1962), 241–59 (252); A. Caquot, 'Breves Remarques Sur L'allegorie Des Pasteurs En Zacharie 11', in *Melanges Bibliques Et Orientaux En L'honneur De M Mathias Delcor* (Kevelaer, West Germany: Butzon und Bercker, 1985): 45–55 (45).

2. *Reading Zechariah 11 in the Light of Jeremiah*

Zechariah 11.4-17 is a series of symbolic acts that the Lord directs an unnamed individual (whom I shall label 'the prophet') to perform. In v. 4, the prophet is told to act out the role of shepherding (רעה) the 'flock of slaughter'.[18] He is apparently performing the role of a chief shepherd, since he exercises authority over under-shepherds (such as 'the three shepherds' he removes in Zech. 11.8). As argued above, the intertextual parallels with Jeremiah suggest that the shepherd whom the prophet is portraying is Yahweh himself. Yahweh is the chief shepherd of his people, who appoints human leaders to his under-shepherds. This imagery is congruent with the picture we see in Ezek. 34.10-12, where Yahweh declares that he is against 'the shepherds [plural] . . . and will remove them from tending the flock' (34.10), and that Yahweh himself will be like a shepherd (רעה) for his flock (34.12).

Verse 5 tells us more about this 'flock of slaughter' – their shepherds (plural) do not spare them, and instead the flock is bought and sold for profit. As noted above, this is exactly the situation as described in Jer. 23.2 – shepherds (רעה) who have not tended (פקד) the flock (צאן). These 'shepherds' are the leadership of Israel. Instead of caring for the flock, they have allowed the flock to be bought and sold – 'Those who buy them slay them and go unpunished; and those who sell them say, "Blessed be Yahweh. I have become rich"' (Zech. 11.5).

In order to understand v. 6 correctly, it is vital that we pay careful attention to the flow in vv. 4–6. Verse 5 is a series of relative clauses introduced by אשר that describe the situation of the flock. Verse 6 then resumes the thought of v. 4, and gives the reason why (כי) the flock is marked for slaughter – 'because I no longer have pity on the inhabitants of this land', declares Yahweh.

At first glance, one might assume that the imperfect/*yiqtol* form of the verb 'pity' (אחמול) means that this symbolic act depicts future events. However, this would be to confuse the timeframe of the symbolic act with the timeframe of that which it depicts. The prophet is being told to perform a symbolic act in which he will – in the immediate future, hence the imperfect verb – be depicting a shepherd (Yahweh) who shows no pity. But this does necessarily mean that his symbolic action is depicting a future act. It is critical that we recognize the difference between 'acted time' and 'actual time'. We see this distinction clearly in the symbolic act in Ezek. 4.4-5. Yahweh tells the prophet Ezekiel:

> Lie upon your left side, and put the guilt of the house of Israel upon yourself;
> for the number of the days that you lie upon it, you will bear their guilt.

---

18. As noted above, the expression 'sheep (צאן) . . . of slaughter (הרגה)' comes from Jer. 12.3.

> I have put upon you a number of days, three hundred and ninety days,
> equal to the number of the years of their guilt.

In these verses, the performance of the symbolic act is future, and so Ezekiel's 'bearing of guilt' is future tense (in 'acted' time). However, in 'actual' time, Ezekiel is depicting a bearing of guilt – of 390 years duration – that has already been running for centuries.[19]

My argument is that the symbolic act in Zechariah 11 functions in a similar way – in vv. 4–6 the prophet is commanded to perform (future) symbolic acts that depict past actual events. Verse 6 describes what the prophet's acts are to symbolize, using a concatenation of imagery from Yahweh's judgments in the past. I agree with Meyers and Meyers that this section has so many resonances with the past judgment and exile because the symbolic act is depicting those past events.[20]

The first of the three symbolic acts involves a shepherd who destroys 'the three shepherds in one month', grows weary of the flock, and abandons the flock to destruction (Zech. 11.8-9). As we have already concluded above, the intertextual connections with Jeremiah suggest that 'the three shepherds' are best understood as the leadership roles of king, priest and prophet. There was one – and only one – instance in Israel's history when king, priest and prophet were entirely cut off in the space of one month – the destruction of Jerusalem in 587 BCE. This was also a time when Yahweh 'grew weary' (cf. Isa. 1.14-15) of the people, and when he abandoned them to destruction.[21]

---

19. Although there are many varied interpretations of the dates and figures in the passage, most commentators view Ezekiel's first symbolic act as depicting Israel's past. For example, M.S. Odell, *Ezekiel* (Macon, GA: Smyth & Helwys, 2005), 63, writes 'The first part of the act, which lasts 390 days, represents the long history of Israel's guilt. The figure of 390 days for 390 years would indicate that Israel's guilt began in 982, or roughly the beginning of the monarchy'. See similarly D.I. Block, *The Book of Ezekiel: Chapters 1–24* (Grand Rapids: Eerdmans, 1997), 178. Cf. W. Eichrodt, *Ezekiel: A Commentary* (London: SCM Press, 1970), 84, who follows the LXX and reads 190 days instead of 390, and notes 'one can assume the forty years of Judah's punishment to be included in the one hundred and ninety years of Israel's punishment . . . One may then reckon backward the remaining one hundred and fifty years of Israel from 586 . . . and thus come to 736 BC'.

20. Meyers and Meyers, *Zechariah 9–14*, 300–301.

21. Compare Zech. 11.9 with Jer. 15.2 and 19.9:

Zech. 11.9b	Let the dying die (המתה תמות), and the perishing perish.
Jer. 15.2	Those for death, to death (למות למות), and those for the sword, to the sword.
Zech. 11.9c	Let a woman (אשה) who remains eat (אכל) the flesh (בשר) of her neighbour (רעות).

The second of the symbolic acts involves the taking and breaking of two staffs (מקל). The prophet takes up the staffs in v. 7, naming them 'Favour' (נעם) and 'Union' (חבלים).[22] We learn the significance of these staffs in subsequent verses, as the staffs are broken. In v. 10, the prophet breaks the staff called Favour, 'revoking the covenant I had made with all the peoples'. There are two main alternate interpretations of 'all the peoples' – either that it refers to all the nations of the earth, and that the first staff thus represents an (implicit) covenant that Yahweh made with all humanity,[23] or that 'the peoples' refers to Israel and Judah or some variation thereon. The intertexts suggest that the second alternative is more likely. The language of Zech. 11.10 closely echoes Genesis 17. In Genesis 17, Yahweh makes a covenant (ברית) with Abraham that he will become the father of many nations. In this passage, 'nations' (גוים) and 'peoples' (עמים) are used synonymously to refer to the descendants of Abraham to whom this covenant will extend – see, for example, the parallelism in v. 16, when it is said of Sarah that 'she will be the mother of nations (גוים); kings of peoples (עמים) will come from her'.[24]

Genesis 17.14 declares that the uncircumcised male 'will be cut off (כרת) from his peoples (עמים); he has broken (פרר *hiph*) my covenant (את־בריתי)'. Zechariah 11.10 echoes all the key terminology: 'to break (פרר *hiph*) my covenant (את־בריתי) which I cut (כרת) with all the peoples (עמים).'

This intertextual connection between Zechariah 11 and Genesis 17 suggests that the breaking of the first staff represents Yahweh's revocation of the Abrahamic covenant.[25] Intertextual connections with the book of Jeremiah help us to understand the timing of this revocation – the prophet pleads in Jer. 14.21 'Remember your covenant (ברית) with us and do not break (פרר *hiph*) it'. The

---

Jer. 19.9   A man (איש) will eat (אכל) the flesh (בשר) of his neighbour (רע).

22. On the names of the two staffs, see further Larkin, *Eschatology of Second Zechariah*, 124–25.

23. Floyd, *Minor Prophets*, 488, takes this to refer to the covenant with all humanity in Gen. 9.8-17. Other scholars take it to be a covenant with the nations which is for the benefit of Israel – see e.g. D.L. Petersen, *Zechariah 9–14 and Malachi: A Commentary* (Old Testament Library; Louisville, KY.: Westminster John Knox Press, 1995), 95–96; cf. M.J. Boda, *Haggai, Zechariah* (Grand Rapids: Zondervan, 2004), 463; and T.J. Finley, 'The Sheep Merchants of Zechariah 11', *Grace Theological Journal* 3 (1982), 51–65 (64).

24. See, similarly, Meyers and Meyers, *Zechariah 9–14*, 270–71. The connection with Genesis 17 is also noted by Mason, 'Use of Earlier Biblical Material', 109, though he interprets its significance differently.

25. So, similarly, Mason, 'Use of Earlier Biblical Material', 108–109.

judgment of exile was the moment when Yahweh revoked the covenant with his people.[26]

The prophet breaks his second staff in v. 14, 'breaking the brotherhood between Judah and Israel'. It is almost universally recognized that this action is related to Ezekiel's symbolic act with staffs in Ezek. 37.16-28, in which the prophet is told to take two sticks – one representing Judah and the other representing Israel – and join them into one stick. Ezekiel's symbolic act was to demonstrate that Yahweh 'will make them one nation in the land . . . they will never again be two nations or be divided into two kingdoms' (Ezek. 37.22).

A common interpretation is that the symbolic act in Zechariah 11 is a direct repudiation of the promise in Ezekiel 37.[27] However, the problem with this interpretation is that it is hard to imagine a historical context in which this symbolic act would have made sense to its original hearers. If we suppose (with most commentators) that Zechariah 11 is addressed to a post-exilic audience, that generation had not seen the restoration promised in Ezekiel 37 – as far as they were concerned, they were still living in the era of 'two sticks', not 'one stick' called union. The prophet's symbolic act in Zechariah 11 would have been breaking what was already broken. This illogicality suggests that we need to seek a different understanding.

The alternate explanation of the relationship between Zechariah 11 and Ezekiel 37 – one which is thoroughly consistent with the other retrospective elements in Zechariah 11 – is that Zechariah 11 explains how there came to be two sticks in the first place. That is, Zechariah 11 depicts the 'brotherhood' being broken, and this is what is restored in Ezekiel's symbolic act. I submit that the breaking of both staffs in Zechariah 11 is looking back to what has already happened in the people's history – Yahweh has revoked the covenant with Israel and Judah, and he has broken the brotherhood between them.[28]

The third symbolic act spans vv. 11–13. In these verses, the 'merchants of the flock'[29] (whom I take to be the same as the buyers and sellers of v. 5) give

---

26. Meyers and Meyers, _Zechariah 9–14_, 269, cite both this verse and Ezek. 16.59. They conclude 'These two prophets of the exilic period indirectly make . . . the claim [that Yahweh has abrogated the Mosaic covenant]'.

27. See e.g. Hanson, _Dawn of Apocalyptic_, 343. Cf. R.L. Smith, _Micah-Malachi_ (Word Biblical Commentary, 32; Waco: Word, 1984), 271; Mason, 'Inner Biblical Exegesis', 349–50; Boda, 'Reading Between', 285.

28. So similarly Meyers and Meyers, _Zechariah 9–14_, 301.

29. My translation of 'the merchants' in v. 11 is based on reading two words in the MT (כן עניי) as one word (כנעניי, 'Canaanite' = merchant). This same two-word combination also occurs in the MT in v. 7, in the form לָכֵן עֲנִיֵּי. Finley, 'The Sheep Merchants', 54–59, demonstrates that the MT reading involves significant grammatical problems, because it is not at all clear how the particle לָכֵן ('for thus') is to function. In both v. 7

the prophet 30 shekels of silver as his pay (שׂכר) for his work as shepherd.[30] According to the MT, Yahweh commands the prophet to 'throw it to the potter (יוצר), the glorious (אדר) value (יקר) at which I was valued (יקר) by them'. The sign act concludes with the prophet casting the silver into the house of Yahweh (בית יהוה) to the potter.

This third sign act raises many questions, only some of which we can find satisfactory answers for. Is it the prophet who says 'the glorious price at which they priced me' or is it Yahweh? Is 30 pieces of silver a suitable remuneration, or is it a pittance? Are the 30 pieces of silver cast to the 'potter' (יוצר) or is this a textual corruption from אוצר ('treasury')? If it is 'potter', then what is a potter doing in the house of Yahweh? And the biggest question of all – what on earth does it all mean?! What is the significance of this symbolic act?

The place to begin our search for the answers to these questions is in the second half of v. 11, which provides the transition between the second and third symbolic acts. Verse 11 tells us that the 'merchants of the flock' watched the prophet break the staff to symbolize the revocation of the covenant, and 'they knew that this was the word of Yahweh'. In my opinion, too little attention has been paid to the significance of this comment in light of the preceding verse. In v. 10, the prophet speaks in the first person about 'the covenant I had made with all the people'. Verse 11 informs us that the 'merchants of the flock' watching this symbolic act realize that this is not merely a prophet acting out a personal

---

and v. 11, the reading of the MT leads to grammatical constructions which are without parallel elsewhere. The LXX suggests a way to resolve the confusion of the MT. At v. 7, the LXX reads εἰς τὴν Χαναανῖτιν ('for the Canaanite [land]'), a literal – if somewhat confused – reading of לכנעני. Similarly, at v. 11 the LXX reads כנעני as οἱ Χαναναῖοι ('the Canaanites'). The word כנעני occurs in the MT of Zech. 14.21 where it is translated Χαναναῖος ('a Canaanite'), demonstrating that this word is part of the vocabulary of Zechariah 9–14. The LXX is clearly the more difficult reading, evidenced by the fact that the LXX translator has struggled to make sense of these verses. Apparently, the LXX translator was not aware of the ancient identification of 'Canaanites' and 'merchants' (see e.g. Ezek. 16.29; Zeph. 1.11), but apparently felt bound to honour the word כנעני in the text before him.

Other scholars who emend the MT in line with the reading suggested by the LXX include S. Feigin, 'Some Notes on Zechariah 11:4–17', *Journal of Biblical Literature* (1925), 203–13 (206); Mason, 'Use of Earlier Biblical Material', 99; Baldwin, *Haggai, Zechariah, Malachi*, 180; Sæbø, *Sacharja 9–14*, 247; Rudolph, *Sacharja*, 202; Finley, 'The Sheep Merchants', 59–60; Laato, *Josiah and David*, 277; and Sweeney, *The Twelve*, 680. For those who retain the MT, see e.g. Baron, *Zechariah*, 390–92; Feinberg, *God Remembers*, 204–205; Caquot, 'Breves Remarques', 49; and Larkin, *Eschatology of Second Zechariah*, 110–11.

30. So also Petersen, *Zechariah 9–14*, 96; *contra* Meyers and Meyers, *Zechariah 9–14*, 273–74, who take it to be 'payment for his prophetic act'.

covenant, but that 'this was the word of Yahweh' – i.e. they realize that the prophet speaks and acts *as Yahweh* as he acts out Yahweh's revocation of his covenant with the peoples. This is critical for our understanding of the third symbolic act which follows in vv. 12–13, because when the 'merchants of the flock' pay the 30 pieces of silver, they know that they are putting a value *on Yahweh* as the shepherd of his people. Thirty pieces of silver may well be an appropriate figure if it is only to remunerate a human shepherd (and is probably an overpayment for a shepherd who has abandoned his flock!). But as a valuation of Yahweh as the shepherd of his people, it is a pittance.[31] According to Exod. 21.32, thirty pieces of silver is what a slave is worth. There may be an echo here of Isa. 43.4, in which Yahweh declares 'Since you are valuable (יקר) in my eyes (בעיני) and glorious, I will give men in exchange for you, and peoples in exchange for your life'. In contrast, Yahweh's value (יקר) in their eyes (בעיניכם – Zech. 11.12) is nothing more than the price of the life of a slave.

Yahweh responds to this paltry valuation in Zech. 11.12, saying 'Throw it to the potter – the glorious value at which I was valued by them!' Though most commentators and translations treat the second clause as a parenthetical aside by the prophet, there is no grammatical or textual reason for this. It naturally reads as the words of Yahweh, and (given the reading of v. 11 above) makes perfect sense to do so in this context.

Before we venture further into the complexities of v. 12, it is important to establish at the outset that the overall meaning of the third symbolic act is (relatively) clear – it depicts the leaders of God's people terminating their relationship with Yahweh as their shepherd, valuing him as though he were worth nothing more than a slave. The significance of the remainder of the symbolic act is not clear, and what follows is admittedly quite speculative. However, whether or not my speculation is found to be persuasive, the overall meaning does not vary.

The complexity of v. 12 arises once we seek to explain the significance of throwing the 30 pieces of silver to the 'potter' who is in the house of Yahweh, since it is not apparent why there should be a potter in the temple, nor what he is supposed to do with the 30 pieces of silver. Meyers and Meyers argue that

---

31. Commentators who understand 30 pieces of silver to be a paltry sum include E. Lipinski, 'Recherches Sur Le Livre De Zacharie', *Vetus Testamentum* 20 (1970), 25–55 (53–55); Rudolph, *Sacharja*, 209; Caquot, 'Breves Remarques', 50; Larkin, *Eschatology of Second Zechariah*, 130; Laato, *Josiah and David*, 284; Petersen, *Zechariah 9–14*, 97; Conrad, *Zechariah*, 175–76.

Commentators who take it be an appropriate sum include Baldwin, *Haggai, Zechariah, Malachi*, 184; Feigin, 'Zechariah 11:4–17', 209; Meyers and Meyers, *Zechariah 9–14*, 276; Sweeney, *The Twelve*, 681.

'potter' (יוצר) is a textual corruption from an original אוצר ('treasury'). This emendation is certainly attractive – casting 30 pieces of silver to the 'treasury' makes much more sense than casting it to the 'potter' – but in my view there is insufficient evidence of textual corruption to warrant an emendation. The LXX renders the word as χωνευτηρίον ('foundry, smelter') from χωνεύω ('molten, molded'), which is apparently an interpretation of the underlying meaning of the Hebrew root יצר ('to form, fashion' – see further below). Similarly, Aquila renders the word as πλάστης ('moulder'). The Vulgate has *statuarius* ('statute-maker, sculptor'). The Targum is highly interpretative and offers no direct support for either יוצר or אוצר. Only the Peshitta provides any support for the emendation, but the Peshitta reading (ܟ݂ܝ ܓܢܙܐ *bēt ganzā*, 'treasury') probably arises from an attempt to wrestle meaning from an obscure verse. The MT reading (יוצר) is the more difficult reading, and it is also the one reading that can explain all of the others,[32] and should therefore be retained.

Retaining 'potter' (יוצר) on the basis of the textual evidence, my (speculative!) interpretation begins with an observation made by C.C. Torrey.[33] Torrey notes that the noun יוצר is the substantive of the verb יצר, meaning 'to form, fashion',[34] and that the meaning of יצר is not necessarily limited to fashioning clay.[35] There are at least three instances where יצר involves fashioning metal – Isa. 44.10, Hab. 2.18 and Exod. 32.4. At this point, Torrey's interpretation and mine diverge. Torrey conjectures that the temple must have had a foundry for the purpose of melting down 'precious metal which was brought to the temple' and that 'the official in charge bore the title יוֹצֵר'.[36] I find this interpretation possible, but it lacks sufficient evidence to support the speculation.

My own (equally speculative) interpretation is based on the observation that the three examples cited above involve not mere metalwork, but the fashioning

---

32. So also Rudolph, *Sacharja*, 202–203.

33. And followed (with variations) by M. Delcor, 'Deux Passages Difficiles: Zach Xii 11 Et Xi 13', *Vetus Testamentum* 3 (1953), 67–77 (76); Rudolph, *Sacharja*, 202–203; C. Stuhlmueller, *Rebuilding with Hope: A Commentary on the Books of Haggai and Zechariah* (Grand Rapids: Eerdmans, 1988), 140; Laato, *Josiah and David*, 277.

34. Rudolph, *Sacharja*, 202, argues that יצר is a variant ('Nebenform') of צור, in the sense that it takes in Exod. 32.4 and 1 Kgs 7.15 where it occurs as וַיָּצַר and means 'to cast or smelt'. (This sense is unusual, as elsewhere צור means 'besiege, contend'.) My alternative explanation is that ויצר in Exod. 32.4 and 1 Kgs 7.15 is in fact the waw consecutive (*wayyiqtol*) form of verb יצר, not צור. The same consonantal form (ויצר) occurs in Gen. 2.19 is this sense (pointed as וַיִּצֶר, and cf. Gen. 2.7 where the same word occurs in the more usual form וַיִּיצֶר).

35. Torrey, 'Foundry', 256.

36. Torrey, 'Foundry', 255–56.

of an idol by casting metal.[37] Isaiah 44.10 refers to the one who 'forms (יצר) a god and casts (נסך) an idol'; Hab. 2.18 asks 'What profit is an idol when its fashioner (יצרו) has shaped it, a cast image (מסכה), a teacher of lies?'; and Exod. 32.4 says that Aaron fashioned (יצר)[38] the gold and 'made a calf, a cast image (מסכה)'. In each of these three examples, the verb יצר is used in association with either the verb נסך ('to cast, to pour') or its cognate noun מסכה ('cast image'). This leads me to offer the suggestion that the יוצר of Zech. 11.12 refers to 'one who forms an idol', on the basis of the similar usage in Isa. 44.10, Hab. 2.18 and Exod. 32.4.[39]

If this speculation is found to have merit, then it helps to explain the significance of the third symbolic act in Zechariah 11. It means that the 30 pieces of silver are being cast to *the one who fashions idols* (היוצר), and this person is making idols in the very place where Yahweh alone ought to have been worshipped. This third symbolic act is thus a depiction of the idolatry that was practised within the house of Yahweh (Jer. 7.30; Ezek. 8.5-6). The use of a mere 30 pieces of silver to make an idol to take the place of Yahweh graphically demonstrates the extent to which 'my people have exchanged their glory for worthless idols' (Jer. 2.11).[40]

As with the first two symbolic acts, the historical background that best resonates with the third symbolic act is the time of the ministry of Jeremiah prior to the destruction of Jerusalem in 587 BC. Jeremiah repeatedly castigates the people for trading the one true God for idols (see e.g. Jer. 2.5; 2.8; 2.11; 4.1; 7.30; 8.19; 10.8; 14.22; 16.18; 18.15; and 32.34).

Each of the three symbolic acts depicts the relationship between Yahweh and his people in the past.[41] The removal of 'the three shepherds in one month' depicts the destruction of the three leadership roles of king, priest and prophet

37. The connection between יצר and casting idols is noted by Mason, 'Use of Earlier Biblical Material', 112–13. Mason argues that Isa. 54.17 is another instance of the verb יצר referring to casting idols.

38. This assumes that ויצר in Exod. 32.4 is from the verb יצר, not צור – see Note 34 above. So likewise Torrey, 'Foundry', 259.

39. I come to the same conclusion as Delcor, though by a different route. Delcor, 'Deux Passages Difficiles', 76–77, argues that the 30 pieces of silver are thrown into the foundry to make a little idol.

40. An idol cast from 30 pieces of silver would have been quite small. By way of comparison, the idol commissioned by Micah's mother in Judg. 17.3 was made from 200 pieces of silver. As Delcor, 'Deux Passages Difficiles', 76, notes, 'Celle que l'on pourrait fabriquer avec trente sicles pèserait seulement 420 grammes, et on aurait ainsi une toute petite figurine d'Astarté ou d'autre divinité.'

41. So also Kimchi, *Zechariah*, 118–27; Meyer, 'Allegory', 232; Meyers and Meyers, *Zechariah 9–14*, 301.

which occurred in a literal period of one month in 587 BCE. The breaking of the two staffs represents the revocation of Yahweh's covenant with his people, and the end of the brotherhood between Judah and Israel, both of which appeared to have come to an end when Yahweh allowed his people to be taken from the land. The symbolic act with the 30 pieces of silver depicts the leaders of God's people terminating Judah's relationship with Yahweh as their shepherd, valuing him as though he were worth nothing more than a slave (and perhaps trading the one true God for a tiny idol).

We must then ask the question: Why would a post-exilic prophet perform symbolic acts depicting the past to his own generation? My answer (following Meyers and Meyers) is that the prophet is 'recapitulating past horrors that have led to the need for restoration',[42] because his present generation is still living with the consequences of those past horrors. The nature of those consequences is explained in the final symbolic act in this chapter, in vv. 15–16. In this final symbolic act, the time horizon shifts from past to present.

This transition from past to present in Zechariah 11 is similar to the time shift in the symbolic acts in Ezekiel 4. The prophet Ezekiel first lay on his left side for 390 days to depict the long history of Israel's guilt. As noted above, this was retrospective in focus. Ezekiel was then commanded to lie on his right side for 40 days for Judah's sins. Most scholars take this period of 40 days to represent Judah's impending exile, perhaps styling the exile as another 40 years in the wilderness.[43] In the same way that Ezekiel uses symbolic acts in two scenes to explain the past and present situation to his generation, so too Zechariah 11 moves from past (vv. 4–14) to present (vv. 15–16). Whereas the symbolic acts in vv. 4–14 depicted past time, this symbolic act depicts the current situation of God's people – 'foolish shepherds'.

3. *A Foolish Shepherd (Zech. 11.15-17)*

Because a previous generation has rejected Yahweh as their shepherd (Zech. 11.4-11), the present generation now experiences 'foolish shepherds' who do not seek the good of the flock, but devour them instead (Zech. 11.15-17). 'Foolish' (אוִלִי) is part of the vocabulary of wisdom literature, in which we discover that a fool despises discipline and correction (Prov. 1.7; 15.5; cf. 14.9). The 'foolish shepherds' of Zech. 11.15 are leaders who have not learnt the lessons from the discipline that Yahweh has brought upon his people in the past.[44]

---

42. Meyers and Meyers, *Zechariah 9–14*, 301.
43. See, e.g., Eichrodt, *Ezekiel*, 85; Block, *Ezekiel 1–24*, 179–80; Odell, *Ezekiel*, 63.
44. Or, worse still, they are fools who do not know Yahweh at all – cf. Jer. 4.22; Ps. 14.1.

The description of 'a shepherd who does not care (פקד) for the perishing (כחד *niph*)' echoes the terminologies from previous verses. When Yahweh judged his people, he said 'let the perishing ones perish (כחד *niph*)' (Zech. 11.9), giving up his care (פקד) for the flock (10.3). The reuse of this language here indicates that the 'foolish shepherd' in Zech. 11.16a is part of Yahweh's continuing judgment on his people. Because the people have rejected Yahweh as their true shepherd, he gives them over to a shepherd of a very different character.

The description of the foolish shepherd in these clauses draws largely on Ezekiel's castigation of the bad shepherds in Ezek. 34.1-14. The key points of comparison are highlighted in the following table:

Zech. 11.16b	Ezek. 34.1-14
Not seek the young (or wanderer)	You have not brought back the strays or searched for the lost (Ezek. 34.4)
nor heals (רפא) the injured (שבר)	You have not strengthened the weak or healed (רפא) the sick or bound up the injured (שבר) (Ezek. 34.4)
nor feeds the healthy (נצב)	cf. Ezek. 34.14 Yahweh says 'I will tend them in a good pasture'
but eats (אכל) the flesh of the fat ones (בריא)	You eat (אכל) the curds . . . and you slaughter the fat ones (בריא) (Ezek. 34.3). [My flock] will no longer be food (אכלה) for them (Ezek. 34.10) Cf. Mic. 3.2 – who tear the skin from off my
tearing off even their hoofs	people and their flesh from off their bones.

This sustained allusion to Ezekiel 34 helps to remind the prophet's audience that their present experience is one of 'worthless shepherds', and that the promise of Ezek. 34.23 – that Yahweh 'will set up over them one shepherd, my servant David, and he shall feed them' – has not yet materialized.

In Zech. 11.17, Yahweh pronounces a word of woe on the worthless shepherd – 'May the sword strike his arm and his right eye!' As Meyers and Meyers note, the arm represents physical power, and the eye represents insight and understanding, and so to remove both is to take away both physical and mental capacity to act.[45] This judgment oracle indicates that Yahweh will – eventually – render the 'the worthless shepherd' powerless. Thus, although this final section affirms that the present experience of God's people is to continue to suffer under a 'bad shepherd', it ends with a (tentative) note of hope for the future.

---

45. See Meyers and Meyers, *Zechariah 9–14*, 291–92.

Conclusion

Reading Zechariah 11 in the light of its intertexts – particularly in light of the book of Jeremiah – has helped to clarify the identity of the three shepherds, the identity of the chief shepherd, and the period of history to which this symbolic act relates.

In Zech. 11.4-14, the prophet depicts Yahweh's relationship with his people in the period leading up to the exile. Though Yahweh was their chief shepherd, he was rejected by his flock, and valued by them as though he were nothing more than a slave. The symbolic acts performed by the prophet depict the consequences of this for the flock. The flock is doomed to slaughter (11.4). Because Yahweh no longer shows them pity, they experience oppression and exploitation at the hands of their leaders (11.5-6). The removal of 'the three shepherds in one month' (11.8) depicts the removal of all of the nation's leadership – king, priest and prophet – in the period of a single month. The prophet enacts the events of 587 BCE, when Yahweh said to his people 'I will not be your shepherd. What is to die, let it die; what is to be destroyed, let it be destroyed; and let those that are left devour the flesh of one another' (Zech. 11.9). The breaking of the two staffs (Zech. 11.10, 14) symbolizes the termination of God's covenant with them and the severing of the brotherhood between Israel and Judah. The symbolic act with 30 pieces of silver (Zech. 11.12-13) depicts the leaders of God's people terminating Judah's relationship with Yahweh as their shepherd, valuing him as though he were worth nothing more than a slave or a tiny idol. The purpose of this recapitulation of the past via this series of symbolic acts is to explain to the prophet's own generation how they had come to be in their present lamentable state.

In Zech. 11.15-17, the symbolic act moves from past to present. Because of their rejection of Yahweh as their shepherd, the people now suffer under 'foolish shepherds'. They are still experiencing the 'bad shepherds' of Ezekiel 34. Yet, despite the present affliction of the flock, the passage ends with a glimmer of hope. In Zech. 11.17, Yahweh promises that he will disarm the worthless shepherd, leaving open the possibility that there may yet be a good Shepherd to rule over the people.

Part III

POETRY

Chapter 10

THE GOLDEN CALF IN THE PSALMS

Gordon J. Wenham
Trinity College, Bristol

The Psalter opens the third division of the Hebrew canon and like Joshua, the first book of the second division, encourages its readers to meditate day and night on the law (Ps. 1.2; Josh. 1.8). By the 'law' is understood not just the legal sections of the Pentateuch, but the whole five books, the narratives as well as the commandments. But in the Psalms these narratives are recalled very unequally. The crossing of the Red Sea and the conquest of Transjordan are mentioned several times (Pss. 66.6; 77.20; 78.13, 53; 106.7; 114.3, 5; 135.11; 136.19). But the episode of the Golden Calf, which occupies three chapters of Exodus (32–34), and nearly two chapters of Deuteronomy (Deut. 9.6–10.11), receives only one brief mention in the Psalms (106.19-23). This essay explores this curious fact, and will suggest that the Golden Calf episode is alluded to in various other places. The effect of these easily overlooked allusions to the Golden Calf incident, as we shall see, is to bring a voice of assurance regarding the forgiveness of sins to those parts of the book that are otherwise dominated by imagery of exile resulting from the people's sin. The Golden Calf allusions in the Psalter point to the ultimate triumph of divine grace rather than divine punishment.

The Golden Calf episode is not the only Pentateuchal episode that seems underplayed in the Psalter. Most striking of all is the omission of the lawgiving at Sinai itself, which immediately precedes the making and worship of the calf. There is theophanic language recalling the Sinai experience (e.g. Pss. 18.8-16; 50.3-6; 68.8-9; 97.2-4; cf. Exod. 19.16-24). There is a quotation from the preamble to the Decalogue: 'I am the LORD your God, who brought you out of the land of Egypt' (Ps. 81.11). There are allusions to various of the commandments (e.g. 50.18-20; 81.10).[1] Psalm 105, which summarizes the history

---

1. Interestingly there is no mention of the Sabbath commandment, nor for that matter are any of the festivals such as Passover mentioned. Given their prominence in the

of Israel from the patriarchs to the exodus concludes with the words: 'That they might keep his statutes and observe his laws' (Ps. 105.45). This enunciates one of the fundamental presuppositions of the Psalter, which constantly relates Israel's successes or failures to their fulfilment of the law, but it makes it the more strange that the positive side of the Sinai experience is not described, and the negative side, the Golden Calf, only once.

1. *Psalm 106.19-23*

Psalm 106 devotes just five verses to this episode.

> They made a calf in Horeb
>> and worshipped a metal image.
> They exchanged their glory
>> for the image of an ox that eats grass.
> They forgot God, their Saviour,
>> who had done great things in Egypt,
> wondrous works in the land of Ham,
>> and awesome deeds by the Red Sea.
> Therefore he said he would destroy them-
>> had not Moses, his chosen one,
> stood in the breach before him,
>> to turn away his wrath from destroying them. (Ps. 106.19-23)

Before examining these verses more closely, we need to set them in context. Psalms 103–106 are a closely integrated group, though only Psalm 103 has a title. Psalms 103 and 104 are obviously a pair. Both begin and end with the command 'Bless the LORD, O my soul'. Psalms 105 and 106 end with 'Praise the LORD', and Psalm 106 continues the story-line of 105. Psalm 105 sums up the story of the patriarchs from Abraham to Joseph and retells the opening chapters of Exodus. Psalm 106 takes up the story of the wilderness wanderings concentrating on Israel's multiple acts of unfaithfulness which eventually led to the exile from which the psalmist prays to be delivered (v. 47). This makes the psalm more like a lament, whereas the preceding psalm retells the history with a very positive spin,

> So he brought his people out with joy,
>> his chosen ones with singing. (105.43)

Pentateuch these omissions are striking. For further discussion see G.J. Wenham, 'The Ethics of the Psalms', in Philip S. Johnston and David G. Firth (eds.), *Interpreting the Psalms* (Leicester: Apollos, 2005), 175–94.

Taken in sequence Psalms 104 to 106 give a summary of saving history from creation to the exile, and by themselves give a very pessimistic sequence. God's marvellous gifts in creation, paeaned in Psalm 104, and the fulfilment of divine promises in Psalm 105, seem to be nullified by Israel's faithlessness in Psalm 106. But as we have already noted Psalm 103 prefaces these three psalms, and its message transforms this gloomy sequence, because the LORD is the one 'who forgives all your iniquity' (Ps. 103.3). And it is this conviction that allows the author or user of Psalm 106 to pray for national restoration.

It is evident that these psalms presuppose the existing Pentateuch, not just one or more of its putative sources. Psalm 104 draws heavily on Genesis 1 and lightly on Genesis 2–3, often supposed to be by different writers. Similarly, Psalm 106 depends on the present Exodus to Numbers with a few deviations.

Sin in Egypt	Exod. 5.20-21	Ps. 106.7
Sin at Red Sea	Exod. 14.11-12	Ps. 106.7-12
Murmuring	Exod. 15.22–17.7; Numbers 11	Ps. 106.14-15
Dathan and Abiram	Numbers 16	Ps. 106.16-18
Golden Calf	Exodus 32–34	Ps. 106.19-23
Spies	Numbers 13–14	Ps. 106.24-27
Baal-Peor	Numbers 25	Ps. 106.28-31
Meribah	Num. 20.1-13	Ps. 106.32-33
Sins in Canaan	Judges	Ps. 106.34-42

The episodes recalled roughly follow the sequence in Exodus to Numbers, but the position of the Golden Calf is the most anomalous, perhaps to highlight it.[2] Seybold holds that the order shows progressive degradation from disbelief at the Red Sea to the nadir of the exile.[3] Though the exile is the endpoint of the sequence, it seems difficult to claim that each sin is worse than the one before. Rather the recitation of past occasions on which Israel has provoked God's anger is a reminder that despite that anger he still saved Israel for his name's sake (v. 8), or because of the intervention of Moses or Phinehas (vv. 23, 30–31), or as a result of the cry of his people and his faithfulness to the covenant (vv. 44–45). This past record gives hope to the final prayer:

Save us, O LORD our God

---

2. See K. Schaefer, *Psalms* (Collegeville: Liturgical Press, 2001), 263.

3. K. Seybold, *Die Psalmen* (Tübingen: Mohr, 1996), 421, but his argument is not persuasive.

> and gather us from among the nations,
> that we may give thanks to your holy name
> and glory in your praise. (v. 47)

Though this list of sins evidently presupposes the narratives in Exodus and Numbers, a careful reading shows that Deuteronomy's retelling of some of these events is also presupposed. Deuteronomic language is present.[4] Only Dathan and Abiram are mentioned as heading the rebellion against Moses. This is in line with Deut. 11.6, which also says nothing about Korah's role. In the spy story the remark 'they murmured in their tents' (v. 25) comes from Deut. 1.27. Like Deut. 1.37 and 3.26, Ps. 106.32 blames the people for Moses' exclusion from the land. Their failure to exterminate the Canaanites and the consequent intermarriage with them (vv. 34–35) is an important theme in Deuteronomy (cf. 7.1-5). Also, the phrase 'They sacrificed . . . to demons' (v. 37) occurs only here and in Deut. 32.17.

This picture of a basic story-line based on Exodus–Numbers supplemented or adorned with Deuteronomic features is confirmed when the account of the Golden Calf in Ps. 106 is analysed.

> They made a calf in Horeb
> and worshipped a metal image. (v. 19)

This verse is an expansion of Exod. 32.8 'they have made themselves a calf, a metal image, and have worshipped it'.[5] But the little addition 'in Horeb' probably betrays the influence of Deuteronomy,[6] which nearly always gives Sinai this name.[7] Exodus 32.8 of course echoes the commandment: 'You shall not *make* for yourself a carved image . . . You shall not *worship* them' (Exod. 20.4-5).

The next verse reads:

> They exchanged their glory
> for the image of an ox that eats grass. (v. 20)

---

4. For example, 'fathers', 'remember', 'rebel' (v. 7); 'forget' (v. 13); 'test' (v. 14); 'Horeb' (v. 19); 'likeness, image' (v. 20); destroy (*hišmîd, hišḥît,* v. 23); 'provoke to anger' (v. 29); 'angered' (v. 32); 'play the whore' (v. 39); 'anger kindled' (v. 40).

5. Cf. Deut. 9.12, 'they have made themselves a metal image'.

6. For further discussion see W.H. Gispen, *Indirecte gegevens voor het bestaan van den Pentateuch in de Psalmen?* (Zutphen: Nauta & Co, 1928), 264–66.

7. But note 'Horeb' is the term in Exod. 33.6.

It is an embellishment of the Exodus account using a key word from Deut. 4.16-18 'likeness'/'image' *tabnît*. The mocking sarcastic tone is unmistakable, and is reinforced by the alliteration between *ʿēgel* and *ʿēśeb*. Then there comes the theological analysis of their behaviour:

> They forgot God, their Saviour,
>> who had done great things in Egypt,
> wondrous works in the land of Ham,
>> and awesome deeds by the Red Sea. (vv. 21–22)

Forgetting God and his gifts is one of Deuteronomy's great worries. 'Remember and do not forget' is one of its refrains. In Deuteronomy it introduces the story of the Golden Calf (Deut. 9.7). Here God's work in redeeming Israel is summed up in three lines. It echoes the earlier, much fuller, description of God's deeds and their reaction in vv. 7–13. Initially

> they believed his words;
>> they sang his praise. (v. 12)

Then they changed their tune. As the psalm puts it:

> they soon forgot his works;
>> they did not wait for his counsel. (v. 13)

This psalm, like the book of Deuteronomy, sees forgetfulness of God's mercy and the consequent indifference and ingratitude as the root cause of Israel's rebelliousness. As the psalm points out, such behaviour prompted divine wrath on each occasion (vv. 15, 23, 26, 29, 32, 40, 43). But twice God's anger was stayed by human intervention. At Baal-Peor Phinehas killed an Israelite having intercourse with a Midianite woman and thereby brought the plague that was decimating Israel to an end (vv. 28–31; cf. Num. 25.1-15). The other successful mediator on Israel's behalf was Moses, who

> stood in the breach before him,
>> to turn away his wrath from destroying them. (Ps. 106.23)

To 'stand in the breach' is a military metaphor. 'Moses confronted God with intercession like the warrior who stands in the breach of the city wall to repel the enemy at the risk of his life.'[8]

---

8. A.F. Kirkpatrick, *The Book of Psalms* (Cambridge: CUP, 1902), 629.

Ezekiel uses the same image to explain why in his day judgment fell on Jerusalem. 'I sought for a man . . . who should . . . stand in the breach before me for the land, that I should not destroy it, but I found none' (Ezek. 22.30). This dramatic figure captures well the tense struggle Moses had to dissuade God from destroying his people. But it slips over the most memorable result of this divine–human debate: namely, the disclosure of God's essential character.

> The LORD descended in the cloud and stood with him there,
>> and proclaimed the name of the LORD.
> The LORD passed before him and proclaimed,
>> 'The LORD, the LORD, a God merciful and gracious,
> slow to anger, and abounding in steadfast love and faithfulness,
>> keeping steadfast love for thousands,
> forgiving iniquity and transgression and sin'. (Exod. 34.5-7)

The term 'steadfast love' occurs twice in this passage, once in the phrase 'abounding in steadfast love' *rab ḥesed*, and secondly in the phrase 'keeping steadfast love' *nōṣēr ḥesed*. The repetition of *ḥesed* makes it prominent in this definition of God's character, but it is the first formula that is more often quoted in the psalms. There is probably an allusion to this great definition of God's character in Ps. 106.7, 45 in the phrase 'according to the abundance of his stead-fast love' *rōb ḥăsādêkā/kěrōb ḥăsādāw* which is very similar to 'abounding in steadfast love' in the Exodus passage.

Steadfast love (*ḥesed*) could well be described as the key word of the Psalter, the majority of its uses (127/245) in the OT are found in the book of the Psalms. It often occurs paired with faithfulness (*'ĕmet*) in the psalms,[9] just as in Exodus 34.6, inviting the surmise that the psalm is alluding to the Golden Calf episode. When the whole formula is quoted, the surmise becomes a strong probability, if not a certainty. Full quotation is found in three psalms, which intriguingly all bear the title 'A Psalm of David'. The first of these is Psalm 86, a solitary Psalm of David interrupting the second collection of Korahite psalms (Psalms 84–88). The next quotation is found in Psalm 103, another isolated Davidic psalm in a section of mostly anonymous psalms (91–106). Finally, in the last Davidic psalm (Psalm 145) there is another quotation of Exodus 34. Not only are all the quotations found in Davidic psalms, but these psalms all occur towards the end of the book in which they are placed.[10] The significance of this position is not very clear, but it could suggest that the editor wished to end each book on

---

9. On this word pair see E. Kellenberger, hesed we'emet *als Ausdruck einer Glaubenserfahrung* (Zurich: Theologischer Verlag, 1982).

10. Psalm 89 ends Book 3, 106 Book 4, and 150 Book 5.

a positive note or at least suggest hope before the bleakness of psalms such as 88 or 89.

2. *David, Aaron and Forgiveness*

The attribution of these psalms to David is also problematic. From the mid-nineteenth century it has been fashionable to dismiss the historical worth of the psalm titles. Their authorship claims are rarely taken seriously. But modern canonical critics point out that even if David or Asaph were not the authors of the psalms attributed to them, at least the editors of the Psalter believed that they were. This means that if we are to understand how the psalms were first read in the context of the whole Psalter, we have to suspend critical doubt about the reliability of the titles and use them to capture the sense of the psalms they head.[11]

Why should the quotation of Exod. 34.6 be found especially in Davidic psalms? Could it be that the editors of the Psalter saw a parallel between his sins and those of Aaron, the first high priest and maker of the Golden Calf? In the opening of David's great penitential Psalm 51 there is a concentration of terms[12] that are also found in the Golden Calf story, especially Exodus 34.6-7.

Ps. 51.3
Have *mercy* on me (Exod. 33.19 [2×], 34.6), O God
　　according to your *steadfast love* (34.6, 7)
according to your *abundant* (34.6, rb) *mercy* (33.19; 34.6, rḥm)
　　blot out (32.32-33) my *transgressions* (34.7)

Ps. 51.4
Wash me thoroughly from my *iniquity* (34.7 [2×], 9),
　　and cleanse me from my *sin* (32.21, 30, 32, 34; 34.7).

Ps. 51.5
For I know my *transgressions* (34.7)
　　and my *sin* (32.21, 30, 31, 32, 34; 34.7) is ever before me.

11. Works that discuss these issues include the commentaries of McCann, Hossfeld and Zenger, and Vesco, as well as M. Kleer, *"Der liebliche Sänger der Psalmen Israels"* (Bodenheim: Philo, 1996); J.-M. Auwers, *La composition littéraire du psautier un état de la question* (Paris: Gabalda, 2000); D. Erbele-Küster, *Lesen als Akt des Betens* (Neukirchen: Neukirchener Verlag, 2001).

12. Noted briefly by J.-L. Vesco, *Le psautier de David* (Paris: du Cerf, 2006), 471 and F.-L. Hossfeld and E. Zenger, *Psalms 2: A Commentary* (Minneapolis: Augsburg Fortress, 2005), 19.

Ps. 51.7
Behold I was brought forth in *iniquity* (34.7 [2×], 9),
    and in *sin* (32.21, 30, 31, 32, 34; 34.7) did my mother conceive me.

Ps. 51.11
Hide your face from my *sins* (32.21, 30, 31, 32, 34; 34.7),
    and *blot out* (32.32-33) all my iniquities (34.7 [2×], 9).

The closeness of these parallels between Exodus 32–34 and Psalm 51 makes it likely that the latter is consciously drawing on the former to strengthen David's plea for forgiveness: if God forgave the great sin of Aaron and the people after Moses' intercession, may he not be willing to pardon David too? Does this principle also apply in the psalms ascribed to David that undoubtedly quote Exodus 34.6? To these we now turn.

3. *Psalm 86*

Psalm 86 is the only psalm ascribed to David in the third book of the psalms.[13] It follows a psalm of the Sons of Korah, which contains a number of allusions to Exodus 32–34, but without any long quotation.[14] This association of ideas and terminology could explain the placing of Psalm 86 at this point in the Psalter. According to Kirkpatrick, Psalm 86 is little more than a catena of quotations from other psalms and some other passages.[15] 'It is the composition of some pious soul whose mind was steeped with the scriptures already in existence, and who recast reminiscences of them into a prayer to suit his own particular needs.'[16] Zenger comments: 'This psalm is conceived as a "recapitulation" of

---

13. Vesco, *Le psautier de David*, 778 notes the similar phenomenon of a messianic psalm inserted into the first collection of Korahite psalms: 'La supplication davidique qu'est le Ps 86 s'insère dans l'ensemble que constitue le second recueil des psaumes des fils de Coré (Ps 84 – 88), comme le Ps 45, messianique, s'insérait dans la première série des psaumes des fils de Coré (Ps 42 – 49).'

14. The allusions are at Ps. 85.3 'You forgave the iniquity of your people . . . all their sin' (Exod. 34.7, 9); 85.4 'you turned from your hot anger' (cf. Exod. 32.12); 85.6 'will you prolong your anger to all generations?' (cf. Exod. 34.7); 85.8 'steadfast love'; 85.11 'steadfast love and faithfulness' (Exod. 34.6-7).

15. 'Psalms 25, 26, 27, 40, 54 are quoted almost verbatim. Pss. 5, 6, 9, 17, 22, 28, 31, 50, 55, 56, 57, 72, 77, 116, 130 seem to have been laid under contribution . . . The use of the two groups 25–28, 54–57 is noticeable' (Kirkpatrick, *Psalms*, 514). Apart from the verbatim quote from Exod. 34.6, Kirkpatrick notes a quotation from Exod. 15.11 and several from Deuteronomy. Most of the psalms apparently quoted are Davidic.

16. Kirkpatrick, *Psalms*, 515.

the two Davidic collections Psalms 3–41 and 51–72.'[17] It is structured by three doxologies in vv. 5, 10, 15. The last is the quotation of Exod. 34.6, and the first seems also to be derived from it.

> For you, O Lord, are good and forgiving,
>> *abounding in steadfast love* to all who call upon you. (Ps. 86.5)

The middle doxology forms the climax of the prayer:

> For you are great and do wondrous things
>> you alone are God. (Ps. 86.10)

As a whole it has the general features of a lament, with requests (vv. 1–4, 6–10), praise (vv. 5, 10, 15), request and lament (vv. 11–14), and a final request (vv. 16–17). As in many Davidic laments the situation of the psalmist is hard to specify. Is he ill, near to Sheol (v. 13) or oppressed by his enemies (v. 14), or is he complaining that his illness is being interpreted by others as a sign of God's displeasure with him?

He recalls a previous situation where he has proved God's steadfast love, rescuing him from death (v. 13). Now he faces 'insolent' and 'ruthless enemies' who seek his life. So he prays for renewed deliverance as he puts it in his closing petition.

> Turn to me and be gracious to me . . .
>> and save the son of your maidservant.
> Show me a sign of your favour,
>> that those who hate me may see and be put to shame
> because you, LORD, have comforted me. (Ps. 86.16-17)

Just preceding this petition is the quotation of Exod. 34.6. It is ultimately to this revelation of God's character that the psalmist appeals. He believes he is godly (*ḥāsîd*), that is someone who shows 'the steadfast love' (*ḥesed*) that characterizes God himself, and he prays that he 'may walk in your truth'. But as in other psalms (e.g. 19.14; 139.23-24) there is the realization that there may well be faults he is not aware of. These faults may deserve divine displeasure. But if God forgave Israel for breaking the first commandment, then surely he can forgive the sins of the psalmist, however black they may be, for as He Himself said: He 'is a God merciful and gracious, slow to anger, and abounding in steadfast

---

17. Hossfeld and Zenger, *Psalms 2*, 370.

love . . . forgiving iniquity, transgression and sin'. It is God's mercy that is the basis of his hope and the presupposition of his prayer.

4. *Psalm 103*

Psalm 103 is aptly termed by Seybold, 'The Song of Songs of Grace' (*Das Hohelied der Gnade*). It praises God for his forgiveness, experienced at the personal, national and cosmic levels. As we have already noted, it heads a group of four psalms which recount the Pentateuchal history from Genesis to Deuteronomy. As told in those books and recounted in Psalms 105–106, it is a distressing story of repeated rebellion and disobedience, provoking God's repeated displeasure. But this psalm prefaces this sad history with a reflection on God's character that provides hope and consolation in the darkest moments of human history. His steadfast love made known to Moses is a rock to rest on.

Formally Psalm 103 is a hymn with features of an individual thanksgiving in the opening verses, which seem to refer to personal deliverance. The title 'A Psalm of David' shows that the editors of the Psalter heard the speaker as David, presumably looking back on his experiences of divine compassion and forgiveness. The title, coupled with the quotation of Exodus, thus underlines that the two leading figures in the Old Testament story, Moses and David, endorse this message of divine mercy.

The psalm itself falls into three main sections, vv. 1–6, 9–14, 17–22, separated by scriptural quotations (vv. 7–8, 15–16). The opening exhortation to 'my soul' to praise the LORD leads to the conclusion 'that it goes back to a personal experience and is intended for personal use'.[18]

The first section (vv. 1–6) focuses on six 'benefits' mostly expressed with participles: forgiving, healing, redeeming, crowning, satisfying and renewing. Already key words from Exodus 33 and 34 anticipate the quotation of 33.13 and 34.6.

Key word	Exodus	Psalm 103
Name	33.12, 17, 19; 34.5, 14	1
Forgive iniquity	34.7, 9	3
Steadfast love	34.6, 7	4
Mercy	33.19; 34.6	4
Goodness	33.19	5

---

18. Seybold, *Die Psalmen*, 403.

The quotation from 33.13 is inexact: 'Show me now your ways' becomes 'He made known his ways to Moses' (Ps. 103.7). The quote from 34.6, however, is precise, if a bit abbreviated: 'The LORD, a God merciful and gracious, slow to anger and abounding in steadfast love and faithfulness' is shortened to 'The LORD is merciful and gracious, slow to anger and abounding in steadfast love'.

However the full passage is evidently known, as the succeeding verses contain further key terms from Exodus.

Key word	Exodus	Psalm 103
Sins	32.21, 30, 31, 32, 34; 34.7, 9	10
Iniquities	34.7, 9	10
Steadfast love	34.6-7	11
Transgressions	34.7	12
Compassion	33.19; 34.6	13
Steadfast love	34.6-7	17
Covenant	34.10, 12, 15, 27, 28	18

It is striking that these terms, which are common to Exodus 32–34 and Psalm 103, do not appear in the parallel account in Deuteronomy 9–10. The command, 'Forget not all his benefits' of course recalls the frequent exhortations in Deuteronomy (e.g. 6.12; 8.11) and the rare term 'diseases' is also found in Deut. 29.21, so it would be wrong to conclude the psalmist does not know Deuteronomy. But whereas Deuteronomy in recounting the Golden Calf story is emphasizing Israel's persistent sinfulness, Psalm 103 is, like the other psalms, using it as a paradigm of God's grace and mercy to Israel. This is the thrust of vv. 9–14. Verse 14 could be an allusion to Genesis 2–3, where the LORD God forms (*yṣr*) man from the dust of the earth (Gen. 2.7) and to which he is sentenced to return after eating the forbidden fruit (3.19), a thought which recurs in Ps. 104.29.

Man's frailty and mortality are expanded on in vv. 15–16, which could be quotations from other Scriptures, should they antedate the composition of this psalm. Close parallels are found in Pss. 90.5, 6; 102.12; Job 14.2; Isa. 40.6-8. The main point in quoting them is to underline the immutability of God's love compared with the fleetingness of human life. But while generations may come and go,

> The steadfast love of the LORD is from everlasting to everlasting
> on those who fear him,
> and his righteousness to children's children. (v. 17)

Once again we have an echo of Exod. 34.7 which affirms that God's love extends to the thousandth generation. This thought prompts the psalmist to urge all creation to bless the king of heaven, and pay him his rightful tribute. And finally he reminds himself to 'Bless the LORD, O my soul'.

To sum up, Psalm 103 uses the Golden Calf episode, not as a demonstration of Israel's sinfulness but as a demonstration of divine *ḥesed*. If God forgave Israel then, and if he forgave David, the named author, later, then who can fail to find mercy at his hands?

> As far as the east is from the west,
>> so far does he remove our transgressions from us. (v. 12)

As Vesco puts it: 'Ps. 103 is a hymn to the glory of the compassionate interventions of Yahweh, an authentic commentary on the divine revelation of Exod. 34:6.'[19] In the time of the exile or soon after, when we assume the Psalter was compiled, this was a message of great reassurance.

5. *Psalm 145*

Psalm 145 is the last psalm to quote Exod. 34.6 and the last in the final Davidic collection. It is a comprehensive paean of praise that introduces the final Hallel collection, five doxologies in praise of the LORD (Pss. 146–150). It is also an acrostic psalm, like Pss. 111, 112 and 119, in that each verse begins with a different letter in the order of the alphabet.[20] This device may aid memorisation but it also conveys the idea of totality, completeness or perfection.[21] So one may surmise that the acrostic form has been chosen to emphasize God's perfections. It divides into an introduction vv. 1–2 and is followed by five sections each of four verses focusing on a particular divine attribute.

1–2	Exhortation to praise the divine king
3–6	God's greatness
7–10	God's kindness
11–13+N	God's kingdom
14–17	God's provision
18–21	God's nearness

---

19. Vesco, *Psautier*, 954 (translation mine).

20. In the MT the verse beginning with N is missing. But on the basis of one Hebrew ms, a DSS, LXX and Syriac, most commentators insert 'The LORD is faithful in all his words and kind in all his works'.

21. Cf. Ps. 119 celebrates the perfection of the law; Prov. 31.10-31 praises the perfect wife; and Lam. 1–4 laments the total destruction of Jerusalem.

The quotation from Exodus comes in the section celebrating God's kindness.

> They shall pour forth the fame of your abundant goodness
>> and shall sing aloud of your righteousness.
> The LORD is gracious and merciful,
>> slow to anger and abounding in steadfast love.
> The LORD is good to all
>> and his mercy is over all that he has made. (vv. 7 – 9)

Here the connection with the Exodus narrative is apparent only in the quotation itself: there are no other verbal linkages with the Golden Calf story. But that does not lessen its significance, as is shown by the use of the story in the previous psalms we have looked at. It is as though the characterization of God in the earlier psalms can now be taken for granted. God is gracious and abounding in steadfast love, and this does not need further demonstration. These attributes of God are, as we noted earlier, frequently mentioned in the psalms, and though it would be going too far to claim that the Golden Calf experience was in the psalmist's mind whenever he spoke of God's *hesed*, it does at least appear that the Exodus version of that event was very influential in their thinking.[22]

Conclusion

This essay has argued that the Golden Calf story as told in Exodus 32–34 was well known to the psalmists, even though the episode is only once explicitly described in Psalm 106. Psalms about God's gracious forgiveness are thick with terms drawn from Exodus 32–34. This is in contrast with Deuteronomy's retelling, which dwells on Israel's persistent forgetfulness and disobedience. For the psalmists the Golden Calf episode shows the depth of God's love and his strength of commitment to his people Israel. Hence they keep praising him for his steadfast love and faithfulness, and invite all those who pray the psalms to do the same. Gordon McConville is one who has modelled this practice in his teaching and writing, and it therefore gives me great pleasure to dedicate this essay to him.

---

22. J.C. McCann, 'The Book of Psalms', in Leander E. Keck, *et al.* (eds.), *New Interpreter's Bible, vol. 4* (Nashville: Abingdon, 1996), 730, has suggested that the Golden Calf episode is alluded to in Pss. 14 and 53. These psalms reflect on the problem of universal human sinfulness using language drawn from Exodus 32–34, as well as Genesis 6–9, 11, 18–19.

Chapter 11

THE HERMENEUTICS OF HUMANITY: REFLECTIONS ON THE HUMAN ORIGIN OF THE LAMENTS

Jamie A. Grant

Highland Theological College UHI

Introduction

Some of the books of the Writings stand out from the rest of the Old Testament Scriptures because they present a perspective that is quite different from the rest of the OT canon. The book of Psalms and the Wisdom Literature (by and large) take a different starting point from the one that characterizes the other books of the Hebrew Bible. Their starting point and perspective is very much that of humanity. The Psalms (again, by and large) are prayers and songs and poems written by people. Clearly, all of the OT is authored by human beings. It was a human hand that wrote every chapter and verse that we find in the books of the Hebrew Bible. However, the difference between the Psalter/Wisdom Literature and the remaining books of the OT is that the other compositions all claim – in some sense, either explicitly or implicitly – the source of their words to be divine.[1] Accordingly, the words of the Torah were clearly written by human hand, however, each of these books claims to present God's perspective on the reality that they discuss. Thus, the Torah (whether written by Moses or by anonymous scribes of a much later era) claims to present divine revelation – these are, indeed, words written by human hands but, ultimately, their source is divine. The Psalms, on the other hand, make no such self claim. There is no attestation inherent to the Psalter claiming divine origin.[2] These are

---

1. Although many of the hermeneutical questions discussed throughout this essay can be applied to both the Psalms and the Wisdom Literature, our focus will be primarily on the Psalms with reference to Job.

2. We should, however, note those psalms that do appear to make some sort of 'prophetic' claim as part of their discourse. For example, Psalms 2 and 110 appear to include

simply the prayers and songs and poems of human beings just like you and me. In this manner the Psalter and the Wisdom Literature set themselves apart from the rest of the Hebrew Bible. They make no claim to divine source, rather they are based in human observation and response to God founded on the authors' responses to the vagaries of life.[3]

1. *Origin and Authority: The Theotropic Nature of the Psalms*

The question to be considered is: What impact does this human origin have upon interpretation? In particular, is there any sense in which the canonical contribution of the Psalms and Wisdom books is demeaned or lessened by the fact that they do not claim to be 'God's' word at source? This consideration is important because, in terms of the rest of the OT, it is the very fact of divine origin that verifies the perspective found within these books. Take, for example, the historical books of the Hebrew Bible. Were we to examine the reign of Ahab son of Omri from a strictly historical and archaeological perspective, we would be inclined to see him as a progressive and 'successful' king who reigned for a lengthy period, engaged in substantial building projects and who was a skilled diplomat and statesman on the international stage of the world in which he lived.[4] However, when we read the words of the Deuteronomistic History (DtrH), we encounter a very different take on King Ahab. 'Ahab son of Omri did more evil in the eyes of the Lord than any of those before him', we are told in 1 Kgs 16.30. So, from one perspective, we are left with a conundrum. Historical and archaeological evidence points to a successful, prosperous king, but the OT's history books describe the same historical figure as the arch-villain of the piece. How then do we resolve the conundrum? From the reader's perspective – be she ancient or modern – there is no tension to be resolved. The historian's implied claim is that his perspective is not simply his own opinion – these are the very words of God.[5] By all means the presentation of Ahab

prophetic-type pronouncements, but such poems are relatively rare within the Psalter and are certainly not typical of the psalms in general.

3. One of the many things that I learned from Gordon McConville throughout my doctoral studies was never to shy away from the difficult questions. Gordon also has a passion for understanding how the Bible speaks as well as what it says. Questions of hermeneutics are important to him, so it is with great joy that I dedicate this essay to Gordon with grateful thanks for his scholarship and his friendship.

4. N.P. Lemche, *The Israelites in History and Tradition* (Library of Ancient Israel; Louisville: WJKP, 1998), 45, 52; I.W. Provan, V.P. Long and T. Longman, III., *A Biblical History of Israel* (Louisville: WJKP, 2003), 263–65.

5. This is, of course, the underlying premise of B.B. Warfield's influential *The Inspiration and Authority of the Bible* (Phillipsburg, NJ: P&R, 1948). The basic idea is

found in the DtrH is perspectival, biased and incomplete. It does not claim to give credit where credit might be due with regard to Ahab's reign.[6] The book of Kings has no desire to present a fully orbed presentation of Ahab the man or even of Ahab the king because these words claimed to present God's perspective on the life of Ahab. They do not need to be circumspect or balanced, they do not need to give anyone what might be considered a 'fair' hearing because this is God's take on the reality of King Ahab and his opinion is the only one that really counts. It is, in fact, the divine origin of these words that makes the opinion regarding Ahab 'reliable'. Our historical/archaeological reading is inherently contentious because that reading is based in the uncertainties of human opinion.[7] For some, no doubt, Ahab was a great king whereas, for others, clearly he was not. The opinion of arguments based in human sources is by nature 'up for the grabs' because it is just that: human opinion. The DtrH's opinion on Ahab carries with it no such frailties because it is firmly based in the revealed assessment of God. 1 Kings 16 claims to give God's opinion on King Ahab and clearly implies that this is the only opinion that counts. So his progressive ideas, his building projects and his international diplomacy count for nothing because Yahweh has declared Ahab wanting.

This, of course, raises profound issues for the very validity of the Psalms and the Wisdom Literature. If human perspectives are by nature suspect because of their lack of divine verification, then why should we listen to the psalms at all? If they are nothing more than prayers and poems and songs *of people*, without any claim to direct divine involvement in their authorship, why then should we listen to these opinions any more than the historical/archaeological evidences that point to the positives in Ahab's reign? The human authors of the books of the Torah and the Prophets (Former and Latter) all claim that the source of

---

that the biblical texts inherently claim an authority above all other sources because of their divine origin. See also J. Barr, *Holy Scripture: Canon, Authority, Criticism* (Oxford: OUP, 1983), 23ff., for discussion of some of the difficulties with such language and understanding. Part of the problem in dealing with history of this type is that 'God' and 'God's opinion' is always mediated to us through the words of the human writer and is, therefore, in some sense also 'under' the hand of the author. However, the implication of these texts is that the human words bear the weight of divine perspectives and the author's expectation (as far as we can ever access such a thing) is that the reader should see these as God's words rather than just his own.

6. A point discussed well by I.H. Marshall regarding Ahab's father Omri in *Biblical Inspiration* (Biblical and Theological Classics Library; Carlisle: Paternoster, 1995), 62.

7. See I.W. Provan, 'In the Stable with the Dwarves: Testimony, Interpretation, Faith and the History of Israel', in A. Lemaire, and M. Sæbo (eds.), *Vetus Testamentum Congress Volume, Oslo 1998* (Leiden: Brill, 2000), 281–319, for a thorough discussion of the question of impartiality in the writing of historical accounts.

their words is found in God himself, thus in some sense validating the authority of their words. There is no such validation with regard to the Psalter, so how then should we read the words of this book? Is everything, therefore, rampantly subjective when it comes to the interpretation of the psalms?

This is particularly significant when it comes to the psalms of lament and imprecation. These particular poems are, in one sense, the most rife with 'human perspective'. The lament psalms are effectively complaints where the poet/speaker protests that God has not kept his side of the covenant relationship (either for the individual or for the community of God's people). In the same vein, the psalms of imprecation present the psalmist's perspective on judgment that should be outworked upon his enemies. The imprecations make it clear that the poet feels wronged by another or others and he calls upon Yahweh to enter into this scenario and to bring punishment upon the wrongdoer. Inevitably both of these types of psalm are absolutely loaded with human perspective and bias. With laments, it is the psalmist's *take* on God's faithfulness. In the imprecatory psalms, once again, we are only party to the poet's perspective on both the wrongs that have been done to him and the appropriateness of the response that he seeks.[8] In neither case is there a self-claim to divine inspiration. There is no assurance that these are 'the words of God' or that this is *the divine take* on the underlying historical reality of the poet's experience. Inevitably these opinions are hugely perspectival. Therefore, what value then can we place on such claims? What impact, then, does the 'questionable' nature of these psalms have upon our interpretation of them?

Nahum Sarna aids our consideration of this issue:

> It will be recalled that the Torah and the Psalms are, in a very real sense, complementary. The former, revelation, is anthropotropic; it represents the divine outreach to humankind. The latter, worship, is theotropic; it epitomises the human striving for contact with God. The Decalogue, commonly known as the Ten Commandments, fittingly opens with 'I am the Lord your God,' and closes with 'Your neighbour' – so the book of Psalms appropriately symbolises movement in the reverse direction by commencing with 'Happy is the one,' and ending with Hallelujah, 'praise the Lord,' marking the direction from humanity to God.[9]

---

8. For further discussion of the imprecatory psalms and the appropriateness of the psalmist's prayers in response to the harm inflicted upon them see D.G. Firth, *Surrendering Retribution in the Psalms: Responses to Violence in the Individual Complaints* (Paternoster Biblical Monographs; Milton Keynes: Paternoster, 2005).

9. N.M. Sarna, *On the Book of Psalms: Exploring the Prayer of Ancient Israel* (New York: Schocken Books, 1993), 27.

Sarna's observation is significant to the task of arriving at a proper understanding of how the psalms communicate. The revelation that we encounter in the majority of the books of the OT is anthropotropic – their source, in some sense, is in God and the direction of communication is towards man. The root of the psalms, however, is to be found in humanity and their direction is Godward. This marks a significant difference in our hermeneutical starting point and gives rise to a whole set of questions specific to the psalms when it comes to interpretation.

A few general observations, at this point, may be helpful to formulate our discussion:

1. If, as suggested above, the divine origin of the anthropotropic revelation that is found in the first two major canonical collections of the Hebrew Bible (Torah, Prophets) is key to the reader's response to those texts, then it seems appropriate to suggest that the human origin of the theotropic worship that we find in the Psalter should also shape the reader's response to the psalms.[10]
2. The theotropic nature of the Psalms also has repercussions with regard to *the effects* of these poems – they are Godward in direction and this has profound implications for all those who voice their perspectives and spirituality through the medium of psalmic prayer.[11]
3. However, by way of the inclusion of the Psalter into the canon of the Hebrew Bible, these prayers that are theotropic in origin, ultimately also become anthropotropic in nature. This appears to be the net effect of canonization and therefore an unusual dynamic is at work in our interpretation of the psalms. They are, arguably, uniquely 'human' in their origin yet, finally, they effectively become just as much the 'Word of God' as are the Ten Commandments, for example.[12]

---

10. See D.G. Firth, 'The Teaching of the Psalms', in P.S. Johnston and D.G. Firth (eds.), *Interpreting the Psalms: Issues and Approaches* (Leicester: Apollos, 2005), 159–74, for discussion of how the psalms teach through testimony, admonition and observation. These approaches are much less directly didactic than law, for example, yet they still effectively communicate with instructive intent.

11. J.L. Crenshaw's discussion of Psalm 1 provides a helpful reminder, 'Nevertheless, that interpretation of torah [proposed by B.S. Childs in his *Introduction to the Old Testament as Scripture*] ignores the explicit designation of Psalms as human prayers and expressions of praise. Such words from below, as it were, may point others in the direction they should go, hence function as torah, but they differ appreciably from divine oracles and legislation. Neither Childs nor Westermann seem to be bothered by this problem. For them, the Psalter comprises a manual of piety with law at the centre. Prayer has therefore been transformed into Yahweh's word for all people' (*The Psalms: An Introduction* [Grand Rapids: Eerdmans, 2001], 100).

12. Therefore, referring back to Note 11 above, both Crenshaw and Childs are correct

These are the issues that we need to take up in our consideration of the herme-neutics of humanity. How are we to understand poetry that is unashamedly human and perspectival in its starting point yet ultimately becomes God's Word to us? How do the prayers of God's people become the revelation of God for that selfsame community?

2. *The Humanity of Lament*

Many of the issues under consideration could be applied to the imprecatory psalms as well, but we will focus attention on the psalms of lament as we con-sider the implications of the human origin of psalmody and, in particular, Psalm 88 will serve as a foil for our discussion. Essentially, lament is the psalmist's accusation of breach of covenant on God's part.[13] Many of the laments are quite unpalatable for the contemporary Christian mind and few of them ever find their way into the worship of the people of God today.[14] Just a few verses of Psalm 88 illustrate the challenge that such psalms present:

> *You* have put me in the lowest pit, in the darkest depths.
> *Your wrath* lies heavily upon me; *you* have overwhelmed me with all your
>   waves. *Selah*

in their assessment of how the psalms communicate. With Crenshaw, we should never forget that the psalms originate in human prayer and praise, but, with Childs, we remem-ber that these prayers and praises *have* become God's word to us. See J.C. McCann, *A Theological Introduction to the Books of Psalms: The Psalms as Torah* (Nashville: Abingdon Press, 1993), 15–16. This is particularly the case given the inclusion of Psalms 1 and 2 as the introduction to the Psalter. Psalm 1 is a Torah-psalm encouraging the reader to meditate of the Scriptures (including the Psalms) as the instruction of the Lord and Psalm 2 includes an element of prophetic decree (see Note 2 above), further emphasizing the revelatory nature of the Psalter. Clearly, the Psalms have become revelation to God's people (J.A. Grant, *The King as Exemplar: The Function of Deuteronomy's Kingship Law in the Shaping of the Book of Psalms* [AB, 17; Atlanta/Leiden: SBL/Brill, 2004], 53–56).

13. P.D. Miller, 'Trouble and Woe: Interpreting the Biblical Laments', *Interpretation* 37 (1983), 32–45; W. Brueggemann, 'The Costly Loss of Lament', *JSOT* 36 (1986), 57–71. See also Robin Parry's forthcoming commentary on the Book of Lamentations in the Two Horizons series for further discussion of covenant disappointment and lament.

14. This is seen both in the choice of psalms to be sung in many psalm-singing con-gregations of the Reformed tradition and in the lectionary readings of other traditions. In both cases the difficult psalms tend to be omitted in practice. As Carleen Mandolfo notes, 'Modern Western Christianity, and Judaism to a lesser extent, have eschewed expressions of anger directed at God' ('Psalm 88 and the Holocaust: Lament in Search of a Divine Response', *Biblical Interpretation* 15 [2007], 155).

> *You* have taken from me my closest friends and have made me repulsive to
> them. I am confined and cannot escape. (Ps. 88.6-8 NIV)

> But I cry to *you* for help, O LORD; in the morning my prayer comes before
> you.
> *Why*, O LORD, do you reject me and hide your face from me?
> From my youth I have been afflicted and close to death; I have suffered *your*
> *terrors* and am in despair.
> *Your wrath* has swept over me; your terrors have destroyed me.
> All day long they surround me like a flood; they have completely engulfed
> me.
> *You* have taken my companions and loved ones from me; the darkness is my
> closest friend. (Ps. 88.13-18 NIV)

There is a directness and forcefulness in these expressions that is entirely alien
to the Christian spirituality of today.[15] Certainly, cultural elements come into
play when we consider the laments of ancient Israel – lament is still a more
common currency in the Middle East today than it is in the West, for example.
However, the question at hand is: How should we view these forceful accusations in the light of *the human origin* of the psalms? The psalmist in Psalm 88
(the otherwise unknown Heman the Ezrahite) makes a number of strong accusations against God, which begs the question: Is he justified in doing so?

In response to that question we encounter one of the most delightful conun-
drums of the Hebrew Psalter – the great question of indeterminacy. Both the
Psalms and the Wisdom Literature are (broadly) indeterminate when it comes
to their historical setting. Just as both Psalms and Wisdom Literature are human
in origin, so also they are remarkably unspecific when it comes to the presentation of the historical reality lying behind their literary expression. Therefore,
when it comes to any assessment of the accuracy of the psalmist's accusations
against God, we must be entirely circumspect in our conclusions. Is Heman the
Ezrahite justified in his claims that God has become his enemy and tormen-
tor? The only reasonable conclusion at which we may arrive is to state that *we
simply do not know*. Indeed, we could probably go further and suggest that it is
impossible for us to know the answer to any such question regarding the legitimacy of claims made in the poetry of the psalms.

---

15. J.A. Grant, 'Psalms 73 and 89: The Crisis of Faith', in C.G. Bartholomew and
A. West (eds.), *Praying by the Book: Reading the Psalms* (Carlisle: Paternoster, 2001),
61–62; N.J. Duff, 'Recovering Lamentation as a Practice in the Church', in S.A. Brown,
and P.D. Miller (eds.), *Lament: Reclaiming Practices in Pulpit, Pew and Public Square*
(Louisville: WJKP, 2005), 3–5.

Often modern Christian readers balk at any accusation of unfaithfulness lev-elled against God. The incongruity of such claims when compared to the rest of Scripture (and, perhaps, more tellingly when compared with our catechetical understanding of God and our experience of worship practice) naturally leads us to position ourselves sceptically towards Heman's accusations. However, in turn, we must ask ourselves whether such scepticism is justified.

2.1 *Heman's Lament*

Many commentators are decidedly uncharitable in the assessment of Heman's prayer. Jaki, for example, suggests that, 'In reciting the psalm we should use it as a gauge to measure the extent to which we have progressed from the Old to the New Testament, or to which we have slided [*sic*], with our groaning and moan-ing, back to the Old again and again . . . The Christian's prayers should never be void of real hope and firm assurance'.[16] Equally, the early Church Fathers saw the despair of Psalm 88 as so bleak that it could not possibly refer to the experience of a person of faith, therefore they read the psalm Christologically as the vocalization of Christ's response to the torment of the cross.[17] Were we to trace the *Wirkungsgeschichte* of this psalm, we would discover that there has been a clear tendency to mitigate the personal darkness of the poet's experience by reading it either as an expression of Israel's exilic suffering (in Jewish inter-pretation) or by seeing it as an expression of Christ's suffering (in the Christian era).[18] Such reading practices, combined with a tendency to shy away from such psalms in the Church, marginalize Heman's 'forceful accusation against God'.[19] However, are we justified in doing so?

2.1.1 Indeterminacy

First, we must remember the reality of indeterminacy. There is not much that we can say about the *Sitz im Leben* (if such a description is in any way appropri-ate) of Psalm 88. Several commentators suggest that this is a notable example of the *Krankenpsalmen*, the 'psalms of the sick', yet even this is uncertain.[20]

16. S.L. Jaki, *Praying the Psalms: A Commentary* (Grand Rapids: Eerdmans, 2001), 164. See Mandolfo, 'Psalm 88 and the Holocaust', 155–57, for further discussion of the tendencies of Church and academy to minimize the dark accusation of Psalm 88 and make it more 'acceptable' to our contemporary Christian ears.

17. Q.F. Wesselschmidt, *Psalms 51–150* (Ancient Christian Commentary on Scripture; Downers Grove, IL: IVP, 2007), 158–60.

18. J.C. McCann, 'The Book of Psalms', in *1 & 2 Maccabees; Introduction to Hebrew Poetry; Job; Psalms* (NIB Vol. IV; Nashville: Abingdon Press, 1996), 1027.

19. W. Brueggemann, *The Psalms and the Life of Faith* (Patrick D. Miller, ed.; Minneapolis: Fortress Press, 1995), 56.

20. See, for example, A.A. Anderson, *The Book of Psalms, Volume II, Psalms 73–150*

Verses 3–5 in the English text certainly imply that the poet is close to death, but whether this is the result of sickness remains an open question. Clearly, the poet sees Yahweh as the source of his torment but the effects of that persecution are, arguably, most clearly voiced in psychological terms (e.g. '*For my soul is full of trouble* and my life draws near the grave' [v. 3] or 'Your wrath has swept over me; *your terrors* have destroyed me' [v. 16]). Could it be that the poet's nearness to death is the result of suicidal thoughts born out of his lengthy experience of darkness (v. 15)? The point is that, as far as we know, the likelihood that the psalmist is contemplating suicide is just as real as the possibility that he has been seriously ill for a lengthy period of time.[21] The 'context-less' expression of despair means that we simply do not (and really cannot) know for sure.

Therefore, were we actually able to sit and listen and empathize with the poet in his bleak experience, is it not just possible that we may actually agree with his assessment of God's treatment? The indeterminacy of the psalms means that we are, in a sense, obliged as readers to accept the poets' assessments of their own reality. They are privileged with information that we do not have and our position as 'reader' is to experience that which they have experienced through their poetic expressions of joy and despair.[22] Part of the 'implied contract' between poet and reader is not to query what lies behind the text, but rather to accept that their words are in fact honest and appropriate response to the realities that they faced.[23] So, why are we normally *acritical* in our reading position with regard

(NCB; London: Marshall, Morgan & Scott, 1972), 623, who is representative of the many commentators who point to the root of Heman's lament in long-term illness. Seybold sees this as one of the *Krankenpsalmen* in *Das Gebet des Kranken im Alten Testament* (BWANT, 99; Stuttgart: Kohlhammer, 1973), 117.

21. Both McCann and Zenger question the origin of Psalm 88 in illness and point to Heman's psychological anguish as a key motivation in his lament (see McCann, 'Psalms', 1027 and F.-L. Hossfeld, and E. Zenger, *Psalms 2* [*Psalms 51–100*] [Hermeneia; trans. Linda M. Maloney; Minneapolis: Fortress, 2005], 391).

22. There is a sense in which the form-critical and cult-functional approaches to the interpretation of the psalms really missed the point. The psalms were not written for the purpose of finding a historical reconstruction. They were written so that the reader can find expression of their own experiences through the words of another. The indeterminacy of the Psalms and Wisdom Literature is, of course, quite deliberate. It is designed to allow adoption by those whose experiences may actually be *quite different* but who find that the psalms express well their emotional response to these (actually different) experiences. See P.D. Miller, *Interpreting the Psalms* (Philadelphia: Fortress Press, 1986), 18–28.

23. Of course, in this postmodern world in which we live, we can choose to adopt any 'reading position' we like with regard to the interpretation of the psalms (see D.J.A. Clines, 'Teaching and Learning the Psalms, Inductively. Or, Keeping Gunkel and Friends out of the Classroom', available online at: http://www.shef.ac.uk/bibs/DJACcurrres/Psalms/TeachingPss.html, for further discussion [accessed 01.02.10]). However, the

to the psalms, except in those cases where the laments (or imprecations) offend our sensibilities? We question the psalmist's complaint in Psalm 88 but not the praise of God's faithfulness in Psalms 103–104 – why so?

2.1.2 Empathy

The by-product of indeterminacy is that we do not get the chance to fully empathize with the poet. If we had the chance to sit with Heman of a pleasant summer's evening over a cold beer and could listen to his 'conflict of faith and experience' (to borrow Craig Broyles' helpful definition of lament[24]), it is entirely possible that we might agree with the psalmist that God – in his mysterious sovereignty – has dealt the poet a pretty rotten hand. This is clearly the case in terms of the OT's most extended lament, that is, in the book of Job. Job, in contrast with the psalms, gives plenty of 'detail' regarding the circumstances of his suffering and the reader is naturally drawn to empathize entirely with Job. I regularly teach a third year, undergraduate class in the Wisdom Literature and, year in year out, students never fail to ask the one question that the book nowhere answers: *Why* did God allow *that* to happen to Job? Seldom, if ever, have I come across a student who would deny Job his right to lament. Instinctively, as readers we are drawn to associate ourselves with Job and – for most readers – there is a real sense in which while we understand the didactic essence of the Yahweh speeches we are actually quite *dissatisfied* with the answer that they supply. Our literary association with Job means that we want to know and ask '*Why? Why did God allow Job to experience that?*'

Thus, when *we know* the historical background we are drawn to associate with the one who laments – why is it then that we tend to be dismissive of the psalmists' experience in poems like Psalm 88 or 44 in our attempt to justify the covenant faithfulness of God? Speaking of the darkness of Psalm 88, Artur Weiser presents a salient warning:

> Psalm 88 is a deeply moving testimony of the grievous temptation into which one who believes in God can fall when he feels God's eye gazing menacingly upon him through the mask of an incomprehensible calamity, and when all his prayers prove unavailing in the face of God's terrible silence. It is not without good reason that such a psalm, so closely akin to the book of Job, has been

poetry and prayers of the psalms naturally imply a reading position wherein the psalmist shares his perspective on life and experience with God in non-specific but emotionally explicit terms, so that the reader can adopt these words of praise or intercession as his own praises and prayers.

24. C.C. Broyles, *The Conflict of Faith and Experience in the Psalms: A Form-Critical and Theological Study* (JSOTSup, 52; Sheffield: JSOT Press, 1989).

included in the Bible side-by-side with that book. The fact that the lament of this godly man fades away without a single word of comfort and that he cannot even nerve himself to make any more direct requests for God's help is a clear warning against any attempt, however well-intentioned, to gloss over with merely human words of slick easy comfort the tremendous seriousness of the problem presented by a God who is hidden behind such suffering instead of facing it with awe, and even with fear and trembling.[25]

Weiser's point is simple: we do a serious disservice to the reality of the poet's experience when we fail to grapple with the reality of his feeling of abandonment by God. Whenever we fail to truly grapple with the imponderable depths of human suffering presented to us by a Job or a Heman the Ezrahite, somehow we deny something of the reality of human experience of life with God. Whenever we skip on too quickly from the laments of Psalms 88 and 89 to the solid assurance of Psalms 90 and 91, we lose an important truth of life in relationship with God – we rob ourselves of part of the fullness of what it is to be in covenant with the Creator God.[26] The book of Job presents the reader with more of an insight into the circumstances that led to his forceful lament and, therefore, with a greater depth of understanding of the fullness of relationship that he experienced with God. How does Job's extended complaint speaks to us about the hermeneutics of humanity and therefore inform our reading of Psalm 88?[27]

3. *Job: A Lament Unpacked*

There is a sense in which the book of Job is dominated by lament. While, of course, we encounter a wide diversity of Wisdom genres throughout the book, much of the story revolves around Job's complaint against God for the cruel suffering that he has experienced without just cause.[28] Equally, it must be acknowledged that there are all sorts of epistemological dynamics at work as

---

25. A. Weiser, *The Psalms: A Commentary* (OTL; trans. H. Hartwell; Philadelphia: Westminster Press, 1962), 586.

26. See Parry's forthcoming commentary on Lamentations.

27. Many of the commentators associate Psalm 88 with the experience of Job: Anderson, for example, describes Psalm 88 as 'the story of Job left half-told' (*Psalms*, 623), but many others make the same association. See McCann, 'Psalms', 1029; J.H. Eaton, *The Psalms: A Historical and Spiritual Commentary with an Introduction and New Translation* (London: T & T Clark International, 2003), 314; A.F. Kirkpatrick, *The Book of Psalms* (Cambridge: CUP, 1910), 524.

28. Murphy is quite correct in pointing out the diversity of literary form in the book of Job ('. . . it is impossible to classify it exclusively as didactic, dramatic, epic, or anything else') but he is clear that 'Westermann is quite correct in underscoring the role of

the argument develops throughout the book's poetic narrative.[29] For example, it seems that Job bows to the sovereignty of God in the Prologue (Job 1–2) and that his complaint against God only arises in response to the friends' logic.[30] In seeking to justify God, it is Eliphaz, Bildad and Zophar who first begin to suggest that Job's suffering is retributive (that is, he suffers because he has failed God in some sense[31]) and the speech cycles of Job 4–27 then begin to revolve around the question of whether or not Job's suffering is justified because of his behaviour.[32] Based on these notions of retributive justice, Job ultimately offers his complaint against God which also stands as one of the most forceful statements of OT ethics in the Hebrew Bible (Job 29–31). While the ethics of the speech are widely addressed in the secondary literature, the implications of the lament in 31.35-37 tend not to receive so much attention. Basically, the secondary literature falls into two groups: 1) those who view Job as an arrogant, self-opinionated fool who needs to be brought down a peg or two; or, 2) those who basically see Job's words as the necessary and logical consequence as a response to his real experience of life.[33]

Essentially, Job's lament revolves around two factors that are key to our understanding of how biblical lament works. First, Job as pray-er claims that God has turned against him (see, for example, Job 29.1-6).[34] And, secondly, Job asserts that the actions of the Divine Being cannot be justified as being a legitimate response to sinful patterns of behaviour on Job's part (this is the very essence of the ethical statement in Job 31).[35] The net effect of these conclusions

complaint in Job . . .' (R.E. Murphy, *Wisdom Literature: Job, Proverbs, Ruth, Canticles, Ecclesiastes and Esther* [FOTL, XIII; Grand Rapids: Eerdmans, 1981], 16–17).

29. R. O'Dowd, *The Wisdom of Torah: Epistemology in Deuteronomy and the Wisdom Literature* (FRLANT, 225; Göttingen: Vandenhoeck & Ruprecht, 2009), 153–61.

30. O'Dowd, *The Wisdom of Torah*, 154–55, 161.

31. See, for example, Eliphaz's speech in Job 4–5.

32. See O'Dowd for fuller discussion of how differing worldviews shape the Joban dialogues (see footnote 27 above). See also J.H. Walton, *Ancient Near Eastern Thought and the Old Testament: Introducing the Conceptual World of the Hebrew Bible* (Nottingham: Apollos, 2007), 23, 106–108.

33. See, for example, Norman Habel who comments that, 'Job's words of remembrance are tantamount to a speech of self-praise . . . Job virtually usurps the functions of God when he reaches the conclusion of his speech' (*The Book of Job* [OTL; Louisville: WJKP, 1985], 406). Whereas, F.I. Andersen states that 'Job's pride in his achievement should not be misunderstood. It was legitimate, not self-righteous' (*Job* [TOTC; Leicester: IVP, 1976], 231).

34. 'Instead of God being an intimate friend (v.4), Job had discovered him to be a violent adversary (13:24–28; 16:9–14; 19:6–12)' (Habel, *Job*, 408).

35. M.H. Pope, *Job: A New Translation with Introduction and Commentary* (AB; New York: Doubleday, 1973), 227.

is that Job offers a forceful charge against God outlining the inequity of his bit-
ter experience and challenging him to justify his actions.[36]

> [35] ('Oh, that I had someone to hear me!
>   I sign now my defence – let the Almighty answer me;
>   let my accuser put his indictment in writing.
> [36] Surely I would wear it on my shoulder,
>   I would put it on like a crown.
> [37] I would give him an account of my every step;
>   like a prince I would approach him.') (Job 31.35-37 NIV)

Although not a direct lament against God, this is a great example of the type of
complaint that we find difficult to palate in contemporary Christian spirituality.
Is Job simply wrong and out of order?

There are a few areas of specific interest when it comes to Job's lament.
First, we should note the sense of critical self-awareness as Job lays out his
challenge to God. He cannot see what he has done to justify this suffering, so
his defence is attack and there is no sense of restraint in the way in which Job
voices his complaint against God.[37] He is absolutely sure that God – whoever
this God might be – has turned against him (29.1-6). Equally, under the influence of his friends, Job has become convinced that God is punishing him for
something – that the Creator is taking him to task in a court of law.[38] Thirdly, we
note the tension in the development of the text in as much as Job both desires a
response from Yahweh (31.35-37), yet elsewhere we also see that he suspects
that at some point God will overpower him with his response and Job resents
the possibility of a divine answer to his questions (see, for example, 9.14-20 or
12.13-25). So we see that Job both *longs for* and yet at the same time *resents*
the possibility of God providing answers to his complaint. Interestingly enough,
when Yahweh replies in 38–41, Job does not resent God's response to his
own accusation, rather he realizes that he was in error in some of his underlying presuppositions (40.3-5; 42.1-6).[39] The divine response brings realization

---

36. 'Job is prepared to defend his integrity to God, and to submit his life to the full-
est examination. Not as a criminal would he appear before God, but as an innocent man
with head held high as a prince' (H.H. Rowley, *The Book of Job* [NCBC; Grand Rapids:
Eerdmans, 1980], 205).

37. 'Far from being abashed, Job is belligerent to the last, eager to have the case settled, confident of the outcome' (Andersen, *Job*, 244).

38. Wrongly so convinced, as it turns out in the Yahweh speeches (see J.G. Janzen,
Job [Interpretation; Atlanta: WJKP, 1985], 241–42).

39. 'In his answers (40:2–5; 42:1–6) Job relinquishes his stance as plaintiff, admits
his ignorance, and declares his willingness to drop his suit' (Habel, *Job*, 529).

that on certain key issues Job simply got things wrong.

So where does that leave us in terms of our understanding of the appropriateness of lament? Job is forceful in his critique of God. His thought processes have been erroneously shaped by the argumentation of his friends, to the extent that he comes to believe that Yahweh (or, at least, God the Most High) has removed his friendship from him and become his enemy.[40] Job longs to know why this has happened because he sees no just reason for this 'divine enmity'. Ultimately, the response comes from Yahweh: 'Enemies?' he asks, 'What makes you think we have become enemies?' *Yahweh denies the very basis of Job's lament as flawed.* At no point has God actually 'removed his friendship from the tent of Job' (29.4) nor have his purposes for Job become evil, and herein lies his gravest error (38.2).[41] Job has called into question the sovereign plan and purpose of God – his *'ēṣāh*, the very order by which God governs the earth. The point of the Yahweh speeches (Job 38–41), of course, is that God's rule within the created order is entirely beyond the ken of humankind. The application of this principle is, clearly, that the same is true of God's control over Job's reality. Both spheres of divine activity are, in a sense, inscrutable.[42] Both God's control over the daily rhythms of the created order and his management of the life and events of each and every individual are shrouded in mystery. But mystery does not equate to enmity.[43] So, although the idea is not entirely original to his own thought processes, nonetheless the root of Job's lament is wrong in fact, even although we would probably acknowledge that he has just cause to offer his complaint anyway.[44]

3.1 *Lament from God's Perspective*
The interesting fact in this equation, of course, is the divine response to Job's lament in the epilogue. As readers, we are drawn into one of the most extended

---

40. O'Dowd, *The Wisdom of Torah*, 153–55.

41. O'Dowd, *The Wisdom of Torah*, 158–60.

42. Andersen, *Job*, 291–92.

43. It is in response to this realization that Job offers his repentance to Yahweh in 42.1-6. Job has realized that his accusation of enmity and his claim that his own design would be better that God's are both wrong and he offers sincere (*contra* Habel) repentance over these matters. He does not, however, repent of his lament and the epilogue makes it plain that he has no need to do so.

44. This is true in the sense that while Job chooses to base his complaint in the incorrect assumption that Yahweh has become his enemy and is punishing him unjustifiably for sin, as readers, we would acknowledge that he retains the right to lament simply on the basis of the suffering that he has experienced at the hands of 'the accuser' (*haśśāṭān*) in Job 1–2. Job retains the right to offer a covenant complaint simply on the grounds of the extent to which he suffered.

and vociferous complaints made out against Yahweh that we encounter in the Hebrew Bible. What is more, we are privileged with 'historical' background information that allows us to judge the justifiability of this forceful lament (an unusual state of affairs when compared to the laments in the Psalms, for example). So, just how does Yahweh respond to the Joban complaint? And what might this tell us about the implications of lament for our contemporary spirituality?

Elaine A. Phillips's recent article in the *Bulletin for Biblical Research* is interesting for our purposes here.[45] Phillips focuses on the dynamics of speech throughout the so-called 'speech cycles' and draws some fascinating conclusions. In particular, she seeks to examine the question of what distinguishes Job from his friends throughout the central text of the book:

> What is a most striking difference, superficial as it might seem, is that the friends talked solely to Job about God in the most pious terms, admonishing him to pray to God in repentance lest the dismal fate of the wicked in a moral universe overtake him as well. Job, on the other hand, talked frankly about God as he attempted to understand the horror that had overtaken him, but he also appealed again and again *to God* and to evidence of his intimate relationship with God.[46]

The significance of Job's habitual practice of *addressing God directly* is seen throughout the whole book but becomes particularly significant when we consider Yahweh's response to Job's friends in the epilogue (42.7-17). Once the debate is done and dusted, and once Yahweh has responded to Job's disputation in a most unexpected manner, he then turns his attention to Job's friends. As readers, we need a definitive statement of who was in the right and who was in the wrong throughout the speech cycles. So detailed and circular is the debate that most readers end up feeling quite unsure as to who ultimately is in the right, therefore the author/editor brings a final definitive statement from God to decide the issue.[47] Job may be in the right on the issue of retributive justice, but did he go too far in his lament? However, it is the friends who are

---

45. E.A. Phillips, 'Speaking Truthfully: Job's Friends and Job', *BBR* 18/1 (2008), 31–43.

46. Phillips, 'Speaking Truthfully', 37–38 (emphasis mine). See also D. Patrick, 'Job's Address of God', *ZAW* 91 (1979), 268–82, who highlights 54 occurrences where Job addresses God directly, whereas he finds no examples of the friends directly addressing the Deity.

47. J.E. Hartley, *The Book of Job* (NICOT; Grand Rapids: Eerdmans, 1988), 540; Habel, *Job*, 583.

thoroughly rebuked and Job is elevated to the status of intercessor. The central question for Phillips, however, revolves around the translation of 42.7. Traditionally this is rendered:

> After the LORD had said these things to Job, he said to Eliphaz the Temanite,
> 'I am angry with you and your two friends, because you have not spoken *of*
> me what is right, as my servant Job has.' (NIV)

However, we should note that the Hebrew simply combines *dābār* plus *'ēl*, a frequently occurring combination which most commonly is translated as 'speaking to' rather than 'speaking about'.[48] Such was their dissatisfaction with the translation of *dibbartem 'ēlay* as 'speaking about me', Driver and Gray suggested that the text should be emended to *dibbartem 'ālay*, which they saw as a more 'normal' means by which 'speaking about someone/something' is rendered in biblical Hebrew.[49] Equally, we should note that Phillips's suggestion is not a uniquely modern one. The Septuagintal text of Job 42.7 translates this phase with the words μη ἐλαλήσατε ἐνώπιόν μου ἀληθὲς (i.e. 'you have not spoken rightly *before* me' or '. . . in my presence', implying direct speech to God rather than debate about God) as do the Syriac and Vulgate texts.[50] Also, the Targum on Job has replaced *'ēlay* with *lᵉwātay*, which would normally be translated as 'unto' or 'towards'.[51] Furthermore, the combination of *dābār* and *'ēl* is used several times elsewhere in Job to refer to 'speaking to' rather than

---

48. Of course, *dābār 'ēl* can refer to 'speaking about someone or something' as is clear from the HALOT entry for *'ēl* (HALOT 491). However, so great is the preponderance of occurrences within the Hebrew Bible where *dābār 'ēl* is translated as 'speaking to' that there should be compelling reasons before the idiom is translated as 'speaking about'. Phillips points out that there are 435 occurrences of this idiom in the MT where the phrase clearly means 'speaking to', whereas there are only seven such instances where the identical phrase must be translated as 'speaking about', and we find a further 13 occurrences where the best translation option is ambiguous (perhaps, deliberately so, see Phillips, 'Speaking Truthfully', 39). Kenneth Ngwa argues that this idiom in 42.7-8 is deliberately ambiguous and is designed to imply both talking *to* and *about* God (*The Hermeneutics of the 'Happy' Ending in Job 42:7–17* [BZAW, 354; Berlin: Walter de Gruyter, 2005], 25).

49. S.R. Driver and G.B. Gray, *A Critical and Exegetical Commentary on the Book of Job, Vol. 2* (New York: Charles Scribner's Sons, 1921), 348.

50. Ngwa, *Hermeneutics of the Happy Ending*, 7.

51. See Phillips, 'Speaking Truthfully', 40, for further discussion. However, it should be noted that although the fragmentary *11QtgJob* does notionally cover this section of the book (37.10–42.11), this verse is not among the fragments recovered (see Ngwa, *Hermeneutics of the Happy Ending*, 31).

'about'.[52] So, there is clearly an argument to be made for translating this verse as: 'you have not spoken to me in the right manner, as has your friend Job.' This is further accentuated in the context of the Epilogue because Job is presented as intercessor in 42.8 – he has spoken in a right manner to God and he continues to speak to God in his intercession for his friends. While we will never be able to answer this question conclusively on its linguistic merits alone, clearly there is a case to be made here.

4. *The Implications of a Lament Unpacked*

The implications of this understanding of the Epilogue for our consideration of the spirituality of lament are marked. A few observations can be made:

4.1 *Right relationship is better than being right*
First, we note that in being elevated to the role of intercessor, Job is commended by Yahweh *because he spoke to him throughout the whole experience*. While the friends deliberated over philosophical questions regarding justice, creation, chaos and the nature of God, Job grappled with God himself while interacting also with the friends. It appears that one implication of Yahweh's commendation of Job, if Phillips's reading is correct, is to be found in the *relational* aspect of Job's lament. The man from Uz did not understand what was happening, he resented God for what he perceived to be his role in his experience of suffering, yet he continued to pray – he continued to address God directly. Although Job was mistaken in some of what he said against God and although he was extremely forceful in voicing his erroneous complaint against God, even so Yahweh commends him for praying rather than condemning him for his prayer. *The essential element of the spirituality of lament as exemplified by Job is found in the express desire to maintain relationship despite the present circumstances.* Phillips, again, is helpful here:

> . . . God declared unequivocally (two times) that speaking correctly meant speaking *to* him, and in the process properly representing both Job's situation and God himself. Job did so; the friends did not, suggesting that, in addition to their limited view of the situation, *they completely lacked the relationship that infused Job's every utterance*.[53]

Furthermore, Phillips adds:

52. Job 2.13; 4.2; 5.8; 13.3; 42.9, etc. See Ngwa, *Hermeneutics of the Happy Ending*, 12.
53. Phillips, 'Speaking Truthfully', 41 (emphasis mine).

On the other side, God's endorsement of Job's words silences those who say that we ought not articulate those difficult truths about the apparently gratuitous evil infesting our fallen world. That had been implicitly the position of the friends who were unnerved by the force of his protest. It is evident that God welcomes the exercise of moral judgement that was the focus of Job's verbal quest. *What Job said represented reality although it was an incomplete picture, as is that of any human observer.* Job's expressed anguish and his refusal to back down were what prompted the unparalleled revelation of God in the whirlwind, and what God said at that point was only that Job spoke in ignorance (38.2).[54]

Surely, this has a significant impact on our thinking when we return to the contextless Psalm 88. There are none of the great statements of faith that we frequently come across in the other psalms of lament, yet the very act of offering a prayer in a time of great despair and disillusionment with God is, in itself, arguably, the greatest act of faith. So, Job's example points to the importance of relationship regardless of knowledge. We see throughout the piece that, although Job was unstintingly forceful in his expression of complaint, he was also aware that there was probably something going on that went beyond his understanding. He knew that God would win in the end (e.g. Job 9.1-20). He sensed throughout that there was an incompleteness about his knowledge of his own situation (e.g. Job 23). Yet, he still protested and, ultimately, he is the one who is declared to 'speak in a right manner to God' and the one who receives God's approbation. The importance of maintaining relationship with God – 'polite' or otherwise – effectively 'trumps' the need to get everything right and in order in our own thinking before approaching the Creator. The friends' desire to justify God by condemning Job actually drew them away from right relationship with God to such an extent that sacrifices had to be offered and a righteous advocate had to be found on their behalf (cf. Job 9.32-35). *When it comes to the spirituality of prayer in general and lament in particular, engaging directly with God is more important than being right.*

Such a realization impacts the way in which we view Heman's prayer in Psalm 88. Our knee-jerk reaction to the bleakness of this poem is to question whether Heman is right or not. The lesson learned from Job's lament is that this question is entirely irrelevant. In certain matters Job is declared wrong, yet still Job is commended because he has *done* rightly in wrestling directly with God rather than withdrawing from relationship. Job accuses, he cajoles, he complains, he charges God with wrong while declaring his own innocence, he accuses God of breach of covenant . . . yet 'he has spoken in a right manner

---

54. Phillips, 'Speaking Truthfully', 42 (emphasis mine).

to me', declares Yahweh following his miraculous self-revelation from the whirlwind. What conclusions then can we draw regarding Psalm 88? It does not matter if Heman is right or wrong. With regard to the spirituality of lament such a question is a category error. Right or wrong must play second fiddle to human observation and experience. If this is how Heman experiences his reality then his lament is 'right'. Honest expression of relationship – even if this amounts to accusation and even if that accusation is 'factually' inaccurate – is more important than saying nothing out of a desire to be sure that one has the facts right.

> From the darkness and the questions believers flee to God, who reveals himself as the faithful One who will not abandon the work of his hands. They keep talking about 'my God', even with a lump in their throat, so to speak. Even in the darkest psalm, Psalm 88, the author calls the Lord 'the God who saves me', though he is overwhelmed by distress. In the midst of Job's despair he keeps trusting in God and appeals 'from him to him'.[55]

4.2 *Honesty is important to God*

Secondly, what we can observe from Job's lament, which provides all the background information that is missing from Psalm 88, is that honesty matters to God more than we realize. At several points throughout the speech cycles, Job warns the friends not to defend God at the expense of a lie (e.g. 13.3-16). The clear point is that something must be skewed in their perspective of cosmic justice if false testimony is required in order to make their case. The ethical irony is unmistakable. How does this speak to our understanding of the spirituality of lament? By and large, we do not associate ourselves with the friends in our reading of the text of Job, yet popular Christianity's desire to defend God in the face of Heman's accusations is alarmingly similar to the friends' intent and purpose. However, it seems that Christians of the twenty-first century fall into the same trap as Job's empty comforters, but for different reasons. The friends succumb to the lie out of a desire to defend God and their understanding of cosmological justice. Modern Christians succumb to the lie out of a false sense of politeness and a shallow understanding of true piety. We simply believe it to be 'improper' to accuse God in the manner characterized by Job or Heman. We elevate politeness over honesty and, in doing so, place ourselves under the need of a Job-like intercessor because well-intentioned but dishonest 'meditation' is offensive to God, whereas forceful and erroneous complaint is

---

55. H.G.L. Peels, *Shadow Sides: God in the Old Testament* (trans. Hetty Lalleman; Carlisle: Paternoster, 2003), 36–37.

not only accepted but also commended by him because it is both *honest* and *relational*.[56]

It is hard for us to be sufficiently objective with regard to the cultural baggage that we carry in terms of 'acceptable means of addressing God'. It is hard for us to allow the Scriptures to confront our paradigms of thought to such a degree that we can fully place ourselves in Job's or Heman's shoes. There is a natural desire to mitigate that is fully apparent in the commentaries on both Job and the Psalms.[57] Why so? The answer lies, probably in equal measure, in an over-developed sense of politeness; an under-developed sense of covenant relationship; and an over-familiarity with the 'white lie'. In short, cultural norms have shaped our spirituality over biblical norms – we do not see the offence that our lamentless spirituality causes the God whom we worship.

Consider the force of Job's lament in 13.3-16, for example. Part of the problem of contemporary perspectives on spirituality is that we are, effectively, quite prepared to 'speak wickedly on God's behalf' (13.7) because of our cultural concept of 'the appropriate'. We fail to see how wayward our thinking is. A 'polite' lie is no less a lie and no less offensive to God. This too is clear from the Epilogue of Job where the rhetorical question of 13.9 ('Would it turn out well if he examined you?') is answered with a clear negative in 42.7-8.[58] The friends are rebuked for their failings and the seriousness of their wrongdoing is marked by the significant cost of their sacrifices for sin.[59] Yet, we tend not to view a lie that is seen as 'polite' to be morally wrong. The moral compass that guides our spirituality is not showing true North. The moral wrong of the lie told should always outweigh any sense of what is culturally appropriate. Lament is not just *an option* in our spiritual vocabulary, it is *a requirement* when disappointment with God fills our hearts – honesty must take precedence

56. This is the lesson confirmed by the Epilogue of Job (see Peels, *Shadow Sides*, 36–37).

57. See, for example, the otherwise excellent H.-J. Kraus, *Psalms 60–150: A Commentary* (trans. Hilton C. Oswald; Minneapolis: Augsburg, 1989), 195, who claims the psalmist's initial call to the God of his salvation shows 'assurance [that] beams through above all the darkness of death. In the OT this extreme lament remains without answer. The NT proclaims that Jesus Christ comes into this worst forsakenness by God and all human beings.' Clearly, the initial prayer is significant and, clearly, the coming of Christ does something to our laments. But neither fact changes the poignant reality that for Heman at that point of time 'darkness was his closest friend'. Moving way too quickly from the depth of the psalmist's anguish does not serve us well as readers.

58. 'God rebukes the friends because they have not spoken rightly to/about God' (Ngwa, *Hermeneutics of the Happy Ending*, 11, but see his broader discussion of blessing and rebuke found in 9–25).

59. Hartley, *Job*, 539.

over that which seems appropriate. The biblical norm (honesty) must outweigh the cultural norm (politeness).

Conclusion

So the task of the interpreter of the Scriptures is not to minimize or mitigate or diminish the voice of Heman the Ezrahite as marginal or extreme. Our task is not to question his starting-point and perspective because of the human origin of the psalms. The inclusion of Psalm 88 into the canon of Scripture places us in a quiescent reading position – we are to accept Heman's take on things as 'accurate enough' to be accepted into the Bible. The pray-er of the psalms must fight the natural tendency that we see to question or explain away the darkness and directness of Heman's accusation against God because one day Heman's words may well express the feelings of our own hearts.

Chapter 12

'I WILL HOPE IN HIM': THEOLOGY AND HOPE IN LAMENTATIONS

Heath Thomas
Southeastern Baptist Theological Seminary

1. *Introducing Hope*

The question of 'hope' in the exilic period has gained prominence in recent years.[1] Is there a kind of expectation held out for exiles facing the aftermath of the deportations and destructions of 597, 587, and 582 BCE, and if so, what is it? This has been answered in various ways.[2] McConville, for one, attends to the question by searching texts that respond to exile.[3] He finds Jeremianic hope to be a recast construction of kingship and renewed relationship in which the people are related faithfully to God in a 'new' covenant (Jeremiah 30–33).[4] By contrast, a portion of DtrH (Kings) conceives of a future hope that 'should not be reposed in any institution or mode of government', and, as a consequence, is not consequent to a return to the land or a messianic kingdom. So 'hope'

---

1. J. Middlemas, *The Templeless Age: An Introduction to the History, Literature and Theology of the 'Exile'* (Louisville: WJK, 2007). Thanks go to Dr Middlemas for reading through this essay.

2. E. Janssen, *Juda in der Exilszeit: Ein Beitrage zur Frage der Entstehung des Judentums* (Göttingen: Vandenhoeck & Ruprecht, 1956); P.T. Ackroyd, *Exile and Restoration: A Study of Hebrew Thought of the Sixth Century B.C.* (OTL; Philadelphia: Westminster, 1968); R. Klein, *Israel in Exile: A Theological Interpretation* (Minneapolis: Fortress, 1979); D.L. Smith-Christopher, *A Biblical Theology of Exile* (OBT; Minneapolis: Fortress, 2002); R. Albertz, *Israel in Exile: The History and Literature of the Sixth Century B.C.E.* (trans. D. Green; Atlanta: SBL, 2003).

3. In light of his interest in hope in the Old Testament, it is with pleasure that I dedicate this essay to Professor McConville.

4. J.G. McConville, *Judgment and Promise: An Interpretation of the Book of Jeremiah* (Winona Lake: Eisenbrauns, 1993), 178–80.

for this segment of DtrH is muted in a way not so in Jeremiah. But far from being without hope, McConville sees expectation in Kings culminating into a vision of radical communion between God and people, wherever God's people might reside, and in whatever political form.[5] This differs from Deuteronomy where hope is countenanced in a kind of Torah-obedience that exhibits political, cultic, and social dimensions which ultimately stands as a totality concept of communal life characterized by faithfulness and worship before God – even beyond exile.[6]

Amidst these various constructions, the book of Lamentations uniquely focuses the issue of hope. I say 'uniquely' because although Lamentations dates to the exilic age, it is Judahite in provenance and attends to a perspective of a 'templeless' people rather than that of an exiled group (like the *Golah* in Babylon).[7] As such, it approaches 'hope' from a particular angle of vision. Lamentations 3 may be an exception. Berges thinks the poem is reflective of those coping with the challenges of the return to the homeland in post-exilic Persian Yehud.[8] Middlemas argues the poem reflects an exilic *Golah* perspective rather than that of Judahites remaining in the land (the 'poor of the land' in Jer. 39.10; 40.7; 52.16). As such, this poem is different from Lamentations 1, 2, 4 and 5 in that it remains more hopeful (like *Golah* writings) than the other 'complaint-orientated' poems.[9] At this point it is sufficient to note that rather than viewing the third poem as deriving from the post-exilic period (Berges) or representing a *Golah* perspective (Middlemas), I will assume its exilic provenance and Judahite outlook, in concord with the rest of the book.[10]

5. J.G. McConville, '1 Kings VIII 46–53 and the Deuteronomic Hope', *VT* 42.1 (1992), 67–79.

6. J.G. McConville, 'Restoration in Deuteronomy and the Deuteronomic Literature', in J.M. Scott (ed.), *Restoration: Old Testament, Jewish, and Christian Perspectives* (JSJSup, 72; Leiden: Brill, 2001), 11–40, esp. 40–41.

7. J. Middlemas, *The Troubles of Templeless Judah* (OTM; Oxford: OUP, 2005); H.A. Thomas, 'The Liturgical Function of the Book of Lamentations', in M. Augustin and H.M. Niemann (eds.), *Thinking Towards New Horizons. Collected Communications to the XIXth Congress of the International Organization for the Study of the Old Testament, Ljubljana 2007* (BEATAJ, 55; Frankfurt am Main: Lang Verlag, 2008), 137–47.

8. U. Berges, '"Ich bin der Mann, der Elend sah" (Klgl 3,1). Zionstheologie als Weg aus der Krise', *BZ* 44 (2000), 1–20.

9. Distinctive motifs in Lamentations 1, 2, 4 and 5 are: a focus upon human suffering, a lack of confidence in a future hope, a deconstruction of the efficacy of confession of sin, the vocalization of pain, and the formulation of grief (Middlemas, *The Troubles*, 197–228).

10. See otherwise in J. Middlemas, 'Did Second Isaiah Write Lamentations III?', *VT* 56.4 (2006), 505–25; *The Troubles*, 197–226; U. Berges, *Klagelieder* (HThKAT;

From this basis, the query is raised, 'What is the substance of hope in Lamentations?' The present essay argues that Lamentations centres its hope in prayer to Yhwh requesting divine action, but the practical extensions of this hope remain multiform due to the logic of prayer and spirituality at work in the book. To show this, I will assess previous conceptions of hope in research, exposing the primacy of penitential prayer in their arguments, and then will attend to the poetics and theology of Lamentations 3 with particular emphasis given to Lam. 3.21-24 and its vision of hope. From this I will turn to the practical extensions of this expectation in relation to the remainder of the chapter and book to highlight the polyvalent nature of appeal (beyond penitential requests for forgiveness) in Lamentations and how that impacts the book's vision of hope and the implications that arise therefrom.

2. *Lamentations' Hope in Previous Research*

Scholars have situated Lamentations' hope in disparate ways. Krašovec assumes that hope appears in Lamentations 3 and anticipates God will be a merciful deity to those who confess sin, demarcated by Lam. 3.21-24.[11] For Childs, these verses provide the central statement of faith in the nature of God's mercy by making free use of Israel's traditional credos (Exod. 34.6-7; Num. 14.18; Ps. 86.15).[12] Tradition-history and redaction-criticism attempt to focus these general views.

Gottwald and Albrektson assess hope through Israel's prophetic traditions and Deuteronomic theology, respectively. Gottwald believes Israel's prophets to be the source of hope in Lamentations, which is predicated upon the grace of God's faithful love (חסד) towards his people (Lam. 3.21-24): 'The ground of hope is in the unshakeable nature of [Yhwh's] justice and love.'[13] What this calls for in return is repentance and conversion to regain the favour and forgiveness of the Lord. This view accords with Israel's prophetic traditions: God will restore the broken sinful people if they will but repent and return to the Lord (Lam. 3.25-41).[14] Deuteronomic theology, by contrast, provides a rationale

Freiburg: Herder, 2002); see also his articles cited in Notes 8 and 17. For my position, see below.

11. J. Krašovec, 'The Source of Hope in the Book of Lamentations', *VT* 42.2 (1992), 224–33.

12. B.S. Childs, *Introduction to the Old Testament as Scripture* (Philadelphia: Fortress, 1979), 594–95.

13. N.K. Gottwald, *Studies in the Book of Lamentations* (SBT, 14; London: SCM Press, 1962), 109.

14. Gottwald, *Studies*, 108–109. He gives Amos, Hosea, Isaiah and Jeremiah as examples.

for divine punishment but not a future hope. Yet Albrektson looks to deutero-nomic thinking to affirm hope in Lamentations. God has destroyed his city and temple, but meaning amidst destruction comes out of a kind of deuteronomic theodicy: God is justified in destroying his city and the people in accordance with his word (c.f. Lam. 2.17). As Yhwh is in control of the events, meaning can be found in them.[15] The people's proper response to judgment is penitential prayer (Lam. 3.21-39).[16]

Conversely, Berges believes Zion theology is foundational for hope in Lamentations, particularly in ch. 3. Yhwh had identified himself with this people and place (the figure of Zion in Lamentations 1–2 as in Isaiah 40–55), and committed himself to the destruction and restoration of this place; it follows then that God had not abandoned his people outright. The destruction/restoration image of Zion in chs. 1–2 reaches its zenith in the 'man' of Lamentations 3. Thus Zion/the man becomes a figure of hope and restoration. Lamentations 3 is exemplary of 'Rollen- oder Problemträger-Dichtungen' in which Zion becomes a model for faithful prayer and hope for those coping with hardships in Persian Yehud; faithful prayer is marked by penitence, in hopes God will forgive (Lam. 3.25-39).[17] While Lamentations 3 may be reflective of 'Problemträger-Dichtungen', Heim rightly notes that 'Dear Zion' (the per-sonification of Jerusalem in Lamentations 1 and 2) functions similarly to the kind of 'role-model' Berges assigns to 'the man' of Lamentations 3, and these poems are firmly dated to the exilic period.[18] Thus there is no need to postdate Lamentations 3, which impacts his view that (this version of) Zion theology informs the logic of hope.

Renkema disputes that Zion theology funds hope. While this tradition pro-vides some background material for the book, trust in God on this basis is, for the poets of Lamentations, distinctly wrongheaded: thinking that Zion was impregnable or that God was always associated with the city has led the people to a dead end. God has destroyed his city and people, so what could they do

---

15. B. Albrektson, *Studies in the Text and Theology of the Book of Lamentations: With a Critical Edition of the Peshitta Text* (STL, 21; Lund: CWK Gleerup, 1963), 236–39.

16. Albrektson, *Studies*, 126–28.

17. Berges, '"Ich bin der Mann, der Elend sah" (Klgl 3,1)', 16–20; 'Kann Zion mann-lisch sein? Klgl 3 als "Literarisches Drama" und "Nachexilische Problemdischtung"', in M. Augustin and H.M. Niemann, *'Basel und Bibel' Collected Communications to the XVIIth Congress of the International Organization for the Study of the Old Testament* (BEATAJ, 51; Frankfurt am Main: Lang Verlag, 2004), 543–46. Note that Berges com-bines tradition-historical insights with redaction criticism.

18. K.M. Heim, 'The Personification of Jerusalem and the Drama of Her Bereavement in Lamentations', in R.S. Hess and G.J. Wenham (eds.), *Zion City of Our God* (Grand Rapids: Eerdmans, 1999), 129–69, esp. 137–44.

now? The only alternative is to turn to him in prayer, trusting that 'misschien is er hoop' (cf. Lam. 3.29b) but this hope is not guaranteed.[19] His later commentary elaborates by saying that hope is found in the essence of the Lord and his faithfulness (esp. Lam. 3.21-24) and the responsible and persistent prayers of the people in crisis, combining Lam. 3.17, 50: 'Gone from peace is my soul; I have forgotten the good [. . .] Until he looks down and sees, Yhwh from the heavens.'[20] This approach helpfully centres hope in prayer rather than Zion, Deuteronomic, or prophetic ideologies.

Tradition-historical research leaves open the question as to source(s) of hope, but redaction criticism has been thought to advance the discussion. Brandschiedt relegates Lam. 3.21-41 to a late stage in the literary development of the book and believes its theological message lies in Lam. 3.21-24.[21] This chapter is 'der Mittlepunkt des Buches und der Kristallisationspunkt seiner theologischen Aussage'.[22] It offers proper response to suffering (repentance) as well as a basis for future hope (Yhwh will deliver). She suggests the poet rejects lamentation and expression of pain (embodied in Lam. 3.1-20 as well as chs. 1–2) as proper religious behaviour: 'Damit sind die anklagenden Partien v. 1–16 und 17–20 als ein für den Frommen inadäquates Verhalten erwiesen worden.'[23] Lament remains 'impious' so Lam. 3.21-24 opens the way to a deeper, more faithful response to Yhwh. But as Westermann rightly recognizes, her view of Lamentations 3 as a theological corrective may derive from a theological devaluation of lament rather than an adequate account of what is going on in the text.[24]

Middlemas helpfully nuances Brandscheidt's line of argument, stating that Lamentations 1, 2, 4 and 5 emphasize suffering and a lack of confidence in a future hope, while Lamentations 3 offers hope based out of parenesis that accepts the just judgment of God due to the people's sin (Lam. 3.19-39), a perspective similar to some *Golah* writings.[25] In short, the third chapter of Lamentations (from an exilic, *Golah* point of view) theologically corrects a

---

19. J. Renkema, *'Misschien is er Hoop . . .' De Theologische Vooronderstellingen van het Boek Klaagliederen* (Franeker: Wever, 1983), 212–96.

20. J. Renkema, *Lamentations* (HCOT; Leuven: Peeters, 1998).

21. R. Brandscheidt, *Gotteszorn und Menschenleid: Die Gerichtsklage des leidenden Gerechten in Klgl 3* (TTS, 41; Trier, 1983), 350–52.

22. R. Brandscheidt, *Das Buch der Klagelieder* (GS, 10; Düsseldorf, 1988), 157.

23. Brandscheidt, *Gotteszorn und Menschenleid*, 66.

24. C. Westermann, *Die Klagelieder: Forschungsgeschichte und Auslegung* (Neukirchener: Neukirchener Verlag, 1990), 50, 78–79.

25. Middlemas, *The Troubles*, 173; see Note 9 above. For Lamentations 3, see her 'Did Second Isaiah Write Lamentations 3?'. This insightful work is limited to Lam. 3.1-39, which impacts outcomes.

Judahite perspective which espouses a 'lack of confidence in a future hope'.[26] To make her argument, she explores the way Lam. 3.1-39 seems to invert the language of complaint in Lamentations 1–2. Middlemas' theory is, to my mind, more plausible and a genuine advance. However, language found in Lamentations 1 and 2 appears throughout Lam. 3.1-66, and all three poems culminate in lament prayer to God (Lam. 1.20-22; 2.20-22; 3.64-66). This evidence detracts from the hypothesis that Lamentations 3 (particularly 3.1-39) stands apart from the rest of the book. Middlemas rightly notes that generic mixture is idiosyncratic in Lamentations 3, which may lend further credence to her view. But generic mixture is not foreign to Lamentations' other poems. City-lament, individual lament, and prophetic genres intertwine in Lamentations 1–2, although the wisdom overtones in Lamentations 3 are distinctive. Even so, Lamentations 3 concludes not with vv. 21–39, but with vv. 64–66, by all counts a petition that God would respond to enemy activity, typical of lament prayer and parallel to the prayer of Lam. 1.22. So the poem concludes in lament rather than the teaching of 3.21-39 and fits with the prayers of the other poems.[27]

From our discussion, a general tendency appears concerning hope in Lamentations. From whatever critical approach, most view hope centred in penitential prayer, particularly located in Lamentations 3: that Yhwh would forgive sins on the basis of his covenant faithfulness. From which particular theological tradition in Israel this view developed (and from when) remains disputed. Renkema diverges somewhat, pushing towards a more robust conception beyond penitential prayer. The next section affirms this insight particularly in conjunction with Lamentations 3. But the final section will build from this and determine that the 'shape' of hope does not exclude penitential prayer but ultimately exceeds its strictures, both for Lamentations 3 and in the book as a whole.

3. *Hope in Lamentations 3*

Although Lam. 3.21-24 is important to Lamentations' construction of hope, one cannot isolate these verses because they sit within a larger context that one must address. In the chapter, vv. 21–24 are a step along a journey from lament (Lam. 3.1-24), to instruction (Lam. 3.25-39), and back to lament

---

26. See esp. Middlemas, *The Troubles*, 202–10. This feature is one of a number of prominent motifs of Judahite thought in the templeless (exilic) age. I will engage this view below.

27. For others taking this view, see: I. Provan, *Lamentations* (NCBC; London: Marshall Pickering 1991), 22, 108–109; and F.W. Dobbs-Allsopp, *Lamentations* (Louisville: John Knox, 2002), 126–28.

(Lam. 3.40-66).[28] Presentation of pain is central as the poem begins, 'I am the man (הגבר) who saw affliction by the rod of his wrath' (Lam. 3.1). This introduction leaves the reader querying the identity of both the speaker 'I', and the antecedent to 'his'.

In the first place, the speaker (הגבר) has been identified variously. Some believe him to be either a (historical) individual or as a communal voice. If an individual, identities range from Jeremiah, a defeated soldier, Jehoiakin, Zedekiah, Seriah the high priest, a general Davidic king, or an anonymous sufferer. If a communal voice, then he may be the persona of Jeremiah to be adopted by his disciples, a paradigmatic and pious sufferer, a literary 'everyman', a collective voice of the suffering community (Zion), the same speaker of Lamentations 1–2 who has not been clearly identified, or a Job-like voice of the exiles. The range of views highlights the elusiveness of the speaker's identity, whose delimitation may diminish its poetic effect. But Renkema gives some direction when he outlines the use of the term גבר in the Psalter. He is as an exemplary figure, a righteous follower of the Lord: 'Taste and see that Yhwh is good; blessed is the man (הגבר) who trusts in him' (Ps. 34.9); 'From Yhwh the steps of a man (גבר) are prepared and he delights (in) his way' (Ps. 37.23); 'Blessed is the man (הגבר) who places[29] his trust (in) Yhwh' (Ps. 40.5). In this light, the 'man' of Lam. 3.1 is a faithful follower, strong precisely because of his devotion, a theme which becomes prominent in Lam. 3.17-39. From this, it is clear that what proceeds is an exposition of a Yahwistic devotee. But who is this devotee precisely? With Berges, the גבר is, at the very least, set alongside Zion in Lamentations 1 and 2, if not identified with her. This point has often been missed, and immediately the גבר and Zion are associated. The language used in Lam. 3.1, 'affliction/misery' (עני), recalls personified Jerusalem's suffering in Lam. 1.3a (מעני), Lam. 7b (עניה) and Lam. 1.9a (עניי). Like Zion, he experiences divine wrath (בעברתו, Lam. 2.2b; עברתו, Lam. 3.1).

From this the antecedent of the pronoun 'his' comes in view: it is God, who is a warrior. The divine warrior breaks the man's bones (שבר עצמותי) in Lam. 3.4, recalling the divine 'breaking' of Zion (שבר) in Lam. 1.15; 2.9a, 11b, 13c. The גבר undergoes the experience of Zion, both of whom receive divine wrath. The

---

28. F. Villanueva, *The 'Uncertainty of Hearing': A Study of the Sudden Change of Mood in the Psalms of Lament* (VTSup, 121; Leiden, Brill, 2008). Note as well the effect of the alphabetic acrostic, which prevents the reader from resting upon the central verses for too long. The acrostic structure creates a steady forward movement for the reader without recourse to rest on one strophe or line. Finally, the repetition of √יחל in Lam. 3.18, 21, 24 and 26, as well as the language of hope in v. 29 (תקוה), lead one away from a myopic isolation of Lam. 3.21-24 from the remainder of the poem.

29. שם is a *qatal* verbal (√שים) rather than a noun, 'the name' (שם), as LXX reads.

Lord is an archer in Lam. 3.10, recalling Lam. 2.4: 'he strung his bow like an enemy, standing strong in his right hand.' But instead of just being tensed ready to fire (Lam. 2.4), Yhwh has made the גבר his target, setting him up to receive arrows of wrath (Lam. 3.12), which have penetrated the man's kidneys (Lam. 3.11). Finally, in Lam. 3.19 (זכר־עניי ומרודי) the גבר proclaims the experience of Zion in Lam. 1.7a (זכרה ירושלים ימי עניה ומרודיה): namely, 'miserable homelessness'. Poetically, the suffering of גבר becomes the suffering of Zion on the day of Yhwh's anger (Lam. 2.1), under the rod of his wrath (Lam. 3.1).

The גבר employs the language of Zion and shares in her experience. The shared experience of pain undergirds his address to God in the next strophe (Lam. 3.16-18):

> He caused my teeth to grind as gravel; he made me cower in the dust.
> And you rejected[30] my soul from peace; I forgot goodness.
> And I said, 'My splendour[31] and my hope are lost from Yhwh'.

The strophe exploits unusual language to depict the difficult experience of the man,[32] and here Yhwh is addressed directly for the first time. The man pronounces what the deity surely knows, based upon his actions described in Lam. 3.1-15: Yhwh has rejected (ותזנח) the man's soul from peace, similar to the way that Yhwh has rejected (זנח) Zion's altar in Lam. 2.7a. Divine activity prevents his worshippers' communion with the deity and therefore there is no way to find peace (שלום) or goodness (טובה). Although he persistently calls to the Lord (אזעק ואשוע; Lam. 3.8a), God has effectively shut off himself from responding to prayer (שתם תפלתי; Lam. 3.8b). This is a profound problem that leads the man to internally reflect that his splendour and hope are lost from the Lord. *Contra* Keil, who believes that the man has moved himself far from the Lord through the complaint, it is apparent that *God* has removed himself far from the *man*, and it is this reality that establishes his statement of loss: gone are

---

30. With W. Rudolph (*Das Buch Ruth, Das Hohe Lied, Die Klagelieder* [KZAT; Gütersloh: Gütersloher Verlaghaus Gerd Mohn, 1962], 231) I retain the MT (Qal 2 masculine singular) ותזנח rather than emendation ('And he rejected', ויזנח, with the LXX) or repointing (וַתִּזְנַח so the subject is נפשי, 'my soul'). Thus the גבר addresses the Lord for the first time directly.

31. נצח may connote either 'glory' or 'permanence'. If 'glory', then the man laments the loss of the Lord's manifest presence and immanence (Renkema, *Lamentations*, 376–78).

32. גרס is only used twice in the OT, here and Ps. 119.20; חצץ occurs only three times (Lam. 3.16; Ps. 77.18; Prov. 20.17); הכפישני is a *hapax legomenon*; and נשיתי is the only instance of נשה in the Qal stem.

his splendour (God's presence) and hope (his expectation of God's goodness).[33] If the poem concluded there, then one could assert the hopelessness of the poem.

But at this moment of radical loss, he turns to the deity directly in defiant faith. Verses 19–21 read:

זכר־עניי ומרודי לענה וראש

זכור תזכור ותשיח עלי נפשי

זאת אשיב אל־לבי על־כן אוחיל

Remember my miserable homelessness, wormwood, and poison.
Surely my soul remembers, and cowers over me.[34]
This I return to my heart; therefore, I will hope.

The imperative זכר, 'remember', presumably is directed towards the Lord, who was addressed in v. 17. As indicated, the גבר urges Yhwh to remember the miserable homelessness that Jerusalem herself has remembered. This repetition rhetorically provides rationale for the deity to respond on behalf of the man, who once again is associated with Zion. The man's soul remembers his miserable homelessness (Lam. 3.19-20) and is disturbed, just as Jerusalem in Lam. 1.7a has remembered her miserable homelessness. By contrast, here Yhwh has not remembered the state of the man (implicating divine forgetfulness of Zion as well); this negligence provides further motivation for his petition.

The strophe then concludes with an abrupt change towards hope and confidence in v. 21, which is both hermeneutically and syntactically difficult. In terms of syntax, על־כן is awkward as the particle normally associates with previous argumentation that gives grounds for a present conclusion ('therefore'), as in Lam. 1.8a. But what prior argument leads him to affirm hope (אוחיל)? His

---

33. Keil, K&D, vol. 8, 513–14. Note similar logic in Lam. 1.16a-b: 'On account of all these things I weep – my eyes constantly flow with water: for far from me is a comforter, the One who restores my soul.'

34. Translating תזכור and ותשיח as Qal imperfect 3 feminine singular verbs from זכר, 'to remember', and חחש or שוח, 'to be bent over/cower' (Kethib), respectively. Moreover, one must read with the supposed scribal change 'my soul', נפשי (*tiqqune sopherim*), over and above the supposed original 'your soul', נפשך, making נפשי the subject of the verbs rather than their object. For a similar construction, see Ps. 42.6: עלי נפשי תשתוחחה על־כן אזכרך, 'My soul bows down over me (my condition); accordingly, I remember you' (Keil, K&D, vol. 8, 515). Alternatively, ותשיח may derive from √שיח, 'to be concerned with something, considering or speaking' (Albrektson, *Studies*, 143), and so coincides with the LXX's καταδολεσχεω, 'to chatter (about)'. Then the line reads: 'Surely you remember and your soul will be concerned over me.' While either the Kethib (ותשיח) or Qere (ותשוח) remains sensible, the Qere reading is preferred here.

present conclusion arrives by returning an unidentified 'this' (זאת) to his heart
(אל־לבי). Its antecedent may be found in Lam. 3.20, with the גבר reflecting upon
the certainty that God surely will remember his 'miserable homelessness' and
God's 'soul will melt over' the man, treating תזכור and ותשׁית as 2nd m. sg. *yiqtol* forms and following the supposed *tiqqune sopherim*: 'Surely you remember
and your soul will melt over me.' God, then, is the subject of the verbs; the text
has been later altered by the scribes to avoid theological affront with the suggestion that God would condescend to humanity.[35] Divine memory of the גבר
is the antecedent of זאת in Lam. 3.21 and then would represent the most explicitly positive and hopeful statement in the book yet.[36] If correct, then this verse
represents a *Heilsorakel*, 'salvation oracle', in the lament genre that prompts a
shift in mood and grounds for hope in Lam. 3.21,[37] which is how Westermann
understands this verse.[38] Most commentators, then, argue that על־כן breaks syn-
tactical convention and refers to what comes after it, namely Lam. 3.22, where
Yhwh's covenant love towards his people is confirmed.[39]

Though attractive, this view is not without problems. McCarthy believes the
evidence of an earlier נפשׁך is tenuous, as does Hillers.[40] The LXX reads נפשׁי
(ψυχή μου), as does the later Targum. Apparently these versions felt no need
to theologically 'correct' the text. Moreover, despite the somewhat awkward
syntax of על־כן and the ambiguous antecedent to זאת, it is conceivable that both
prepare the reader for the positive portrait of Yhwh in Lam. 3.22-24. Following
most commentators, LXX and the Targum, the reader must face the reality that
Yhwh either has punished the man (Lam. 3.1-18), which in turn leads the man
to complain (Lam. 3.19-20), only to then express an abrupt and unsolicited confession of hope (Lam. 3.21). In this interpretation, the reader is left wondering
how the man changes his perception, as the concept has been central from v. 18b
(ואמר אבד נצחי ותוחלתי מיהוה) but nothing prepares the reader for this unexpected
shift to trust Yhwh. It may be that the ambiguous referent to זאת and the awkward syntax of על־כן is designed to exhaust the reader's search for something
that brings hope in vv. 1–21 (there is simply nothing there) only to work alongside the alphabetic acrostic and create a forward impulse: the reader must move

35. Gottwald, *Studies*, 13.

36. Albrektson, *Studies*, 142.

37. J. Begrich, 'Das presterliche Heilsorakel', *ZAW* 52 (1934), 81–92.

38. Westermann, *Die Klagelieder*, 145.

39. See Albrektson's overview (*Studies*, 143–45).

40. D. Hillers, *Lamentations* (AB; New York: Doubleday, 2nd rev. edn, 1992),
114; C. McCarthy, *The Tiqqune Sopherim and Other Theological Corrections in the
Masoretic Text of the Old Testament* (OBO, 36; Göttingen: Vandenhoeck & Ruprecht,
1981), 120–23.

to the following verses to understand what grounds this hope.

Verses 22–24 partially satisfy the reader's query, as the speaker describes God's faithful love and covenant loyalty. The text reads:

חסדי יהוה כי לא־תמנו כי לא־כלו רחמיו

חדשים לבקרים רבה אמונתך

חלקי יהוה אמרה נפשי על־כן אוחיל לו

[It is due to] Yhwh's proofs of faithfulness[41] that we are not consumed;
indeed his mercies do not fail.
[They are] new every morning; great [is] your faithfulness.
'Yhwh is my portion,' my soul says, 'therefore I will hope in him'.

The first verse is difficult for a number of reasons. Some emend כי לא־תמנו, 'that we are not consumed', to read תמו, 'they have (not) ceased'. Hillers understands both instances of כי asseveratively (following Gordis) and חסדי יהוה as the subject of the verb: 'surely the lovingkindness of [Yhwh] has not ceased, nor have his mercies ceased', which reveals chiasm: (A¹) לא־תמו (B) כי לא־כלו (B¹) רחמיו כי (A) חסדי יהוה.[42] The Targum and possibly the Peshitta read תמו. The impetus for emendation stems in part from a view that the clause is supposedly illegible without it.[43] Albrektson believes the emendation belies a prejudice against a corporate understanding of the speaker in the poem[44] yet corporate connotations of the גבר already have been introduced effectively up to this point by associating him with Zion, and some versions read תמנו.[45] The shift from a singular to plural perspective further blends the perspective of the man to the community, but here the man becomes a spokesman for the community. In terms of syntax, Keil and Albrektson rightly translate on the basis of תמנו and surmise כי introduces a subject clause: '*that* we are not consumed.'[46]

The phrase חסדי יהוה is important but rare, occurring only here and Pss. 89.2; 107.43; and Isa. 63.7. In every instance the phrase depicts divine activity that

---

41. *HALOT* translates the pl. construct form of חסד as visible or tangible 'proofs' or 'acts' of faithfulness, as in Ps. 89.2 and esp. Isa. 63.7. The term חסד 'describes the disposition of and beneficent actions of God toward the faithful, Israel his people, and humanity in general' (*NIDOTTE*, 2: 211).

42. Hillers, *Lamentations*, 115; R. Gordis, *The Song of Songs and Lamentations* (New York: KTAV, rev. and expanded edn, 1974), 179.

43. For further rationale for תמו, see H. Gottlieb, *A Study on the Text and Theology of Lamentations* (trans. John Sturdy; AJ; Århus: Århus Universitet, 1978), 45–46.

44. Albrektson, *Studies*, 145.

45. Aquila, Symmachus, Old Latin, Vulgate.

46. Albrektson, *Studies*, 145; Keil, K&D, vol. 8, 515.

demonstrates Yhwh's faithful *actions* toward the parties with whom he is in relationship: the king and his royal line (Ps. 89.2), Israel (Ps. 107.43), and remnant Israel (Isa. 63.7). Especially in Psalm 107, the phrase is a summary of Israel's history of God's redemptive and salvific activity, indicating the expectation of real, tangible and 'earthy' divine actions. In its stilted, initial position directly following על־כן אוחיל (Lam. 3.21b) חסדי יהוה responds to the grounds for hope that was broached in v. 21: the גבר's expectation of physical proofs of divine deliverance. This is covenant language that points back to the man's/ Zion's experience of pain, but points forward to an expectation of *future* divine activity.

The covenant language represents more than a mere reflection upon what God has done in the *past*. It anticipates divine activity in the future as well. This hope is reflected in על־כן אוחיל (Lam. 3.21b, 3.24b), which provides a structural *inclusio*:

Lam. 3.21 (על־כן אוחיל) ⎤
Lam. 3.22   ⎥
Lam. 3.23   ⎥
Lam. 3.24 (על־כן אוחיל לו) ⎦

The acrostic provides a forward movement that is met with a reflexive movement through על־כן אוחיל, emphasizing the entire ה strophe within the *inclusio*. The progress of the acrostic retards, and the reader is left to consider how divine acts of faithfulness (amongst other characteristics) may bring the man (and Zion by extension) hope.

Thus Lam. 3.21-24 *partially* satisfies the reader's search for the man's ground for hope. What remains unstated in this construction is significant. That is to say, placing hope in 'Yhwh's proofs of faithfulness' gives little specificity as to its particular shape, other than to say that it expects some sort of divine activity. Here we approach the query raised at the introduction of the essay. What is the substance or shape of hope in Lamentations? Once one sees Lam. 3.21-24 as central to the logic of hope, one must press further to contextualize these verses within the poem and book to uncover the ways in which hope finds its meaning.

4. *'Shape(s)' of Hope in Lamentations*

For some, the 'shape' of hope remains somewhat abstract. It supposes that adopting a theological *conviction* about the Lord's character expressed in Lam. 3.22-24 will move the community out of suffering in some way. By meditating upon the mercies of God the sufferer will transition out of his state of pain and into an acceptance of Yhwh being the man's 'portion' (חלק) as in Lam. 3.24. 'In this way the poet gains new courage and new hope (v. 24b) and this he longs to impart to his congregation – "God is our only hope, in this hopeless situation".'[47] Yet such abstraction does not comport with the 'earthy' overtones resonant in the phrase חסדי יהוה, as discussed above. Rather, hope lay in an expectation that Yhwh will demonstrate his faithfulness through physical, tangible proofs which are yet to be experienced. This anticipation runs throughout the rest of the chapter and book.

Set alongside vv. 1–20, vv. 21–24 centre upon a hope for reversal of God's negative actions against the man/Zion which have already been addressed in prayer (Lam. 3.19). The negative acts of Yhwh are figured through a variety of metaphors throughout Lam. 3.1-15: anti-shepherd (vv. 1–3), jailor (vv. 5, 7), warrior (vv. 4, 11–12), bear (v. 10a), lion (v. 10b), and grim party host serving horrible food (v. 15).[48] This abuse leads the man/Zion to state that Yhwh has rejected his soul from peace (v. 17) and ultimately to pray that God would reverse the miserable homelessness of the man/Zion (v. 19). In its immediate context then, חסדי יהוה (v. 21) is semantically 'filled' with an expectation of reversal from real suffering (or deliverance out of it) caused by God which has been expressed to God through prayer. Hope here lay in the possibility that God would act (in a sense) against himself, that his salvific acts would counteract his punitive acts. This 'shape' of hope recurs in Lam. 3.43-5 and will be explored below.

And yet this view does not explain the shift to wisdom instruction in Lam. 3.25-39, which deserves attention. As has been shown, many think the 'shape' of hope is related to exactly this section of the poem and equates to the possibility of forgiveness from sin on the logic of 3.25-39. On this view, the man/Zion is instructed to be silent before the Lord, and hope (ויחיל, v. 26) for his salvation. Silence, sitting alone, putting his mouth in the dust, giving his cheek to the one who strikes him (vv. 28–30) comprise acts of penitence for sin. The man/Zion hopes for God's forgiveness as the community humbly and patiently waits for divine mercy. Thus 'forgiveness from sin' comprises the semantic referent for the clause חסדי יהוה.

There is some evidence for this. Middlemas recognizes the wisdom-like instruction of vv. 25–39 inverts some of the cries of Lamentations 1–2, as intimated above. '[T]he admonitory section refutes the speeches made by Lady Jerusalem [in Lamentations 1–2], the stance taken by the eyewitness reporter

---

47. R. Martin-Achard and S.P. Re'emi, *God's People In Crisis: Amos and Lamentations* (ITC; Edinburgh: Handsel, 1984), 108.
48. On 'Gastgeber' imagery, see Rudolph, *Klagelieder*, 239.

towards her and corrects the (mis-) understanding of Yhwh.'[49] Because the parenetic section affirms the Lord's sovereignty, power, and salvific dispo-sition (cf. Lam. 3.26, 31–36), it counters the strident prayers of the previous poems, especially Lam. 2.20-22. In Lam. 3.21-39, among other related themes God is pictured as a 'divine saviour' whereas in Lamentations 1–2, God (often) is depicted as a 'divine warrior'.[50] For Middlemas, then, these central verses, coupled with Lam. 3.1-24, are the *Golah* perspective on hope: because God is faithful to his covenant love (Lam. 3.21-24), acts of penitence (Lam. 3.25-30) will lead God to move out of his covenant faithfulness to forgiveness (Lam. 3.31-39).

While this thread should not be pulled out of the tapestry of Lamentations, it nonetheless cannot be construed as the only tie that draws the concept of hope in ch. 3 (or the book) together. Lam. 3.43-45 builds upon previous language used to depict judgment against God's people described in chs. 1 and 2; this deployment of intertextuality essentially works to invert the logic of Lam. 3.25-39 by returning to the kind of pain and lament expressed in Lam. 3.1-19. Note, for example: סכך (Lam. 2.1a//3.43a), הרג (Lam. 2.4b, 20c, 21c//3.43b), and לא חמל (Lam. 2.2a, 17b, 21c//3.43b). These verses also exploit language used for enemies who *pursued* Jerusalem's inhabitants in Lam. 1.3c (כל־רדפיה), 6c (לפני רודף)//3.43a (ותרדפנו). The implications are clear: the Lord has once again become an enemy pursuer by 'covering himself' in a cloud, rebuffing prayers, slaughtering, and not pitying his people. This divine activ-ity, employing 'Day of Yhwh' language from Lam. 2.1-9, leaves his people as 'offscouring and rubbish' (Lam. 3.45) once again 'in the midst of the peoples (בקרב העמים)' (Lam. 3.45b), or as Lam. 1.3b states, 'among the nations (בגוים)'. Middlemas' insight on intertextual connections between the first three poems of Lamentations is a welcome contribution but does not go far enough to rec-ognize that these connections proceed throughout the whole of Lamentations 3 and help shape the concept of hope. Repetition of language correlates the com-plaints of personified Zion in the first two chapters with the suffering man of Lamentations 3.

As in Lamentations 1–2, the rhetorical function of this complaint in ch. 3 is to present the current plight (namely Yhwh's own activity) before the deity so that he might transform the negative situation (divine judgment) into a positive situation (divine mercy) – a most basic function of lament. Lament does more than generate catharsis or ruminate on the shards of existence. It is persuasive

---

49. Middlemas, 'Did Second Isaiah Write Lamentations III?', 515. She notes particu-larly Lam. 1.14//3.27, 28 in the repetition of the term על, 'yoke'; Lam. 2.18-19//3.26-30 in the repetition of the two roots דמם, 'to be silent' and נתן, 'to give'.

50. Middlemas, 'Did Second Isaiah Write Lamentations III?', 518–19

speech designed to gain the deity's attention.[51] In this way, the metaphor of the divine enemy warrior is juxtaposed against the metaphor of the just judge who will hear the complaint (about his own activity) and respond justly.[52]

On the one hand, this may not be conceived of as hope as it is too virulent and impious (so Brandscheidt). But on the other hand, the return to lament in Lamentations 3 and the juxtaposition of 'God as warrior' against 'God as judge' actually reinforces the logic of spirituality and faith *through* lament prayer, though the sources of pain that ground appeal may be multiform. Miller rightly sees that *expectation* and *hope* is built into lament prayer that expressions of grief, catharsis, protest, or doubt may not share: 'There is, therefore, in the character of Scriptural prayer a powerful suggestion that the one who prays can truly engage the deity, can urge reasons upon God for acting in behalf of the one in need, just as God in giving the law urges reasons upon the people for responding and obeying.'[53] In light of the 'shape' of hope through lament, it appears that the majority scholarly view – that hope in Lamentations is found in parenesis and confession (Lam. 3.25-39) – becomes relegated to only *one* possible 'shape' for hope in the poetry, as it is surrounded by lament. The call for confession (or its enactment) reappears in Lam. 1.18; 2.14; 4.13-15; and 5.16, and so this shape of hope is not *contravened* as much as it is coupled with lament.

Through lament, Lamentations reinforces a theology of covenant. On the basis of his covenant with his people, Yhwh's proofs of faithfulness (חסדי יהוה) will be actualized in response to their specific pleas. This theology undergirds the structure of ch. 3 (lament-parenesis-lament) as well as the recurrent use of prayer in and through the book that exhibit a variety of appeals: Lam. 1.9, 11, 20-22; 2.20-22; 3.19, 42-66; 5.1-22.[54] The appeals actually present divergent expectations of Yhwh beyond his forgiveness of sin: countering divine

---

51. P.D. Miller, *They Cried to the Lord: The Form and Theology of Biblical Prayer* (Minneapolis: Fortess, 1994), 55–134, esp. 57, 126.

52. So Middlemas' distinctions between 'divine warrior' and 'divine saviour' become somewhat blurred theologically. She may view Lam. 3.40-66 to be a Judahite redaction of the *Golah* poem (Lam. 3.1-39), which would be sensible enough, but then one would have to (a) explain the range of negative divine metaphors in 3.1-15, and (b) prove that the careful intertextual links that exist not only between the first three chapters, but also throughout the corpus of Lam. 3.1-66, are in fact the work of Judahite redaction rather than the work of an intentional composition written from a Judahite perspective. Note as well: Lam. 3.8b (תפלתי)//3.44b (תפלה); Lam. 3.30b (בחרפה)//3.61a (חרפתם); ראה√ (Lam. 3.36b//3.59a, 60a); Lam. 3.35a (משפט־גבר)//3.59b (משפטי).

53. P.D. Miller, 'Prayer as Persuasion: The Rhetoric and Intention of Prayer', *Word and World* 13.4 (1993), 361.

54. Thomas, 'Liturgical Function', 139–47.

punitive activity,[55] delivering from – or punishing – enemies of Zion,[56] or restoring Zion's dignity and removing disgrace.[57] Further, the hope may be that God would relieve 'miserable homelessness' experienced by the man/Zion (Lam. 3.19//1.7). In its immediate context, this petition requests that Yhwh would no longer punish the man/Zion, but as it is situated within the book, the plea may be extended to express a desire to be liberated from a state of home-lessness in destroyed Judah and restored to a place of rest and security. If so, then this connotes a practical expectation that God would provide a means for rebuilding and restoration to a sense of selfhood and identity associated with the notion of 'place' (Lam. 2.1-9; 4.1; 5.2, 18) and 'peace' (Lam. 3.17) with an anointed king (Lam. 4.20).

Further, the 'lament-shape' of hope gives a certain earthiness to a poignant verse: השיבנו יהוה ונשובה[58] חדש ימינו כקדם, 'Restore us to yourself, O Yhwh, and we will return; renew our days as of old' (Lam. 5.21). At first blush, this verse longs for a return back to what had been prior to destruction. But there is more here than meets the eye. As it is the penultimate verse in the book, the prior poems have shown the status quo of the former days contributed to Jerusalem's demise. Confessions of faulty political alliances (Lam. 1.19; 4.17; 5.6), the sins of priests and prophets (Lam. 2.14; 4.13-15), and Zion's sins (Lam. 1.10, 13–15; 2.1-9, 20–22; 3.1-18, 42b-45; 4.6, 22; 5.16) portray a former way of life that cannot be reinstated without modification – socially, politically, and theologi-cally. So the prayer for renewal in 5.21 cannot mean hope in restoration to the status quo prior to Jerusalem's destruction.

Hope for the return and restoration, and renewal to 'days as of old' found here is resonant with, and is indeed unique to, language of restoration in Jer. 31.17-22, esp. v. 18c (השיבני ואשובה), as well as Jer. 30.20 and Ezek. 36.11 (קדם + כ). This hope for return and renewal lay in an idealized and future portrait of covenant relationship between God, people and land, where sin and corrup-tion do not sully any portion of the triad. Further, this return and renewal is an act of God (note the Hiphil in השיבני and השיבנו in Jer. 31.18c and Lam. 5.21a, respectively) that is anticipated in and through prayer. So the appeal to 'renew our days as of old' looks to the past at how God has worked to re-establish jus-tice with his people in proper relationship and anticipates that same enactment of justice in an unspecified, but hoped for, future reality. McConville's com-ments on Jeremiah 30–31 are equally apt for Lam. 5.21:

---

55. Lam. 1.10, 13–15; 2.1-9, 20-22; 3.1-18, 42b-45.
56. Lam. 1.9c, 21a-b, 22a-b; 3.46-66.
57. Lam. 3.61; 5.1-12.
58. I follow the Qere (ונשובה) rather than the Kethib (ונשוב).

The picture of a new life of Israel with [Yhwh], therefore, does not merely turn the clock back. All will be restored, indeed, but the prospect is not one which simply ignores the need to create a real, responsive relationship between the two parties to the covenant [. . .] His 'bring me back that I may be restored' rests on a play on the verb [שׁוּב, Jer. 31.18c] which is at the heart of the great solution, and indeed of all theological wrestling with the relationship of divine enabling and human responsibility in adequate human response to God.[59]

The prayer of Lam. 5.21 reflects upon the problems which led to destruction, gazes upon the present condition of misery, but yearns for a future in which God really will restore the people to himself in a move that is at once spiritual and physical. The physicality of the restoration encompasses a reversal from a myriad of points of pain already highlighted in the poetry: disgrace, activity of enemies, internal strife (Lam. 1.20), and a relinquishing of present divine punishment.

But is the sense of expectancy in lament a sure bet? The major difference between Jeremiah and Lamentations' conception of hope is that the latter does not share the same optimism as the former. In her assessment of Lamentations 1, 2, 4 and 5, Middlemas rightly brings to the fore the *un*certainty regarding God's presence or activity on behalf of Judahites in the land, thus leading them to pray to – or on her reckoning, protest to – God about re-engaging Judahites at the point of their sustained attention to, and vocalization of, pain and suffering.[60]

While not characterizing it as protest in which Zion walks away from God, the petitions of Lamentations provide only a *glimpse* of what is hoped for beyond various sources of pain. But this is not an actualized picture. Hope here is not certainty.[61] Rather it is an anticipation that חסדי יהוה provide the possibility of a future life beyond lament. As Middlemas recognizes, this cannot be equated to confident affirmations of hope found, for instance, in Isaiah 40–55 in particular. This hope depends upon God, but because it is prayer, it is tempered by the recognition of its potentiality: אולי יֵשׁ תקוה, *'perhaps* there is hope' (Lam. 3.29b). Lamentations looks for the חסדי יהוה to be made manifest in the life of the man, in the experience of Zion. But nonetheless it remains a

59. McConville, *Judgment and Promise*, 97.
60. Middlemas, *The Troubles*, 198–228.
61. Even the most hopeful statement of the book, 'Rejoice and be glad, O Daughter Edom, O resident in the land of Uz! For the cup will pass to you; you will get drunk and expose yourself. Your punishment is complete, Dear Zion; he will not add to your exile. But he will punish your iniquity, O Daughter Edom; he will expose your sins' (Lam. 4.21-22) is tempered by the final chapter which casts a rather ominous and uncertain tone over the declaration.

question begging for an answer: 'Unless you have rejected us utterly, and are exceedingly angry with us forever' (Lam. 5.22).

Conclusion

The substance of hope in Lamentations is found in the logic of prayer: 'I will hope in Him' (Lam. 3.24b). This is true in Lamentations 3 but throughout the book as well. Without recognition that Yhwh remains vital to the life of Judahites in the land during the exilic age, the prayers of Lamentations essentially fall flat. This presupposes a view of divine potency that mobilizes Lamentations' prayers and grounds expectancy that he would *do* something on behalf of his people. Incidentally, this logic counters other sentiments among other ANE people in their city-laments whose patron deity has been defeated by a rival army (and god). The logic of prayer in Lamentations runs against this tendency, conferring upon Yhwh a potency that not only can he counteract the work of enemies and sin, but even his own punitive action.[62] The responsibility for the people, then, is to pray. Searching for hope apart from this basic construct, while not unfruitful, in the end may overextend the evidence in Lamentations.

The shape of this prayer, it has been shown, cannot be reduced to an expectation of divine forgiveness (and a concomitant set of penitential acts). This thread runs throughout the tapestry of Lamentations but cannot be said to be the only one. Hope is also shaped in the tears and pain of recurrent lament prayers that conclude both Lamentations 3 and the book as a whole. Their petitions are multiform and provide an 'earthy' set of expectations regarding Yhwh's deliverance. Such a range is understandable for a people who lived in a time of enormous upheaval and change for Judah. The poetry, then, provides a variety of ways for Judahites to engage the deity in prayer, both in lament and penitence. Research that polarizes lament prayer against penitential prayer, then, under-reads the diverse shapes of hope in Lamentations. Lamentations' expectancy centres upon what God may do when his people appeal to him. In a sense this comprises the essence of *faith* as opposed to certainty.

Finally, Lamentations belongs to a canon that interacts with it. Its interchanges with Isaiah 40–55, Zechariah 1–2, Jeremiah and even the Psalter

---

62. See F.W. Dobbs-Allsopp, *Weep, O Daughter of Zion: A Study of the City-Lament Genre in the Hebrew Bible* (BibOr, 44; Rome: Pontifical Biblical Institute, 1993), 45–75. Lamentations merges the presentation of the high-god of the pantheon (who decrees destruction via an invading army) with the patron deity (who must vacate his/her shrine at the command of the high-god). As such, Yhwh (as the patron-deity of Jerusalem), while abandoning his temple and land, remains potent to hear the pleas of his people (figured as the high-god who decreed destruction).

highlight that the petitions of Lamentations are heard by God in these other texts.[63] This canonical dialogue frames the hope that exile, destruction, misery and abuse in the world do not have the final say. But Lamentations' petitions do not diminish, as God's people continue to ask him to step into the breach of the broken world: 'Your kingdom come, your will be done, on earth as it is in heaven' (Mt. 6.10). These prayers will take various shapes, but will remain rooted in a tacit and tenacious hope in God's salvation.

63. P. Willey, *Remember the Former Things: The Recollection of Previous Texts in Isaiah 40–55* (SBLDS, 161; Atlanta: Scholar's Press, 1997); C.R. Seitz, *Word without End: The Old Testament as Abiding Theological Witness* (Grand Rapids: Eerdmans, 1998), 130–49; C. Mandolfo, *The Singers of Lamentations: Cities under Siege, from Ur to Jerusalem to Sarajevo* (BIS, 60; Leiden: Brill, 2002); Renkema, *Lamentations*.

CPSIA information can be obtained at www.ICGtesting.com
Printed in the USA
LVOW07s0140230713

344147LV00002B/46/P

9 780567 642752